Streetsmart Guide to

Managing Your Portfolio

An Investor's Guide to Minimizing Risk and Maximizing Returns

Frank Yao, Bret Xu, Patrick Adams, and Kenneth Doucet

McGraw-Hill

New York   Chicago   San Francisco   Lisbon
London   Madrid   Mexico City   New Delhi
San Juan   Seoul   Singapore   Sydney   Toronto

McGraw-Hill

A Division of The **McGraw·Hill** *Companies*

1 2 3 4 5 6 7 8 9 0   AGM/AGM   0 9 8 7 6 5 4 3 2

ISBN 0-07-138051-5

Printed and bound by Quebecor World.

This publication is designed to provide accurate and authoritative information in regard to the subject matter covered. It is sold with the understanding that neither the author nor the publisher is engaged in rendering legal, accounting, or other professional service. If legal advice or other expert assistance is required, the services of a competent professional person should be sought.

> *—From a Declaration of Principles jointly adopted by a Committee of the American Bar Association and a Committee of Publishers*

McGraw-Hill books are available at special quantity discounts to use as premiums and sales promotions, or for use in corporate training programs. For more information, please write to the Director of Special Sales, Professional Publishing, McGraw-Hill, Two Penn Plaza, New York, NY 10121-2298. Or contact your local bookstore.

Contents

Preface

nstitutional investors, retail investment advisors, and self-directed individual investors face the same challenge in planning, implementing and monitoring portfolios. Each must delicately balance risk and return across all assets in his or her portfolio. As important as any one holding can be to an investor, it is the performance of the entire portfolio that ultimately defines success.

Traditionally, large institutional investors have had two advantages over retail investment advisors and self-directed individual investors in managing portfolios: Know-how and the tools to apply that know-how. *Streetsmart Guide to Managing Your Portfolio* levels the playing field, providing not only valuable insight into the techniques that have long been used by Wall Street pros (the know-how), but also guidance on inexpensive tools available to retail investment advisors and self-directed individual investors to implement that know-how. The authors show retail advisors and individual investors how to employ Noble-prize winning methodologies and leading Wall Street practices, and the book is comprehensive in guiding the reader from early-stage asset allocation strategy, to asset selection and portfolio construction, to late-stage performance measurement and style analysis.

Investment literature dedicated to tools and techniques for investment decision-making has traditionally focused on fundamental and technical analysis. *Streetsmart Guide to Managing Your Portfolio* fills a void in that body of literature, providing guidance to retail advisors and individual investors in the use of Modern Portfolio Theory (MPT). As MPT has developed over the years, it has come to be widely accepted by many major financial institutions worldwide. The rapid advancement and spread of technology, and the Internet in particular, has made the tools and techniques of MPT available and accessible to small institutional investors and individual investors alike. To effectively incorporate MPT into one's investment decision-making process, that process must be highly disciplined and consistently applied over time. This book provides a means of doing that.

In this book, we begin by addressing the two most important concepts of MPT: the tradeoff between risk and return and the benefits of diversification. We then present a top-down investment process for active investment management, which we divide into three stages: planning, implementing, and monitoring. The Nobel-prize winning methodologies and professional practices used in many leading Wall Street institutions, such as asset allocation, financial planning, fundamental and quantitative asset selection, portfolio optimization (tactical asset allocation), performance measurement, style analysis and investing, and performance attribution are all discussed in detail. For each technique, in addition to showing what it is and how it works, we also show why it is important for investors and how it can be applied to real life problems throughout the investment process.

The book should be used as a resource throughout the life of an investment portfolio. As the techniques described will never grow old, self-directed individual investors, broker-dealers, traders, consultants, money managers, plan sponsors, and, for that matter, anyone interested in employing a proven, disciplined approach to investment decision-making should find much of interest in this book.

Finally, this book is the result of tremendous collaboration and teamwork on the part of its authors. In his role as lead author, Frank Yao defined the book's overall structure and organization and contributed chapters on risk and return, performance measurement, style analysis, and performance attribution. Patrick Adams contributed chapters on the benefits of diversification, stock selection, and mutual fund selection. Bret Xu contributed chapters on strategic asset allocation, quantitative asset selection, and tactical asset allocation (portfolio optimization). Kenneth Doucet contributed the chapter on investment planning and served as editor for the entire book.

Acknowledgments

FRANK YAO—I owe thanks to so many people that it is difficult to come up with a complete list. Special thanks to my wife, Ying Chen, and my children, David and Daphen, who have always been there with support, understanding, and love. I would also like to thank my parents, Shihua Yao and Juhong He, and my in-laws, GenFu Chen and Rongxian Ma, for all their love and constant support over the years.

This book is also a rare opportunity to look back on my career in the financial industry and to express my gratitude to those who helped and educated me. I have been fortunate to have the opportunity to meet and work with a tremendous group of people in the financial industry over the years. Linda Becker, my mentor at Dow Jones, introduced me to the financial industry. I would like to thank Phil Enny and Larry Landau for their encouragement and support while I worked at the Mortgage-backed Securities Division of Dow Jones as a newcomer to the financial industry. My experience at Goldman Sachs's Firmwide Risk Department owes a lot to working in a team with such brilliant professionals as Bob Litterman, Guangliang He, Steve Lucas, Ravi Narula, Jae Sang, and Jeff Weiss, among many others.

BRET XU—I would like to thank my parents, John Xu and Grace Zhou, for introducing me to the joys of financial investing at an early age. I am forever grateful to their love, guidance, and support over the years. I would also like to thank Frank Yao, who taught me intricacies of finance that I could not have learned in a classroom. Finally, I would like to thank the faculty at the Cooper Union and Carnegie Mellon GSIA for giving me a top quality education, not only in academia but also in life.

PATRICK ADAMS—In writing this book, I recall many a conversation with my father, Walter Adams, who has taught me most of what I know about investing. I owe him a huge thanks. His guidance together with the support of Mom, Chris, Laura, and Grandma provide me with a great foundation.

Writing this book would not have been possible without Alyssa Rockland's encouragement and inspiration. And the quality of this book depends on the insight of good friends Colin Clark, Marc Aylett, and Helen Vlassis. Finally, I owe thanks to former colleagues at Alex Brown & Sons, Marc Rich Holding, and Goldman Sachs, and to the faculty at Claremont McKenna College and NYU Stern.

KENNETH DOUCET—My chief thanks in this endeavor goes to my wife, Wenyan. Always by and on my side, she inspires me in so many ways. Special thanks too to my parents, Catherine and Russell Doucet, who kindled my interest in investing at a very early age and instilled in me the intellectual curiosity and lust for learning that are essential for high-quality, original work. Thanks also go out to the world-class MBA faculty at NYU Stern School of Business, whose classroom lectures and real-world experience continue to guide and instruct me in the business world. Finally, I would like to thank my co-authors on this book project. Our collaboration has been both intellectually stimulating and personally rewarding.

The authors would especially like to thank Ela Aktay, acquisitions editor, for her professional work. This book would not have been possible without her constant support.

Introduction

The art of investing is evolving into the science of investing. As modern portfolio and investment theory has developed over the past several decades, it has come to be widely accepted by financial institutions worldwide, from the largest Wall Street firms to the not-so-large Main Street banks. In recent years, PC-based software resulted in wide acceptance of modern portfolio and investment theory-based financial and investment advisors. In addition, the Internet makes the tools and techniques of modern portfolio and investment theory available and accessible to individual investors.

Not a moment too soon, either. With the rapid advancement and spread of technology, easy access to mountains of investment-related information, and the emergence of inexpensive self-directed trading, investors have more power than ever before. Along with that power has come increased sophistication, and the understanding that stock tips and intuition need to give way to a more systematic, disciplined approach to investing.

Anyone with experience of building a house (or having one built) knows how important it is to start with a sound architectural design and then follow through with systematic, disciplined execution of those plans. This helps to ensure that the end product meets all of the designer's expectations in terms of the realization of the original vision, materials used, and total budget planned. Poor design, poor execution, or a combination of the two, offers no such assurance, and can lead to unexpected or even disastrous results, both physically and financially.

When investing, it is equally important to have a framework that allows an investor to systematically relate raw materials (i.e., stocks, mutual funds, etc.), construction techniques (investment implementation approaches), and associated costs (risk) to an end product—the investment portfolio. Such a framework is called an investment process, and can serve as a blueprint for investment decision-making.

An Investment Process for Active Investment Management

An investment process is a plan of action for implementing an investment philosophy. We believe that to be successful, an investment process must be highly disciplined and consistently applied over time. In this book, we outline a top-down investment process for active investment management, which we divide into three stages.

- Stage 1—Planning
- Stage 2—Implementing
- Stage 3—Monitoring

Figure 1 illustrates the three stages of the investment process, plus the foundation (i.e., knowledge and understanding) that is required to successfully navigate through that process.

Foundation

At the very core of the investment process is the need to choose from among alternative investments. Selecting assets for an investment portfolio requires the investor to understand the risk–return tradeoff for the alternative investments available. This risk–return tradeoff is central to modern portfolio and investment theory.

To effectively incorporate modern portfolio and investment theory (see Figure 1) into the investment decision-making process, we need to be able to estimate and evaluate the expected risk and return for individual investments, for investment portfolios, and for broad asset classes. To that end, Chapter 1 explains how to measure and calculate expected return and risk, and discusses the risk and return characteristics of various major asset classes. To supplement the

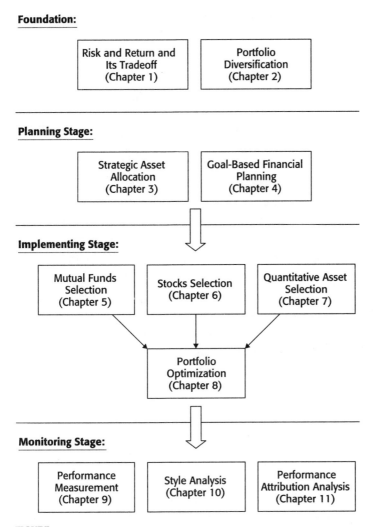

Foundation:

Risk and Return and Its Tradeoff (Chapter 1)

Portfolio Diversification (Chapter 2)

Planning Stage:

Strategic Asset Allocation (Chapter 3)

Goal-Based Financial Planning (Chapter 4)

Implementing Stage:

Mutual Funds Selection (Chapter 5)

Stocks Selection (Chapter 6)

Quantitative Asset Selection (Chapter 7)

Portfolio Optimization (Chapter 8)

Monitoring Stage:

Performance Measurement (Chapter 9)

Style Analysis (Chapter 10)

Performance Attribution Analysis (Chapter 11)

FIGURE 1

understanding of risk and return, Chapter 1 presents research results that show how risk and return have evolved during the 20th century.

Diversification is another cornerstone of modern portfolio theory. Chapter 2 explains how investors can benefit from diversification without compromising the goal of high returns. Many investors believe diversification is simply a matter of holding a number of different assets, but we show that two portfolios with the same number of assets can differ significantly in terms of *quality of diversification*. The quality

Harry Markowitz and Modern Portfolio Theory

Modern portfolio theory (MPT) was developed in the 1950s by Harry Markowitz. His book, *Portfolio Selection: Efficient Diversification of Investments* (1959, New York: John Wiley & Sons), was an extension of his PhD thesis at the University of Chicago and an article that appeared in the *Journal of Finance* (Harry Markowitz, "Portfolio Selection." *Journal of Finance,* Vol. 7, No. 1, pp. 77–91, 1952). Modern portfolio theory is regarded as one of the most important financial analytical tools developed in the 20th century. In 1990, Markowitz shared the Nobel prize in Economics with Merton Miller and William Sharpe for what has become a broad theory for portfolio selection and corporate finance.

Markowitz is a scholarly academic and "computer techie" type person with a varied background. He has always been eager to apply his theory to solve real-world problems. His experience ranges from teaching at business schools to designing a computer language at RAND Corporation and helping a Japanese bank develop large-scale portfolio optimization by computer program.

The mathematics of modern portfolio theory is rather technical and challenging; it has kept a lot of academics busy. Fortunately, there is no need to lead the reader through the technical details of the mathematics, such as quadratic programming or separation theorem, to understand the essence of modern portfolio theory. Simple explanation or examples will make it clear. Imagine that a portfolio consists of two risky assets: One that pays off if the sun shines, another that pays off if it does not. This portfolio containing two assets will always pay something whether the sun shines or not. Therefore, adding one type of risky asset to another can possibly reduce the overall risk of our simple all-weather portfolio.

Although some investors can take more risk than others, MPT reasonably assumes that all investors are risk averse. A risk-averse investor is one who will choose the asset with the lowest risk given the same expected return.

We cannot be sure about the future return on any assets. However, we can use past return history to project the future and determine the likelihood or probability of a certain

---

of diversification in a portfolio depends on more than the number of stocks alone. It also depends heavily on how the individual stocks within the portfolio correlate to one another. Therefore, we discuss asset correlation in depth.

Chapters 1 and 2 provide a basic grounding in the concepts of modern portfolio theory, and the foundation on which to build a disciplined framework for investment decision-making.

return. The expected return on a risky asset is based on the probabilities associated with all possible future returns. You might refer to Chapter 1 for a detailed discussion on this subject. MPT explores how risk-averse investors construct portfolios to achieve the best risk–return trade-off or to have optimal market risk against expected returns.

Unlike traditional asset management theory and practice, which involves the use of technical or fundamental analysis to predict individual stock price movements, Markowitz's MPT concentrates on the performance of a portfolio of assets based on the risk and return behavior of its combined holdings.

Markowitz's most original contribution was his insistence on distinguishing between the risk of an individual asset (such as a stock) and the risk of an entire portfolio. The crucial insight of MPT is this: The risk of an individual asset is of little importance to the investor; what matters is its contribution to the entire portfolio's risk. The risk of a portfolio depends on the covariance between its individual asset holdings, *not* on the average risk of the individual investments or assets. A combination of very risky assets may still comprise a low-risk portfolio as long as they have low covariance. MPT has shown that even a random mix of assets is less risky than putting all your money in a single asset or stock.

True diversification depends on having assets in your portfolio that are not all dependent on the same economic variables (consumer spending, business cycle, housing, fiscal and monetary policy, etc.). Wise investors will diversify their portfolios not by name or industry but by the determinants that influence the fluctuations of various assets.

In order to increase portfolio returns, investors have to take on greater risk, which could translate to a bumpy ride in the investment journey. To smooth out the bumps, you will have to diversify your investments across various asset classes (for example, domestic stocks, international stocks, domestic bonds, emerging stock and bonds markets, and cash) and discipline your investment process, as discussed extensively in this book, over a long time period. You may not win the Nobel prize, but you will be on the right road to investment success.

Planning Stage

In planning investments, which more than likely are tied to some goal or a number of goals, the first step is to determine an appropriate asset allocation, given the individual risk tolerance, investment time horizon, financial "big picture," and the nature of the goal(s) for which a person is investing. Asset allocation is essentially how we divvy up our money across a broad set of asset classes, such as domestic stocks, international stocks, bonds, and cash. We cannot overstate the importance of getting the right mix of assets in a portfolio, since widely cited academic research has found that over 90 percent of a portfolio's return variability can be explained by the portfolio's asset allocation.[1] Over time, a portfolio's performance will be most heavily influenced by the types and relative weightings of asset classes within it, and less influenced by market timing or individual stock or mutual fund selection.

Chapter 3 carefully investigates various methods of asset allocation, including simple asset allocation, naïve asset allocation, and optimal asset allocation, and demonstrates the benefits of asset allocation for long-term investing. Given the lively debate currently surrounding international diversification, this chapter also examines the correlation between the U.S. equity and international stock markets, which has steadily increased in recent years, most likely due at least in part to the globalization and integration of world economies. The conclusion is that such rising correlation may reduce the benefits of international diversification.

Planning for any goal involves determining the target dollar amount we are striving to accumulate, and the amount we can contribute today and each year along the way. The target may be a lump sum to purchase a home, or an annual amount to live on in retirement, and we need to be disciplined in choosing the investments to help achieve that goal. As tempting as a high-risk, get-rich-quick investment may look, an investor cannot lose track of the investment goal and the risk he or she is willing to bear to achieve it. Once invested, patience is essential. Some months, quarters, or even years may be disappointing, but over the long-term, if investments are allocated appropriately and reasonable goals were set, those goals ought to be achievable.

Chapter 4 explains *why* investment planning is so essential, and *how* it can be effectively incorporated into one's investment process. We first examine the "drivers" behind investment planning (i.e., those needs that only investment planning can satisfy); then identify the

---

[1] See, Gary Brinson, Hood Randolph, and Gilbert Beebower, "Determinants of Portfolio Performance," *Financial Analysts Journal,* July/August, 1986. Gary Brinson, Brian Singer, and Gilbert Beebower, "Determinants of Portfolio Performance II: An Update," *Financial Analysts Journal,* May/June, 1991.

tools and techniques for addressing those needs; and finally, present a disciplined process for investment planning using those tools and techniques.

The ultimate goal of investment planning is to achieve a balance between goals and investments, and the first step toward measuring (and ultimately achieving) that balance is to quantify *both* the goals and investments. With goals and investments that have been quantified, we are able to construct a simple cash-flow model that can show an investor, on average, whether or not the goals are likely to be achieved with the investments dedicated to them. However, a cash-flow model, as useful as it can be, still has its weaknesses. For that reason, we turn our focus to a technique called Monte Carlo simulation, which, when applied to financial planning, helps us to understand the statistical likelihood of successfully achieving our goals.

Implementing Stage

Once we have determined our asset allocation strategy, we turn our attention to selecting individual assets for each portion of our portfolio. This can be one of the most interesting and challenging parts of the investment process.

There are several methods of building a portfolio. The simplest and most effective way of filling in each section of the portfolio pie is to buy index funds or ETFs (exchange-traded funds). An index fund is a mutual fund with an investment objective of replicating the performance of a market index. One example of an index fund is the Vanguard S&P 500 Fund (ticker symbol: "VFINX"), which tracks the performance of the Standard & Poor 500 market index. An ETF is a special type of mutual fund called a unit investment trust (UIT), and trades like a single stock. An ETF is a basket of stocks that reflects the composition of an index, like the S&P 500. Investors can buy and sell the ETFs throughout a trading day at a price determined by the net asset value of the underlying basket of stocks. The most widely traded and well-known ETF is the SPDR (pronounced *spider,* Standard and Poor's Depository Receipt; ticker symbol: "SPY"). For most asset classes there are funds or ETFs that replicate the performance of the various asset classes. For example, an index fund that tracks the S&P 500, or an ETF that replicates the S&P 500 performance (SPY), will fulfill the large cap stock portion of a portfolio. Chapter 5 shows in great detail how we can use index funds or ETFs to implement a target asset allocation.

If the idea of investing in index funds or ETFs seems too remote from direct asset classes, an investor can decide to pick individual stocks and mutual funds. Mutual funds enable investors to pool their money in the hands of a professional investor or fund manager. In Chapter 5, we closely examine the advantages and disadvantages of mutual fund investing. Based on that analysis, we recommend four key selection criteria that ought to be considered when evaluating "actively managed" mutual funds for possible inclusion in a portfolio.

- Risk-adjusted return
- Style
- Low expense ratio and low turnover
- Manager's experience

For passive investing, using index funds and ETFs is just what we're looking for. The key determination of which funds we ultimately hold will be based on the asset allocation we choose to pursue. Asset allocation is discussed at length in Chapter 3.

How can we take advantage of the limitless information on sectors, industries, and individual companies to make intelligent decisions about the value of a stock? Chapter 6 introduces a basic technique for stock valuation and several factors that impact the price of a stock, including:

- Economic forces, such as the business cycle, economic growth, interest rates, oil prices, etc.
- Market movement and firm-specific factors, such as management and corporate strategy.
- Fundamental factors, such as relative price earnings (PE) ratio and PE growth ratio.

There are many ways to choose stocks and mutual funds. In Chapter 5, we discuss how to choose great-performing mutual funds, and in Chapter 6 we discuss how to select individual stocks that are likely to earn the best returns. Will every high return stock or mutual fund be a good fit for a portfolio? The answer, of course, is "no," and because of that, the objective in selecting assets should not be to choose the best-performing stocks or mutual funds, but to choose assets that best fit into the portfolio. In Chapter 7, we use a set of interesting examples to demonstrate how to choose the best-fitting assets for a portfolio (based on quantitative criteria) and conclude that the following factors should be considered *together* when selecting assets for a portfolio.

- Stocks or mutual funds with high returns can increase the portfolio return.

- Stocks or mutual funds with low risks can reduce the portfolio risk.

- Stocks or mutual funds with low correlation to an existing portfolio can reduce that portfolio risk.

We want to emphasize that investors should consider all of these factors together when conducting quantitative asset selection, because all of these factors will have an impact on the return and risk of investment portfolios.

Once we have selected the individual stocks and mutual funds that will make up the portfolio, the next natural step is to determine how much of each asset ought to be included in the portfolio. Chapter 8 presents a technique called portfolio optimization or tactical asset allocation that allows us to shoot for the *additional* possible return available at any given level of risk, given the assets that are held. We use a simple stock portfolio example to demonstrate how tactical asset allocation can provide a means of generating higher expected return over a naïve diversification strategy, an all too common strategy that involves simply investing one's money equally across all portfolio assets.

Since tactical asset allocation is very sensitive to inputs, such as expected return, we cannot simply use historical average return. In this chapter, we discuss extensively how we can use the capital asset pricing model (CAPM) to estimate expected return and get better results from tactical asset allocation. We also discuss the benefits of setting constraints on individual portfolio assets to promote broader diversification. Although individual asset constraints can limit the potential upside return, when used properly, the benefits of the resulting diversification can outweigh the cost associated with reduced return.

Monitoring Stage

An investment process for active investment management requires ongoing and regular monitoring, as well as feedback on performance. In our discussion of the monitoring stage, we provide a guide to performance analysis, style analysis, and performance attribution analysis techniques, and the insights they can provide.

Evaluation of portfolio performance, the bottom line of the investing process, is naturally of interest to all investors and money managers. The framework for evaluating portfolio performance consists of measuring both the realized return and the differential risk of the portfolio relative to a benchmark, which enables comparison of the portfolio's performance with that of other portfolios. Many advances have been made over the past few decades in the measurement and attribution of investment performance. A field that began with the simple regression of a managed portfolio return on the return of a single benchmark portfolio (a single index model) has transformed into one that invokes multiple style benchmarks and advanced econometric techniques to determine the statistical significance of a manager's investment ability.

In Chapter 9, we present two techniques for measuring performance for a multi-period investment: Dollar-weighted return and time-weighted return. We then provide broad and practical coverage of the risk-adjusted performance evaluation techniques that are available today.

Since the early 1970s, when researchers determined that there were categories of stocks with common characteristics and similar return patterns, style has played a major role in asset classification. Essentially, that research uncovered that categories of stock tended to perform differently from one another in terms of return behavior, but that within any given category, stocks tended to be highly correlated.

Today, assets are classified as stocks or bonds (fixed income securities), and stocks are likely to be classified as domestic or international, small or large, growth or value. Such groups of assets with similar or common characteristics are often called "asset classes" or "styles." Portfolio investment based on selection among styles or asset classes rather than among individual assets is called "style investing." Chapter

10 presents a simple equity classification system and discusses how the various styles have behaved historically. Because different style stocks have different performance cycles, both in length and magnitude, one might be able to develop a style investment strategy to capture such a trend. We use a detailed example of two timing-based style investment strategies to illustrate the potential impact of shifting a portfolio's style between the four major stock style indices, small cap value, small cap growth, large cap value and large cap growth, between 1981 and 2000. The example leads us to conclude that style-based momentum trading, while admittedly mechanical, can be more effective than investing in and sticking to any one style.

It is critical to understand an investment portfolio's style. This becomes even more important for those who invest in mutual funds, whether for understanding the style of an individual fund (which after all is a portfolio of stocks) or a portfolio of funds. Style analysis is an important tool to help us understand a mutual fund's investment policy and objective. To analyze the true source of an investment performance, we turn to William Sharpe's Nobel prize-winning returns-based style analysis technique, discussed in a great detail in Chapter 10. This enables us to determine what mix of a given set of benchmark indices would be necessary to replicate the historical return pattern of the investment.

Anyone who has been invested in the market long enough to receive a monthly or quarterly brokerage statement inevitably wonders (or should wonder), "How have I achieved my investment performance and where have these returns come from?" For mutual funds, we might also want to know whether a fund's manager delivered any added value over some index or benchmark investment. Simply speaking, if a fund performs well, we want to know whether the fund manager is smart or just lucky. In Chapter 11, we discuss a technique called performance attribution analysis, which helps to explain to what extent an investment portfolio's return differentials (relative to an index or benchmark investment) are caused by such factors as country selection, asset allocation, security or stock selection, and other attributes. In this chapter we also use Sharpe's returns-based style analysis to provide insights into the sources of a fund's historic returns, expressing them as a combination of benchmark returns that best represents the fund's overall returns.

Performance attribution analysis has great benefits to investors, allowing them to:

- Identify the detailed and key performance drivers of a portfolio.
- Highlight a potential money manager's strong and weak points, thereby facilitating the choice of manager.
- Separate those performance and risk factors that are within a money manager's control from those that might be outside his or her control due to a client's investment mandate or prospectus limitations.
- Ensure that the portfolio performance or money manager's performance remains within our investment mandate.

By planning with care, investing with discipline, and monitoring investments, investors can navigate the investment process with confidence, and achieve the goals of investment.

Understanding Risk and Return

A t the very core of the investment process is the need to choose from among alternative investments. Selecting assets for an investment portfolio requires that an investor understand the risk-return tradeoff for the alternative investments available. This risk-return tradeoff is central to modern portfolio and investment theory, which underlies the techniques for professional portfolio management presented in this book.

To effectively incorporate modern portfolio and investment theory into the investment decision-making process, investors need to be able to estimate and evaluate the expected risk and return for individual investments, for investment portfolios, and for broad asset classes. To that end, this chapter provides answers to the following questions:

- How do investors measure expected return and risk?
- What are the risk and return characteristic of various major asset classes?
- What are some various alternative risk measures?

To supplement an understanding of risk and return, this chapter also introduces the latest research results on the evolution of risk and return in the 20th century.

Perceptions of Return and Risk

Investing in two different short-term periods could result in completely different experiences for an investor, and quite possibly very
different perceptions of risk and return. For example, if someone
invested in the U.S. stock market in 1999 only, he or she might think
that 30 percent or 40 percent annual return with 25 percent volatility
should be easily achieved. However, if someone started to invest in the
market in early 2000, he or she might think it is very difficulty to
achieve an annual return of 15 percent with 20 percent volatility. So the
question is this: What should investors consider to be reasonable
return and risk over the long run? The fact is there is no definitive
answer. However, by understanding how return and risk are measured, and knowing how major asset classes have behaved in terms of
risk and return over time, each investor ought to be able to answer this
question for himself or herself.

Historical Measurements of Return and Risk

We focus on historical measurements of return and risk because many
financial publications, ranging from mutual fund prospectuses to periodic brokerage statements, present return and risk in this way. It is
also important to understand these measurements because historical
results often provide a good basis for estimating the expected return
and risk for an asset or an asset class. Most of the calculations in this
chapter can be carried out in popular spreadsheet software, such as
Microsoft Excel.

Measuring Return

In terms of return, the first measurement to look at is the historical
return on an investment over a given single time period (or holding
period return). Following that, we explain how to measure the average
historical return for an investment over several periods. Finally, we
consider the annualized holding return over a few periods (or annualized total return).

Single Period Holding Period Return

If an investor commits $100 to an investment at the beginning of the period and receive back $120 at the end of the period, what is the return for the period? The answer is the holding period return.

The period during which investors own an investment is called its investment holding period. The return for that period is the holding period return (HPR), or holding period total return. The HPR is defined as the percentage change of the investment for this period. In this example, the HPR for this single period is calculated as follows.

$$HPR = \frac{\$120 - \$100}{\$100} = 0.20 = 20\%$$

As this simple formula suggests, the HPR can be positive, zero, or negative. An HPR greater than zero reflects an increased value in the investment for the period; an HPR of zero indicates that the investment value remained unchanged for the period; and an HPR less than zero indicates a loss.

The holding period in the example just cited can be a month, a quarter, a year, 2 years, or any other time period. In order to compare alternative investments with varying holding periods, investors typically need to evaluate returns on an annual basis.[1] This can be tricky. Consider the following two examples.

Example 1: An investment that starts with $100 is worth $150 after a 2-year holding period.

$$Annual\ HPR = \left(1 + \frac{\$150 - \$100}{\$100}\right)^{1/2} - 1 = 1.5^{1/2} - 1 = 22.47\%$$

Example 2: An investment that starts with $100 is worth $110 after a 3-month holding period.

$$Annual\ HPR = \left(1 + \frac{\$110 - \$100}{\$100}\right)^{1/0.25} - 1 = 1.1^{1/0.25} - 1 = 46.41\%$$

---

[1] In general, annual HPR can be computed by:

$$Annual\ HPR = (1 + HPR)^{1/n} - 1$$

where n = the number of years the investment is held.

Note that the above calculations for annualizing HPR assume a constant annual return, as well as compounding from period to period. In the first example, we calculate a compounded annual return of 22.47 percent per year. In the second example, assuming that the 10 percent return earned during the first quarter of the year will be replicated in each of the following three quarters, with compounding from quarter to quarter, we calculate an annual return of 46.41 percent for the entire year.

Can we say for sure that Example 2 illustrates the better investment? In terms of the annual HPR, 46.41 percent is clearly greater than 22.47 percent, but the fact is, we cannot say for sure which will prove to be the better investment. The returns on both investments have been restated in annual terms and, therefore, can be compared. The annualized partial year HPR in Example 2 needs to be considered in the context of our assumption that the 10 percent return earned during the first quarter of the year will be replicated in each of the following three quarters. Since it is quite possible that the investment in Example 2 will incur losses in the subsequent three quarters, the annualized partial year HPR can prove to be quite misleading.

Average Historical Multiperiod Returns

Over a number of years, any given investment will likely have good years with high positive returns, flat years with low positive or zero returns, and even bad years with negative returns. While investors should analyze each of these returns, they also need some summary measurement to analyze the investment's performance over time, and can gain a better understanding of what kind of returns investors should expect to receive if they were to hold the investment going forward. We can derive such a summary figure by calculating the average historical returns for our investment over a period of time.

Given a set of HPRs for an investment, there are two important summary measurements of historical returns: the arithmetic mean of returns (or average return) and the geometric mean of returns. To compute the arithmetic mean, the sum of HPRs is divided by the number of periods.[2] Alternatively, the geometric mean is the nth root of the product of the $(1 + HPR)s$ for n periods.[3]

To illustrate these two means, consider an investment with following historical returns.

Period	Beginning Value	Ending Value	HPR
1	$100	$150	50.00%
2	$150	$100	−33.33%
3	$100	$120	20.00%

The arithmetic mean of return (average return) and geometric mean of returns are computed as follows:

$$\textit{Arithmetic Mean for 3 Periods} = \frac{0.50 - 0.3333 + 0.20}{3} = 12.22\%$$

$$\textit{Geometric Mean for 3 Periods}$$
$$= [(1 + 0.5)(1 - 0.3333)(1 + 0.2)]^{1/3} - 1 = 6.27\%$$

Although the arithmetic mean provides a good indication of the expected rate of return for an investment in the future, it is biased upward if you are trying to measure an investment's performance. This is particularly true in a volatile market. We can illustrate this by computing the arithmetic and geometric means for the first two periods only from the prior example:

$$\textit{Arithmetic Mean for First 2 Periods} = \frac{0.50 - 0.3333}{2} = 8.34\%$$

---

[2] The arithmetic mean can be computed by:

$$\textit{Arithmetic Mean} = \frac{HPR_1 + HPR_2 + \cdots + HPR_n}{n}$$

where n = the number of periods for the investment
    $HPRi$ = the return for period i.

[3] The geometric mean is the nth root of the product of the $(1 + HPR)s$ for n periods:

$$\textit{Geometric Mean} = [(1 + HPR_1)(1 + HPR_2) \ldots (1 + HPR_n)]^{1/n} - 1$$

The value of this investment remains unchanged after two periods, yet the arithmetic mean rate of return is computed as 8.34 percent:

Geometric Mean for First 2 Periods $= [(1 + 0.5)(1 - 0.3333)]^{1/2} - 1 = 0\%$

The resulting 0 percent rate of return from the geometric mean calculation accurately measures the fact that there has been no change in wealth from this investment after two periods.

Annualized Total Return

The geometric mean rate of return gives the compound rate of returns based on the ending value of the investment against its beginning value. Therefore it is a superior measure of long-term investment performance. Specifically, in our previously cited 3-year investment example, if we compounded the 6.27 percent geometric mean return for three periods, $(1.627)^3 - 1 = 20\%$, the ending value of investment would be $100 * (1 + 20\%) = \$120$. As is seen, this is exactly the same as our ending value after year 3.

Now let's turn to a real life example. Assume that we are invested in the U.S. equity market (e.g., an S&P 500 index fund) for 2 years from January 1999 to December 2000. The value of the investment begins at 1229 and ends at 1320. See Table 1.1.

At the bottom of the table are several results of historical return means. (We will discuss the two volatility statistics shortly.) The arithmetic monthly mean return is 0.39 percent and its annualized arithmetic mean return is 4.72 percent ($0.39\% \times 12 = 4.72\%$). Annualized HPR or annualized geometric mean is 3.64 percent. If we compound the 3.64 percent for two years, $(1 + 3.64\%)^2 - 1 = 7.41\%$, the ending value of the investment works out to be $1229 * (1 + 7.41\%) = 1320$. That's right on the money!

Calculating Expected Return

Risk means uncertainty about future rates of return. Since uncertainty will always exist as to the future value of any investment (unless investors put their money into a CD account), investors need to have a means of calculating expected return. Investors can quantify that uncertainty and calculate an expected return using probability (or likelihood) distributions.

TABLE 1.1   S&P 500 Index Monthly Return (1/1999–12/2000) and Historical Mean Return and Risk

Month	Beginning Level of Each Period	Ending Level of Each Period	Monthly Return (HPR)
Jan-99	1229	1280	4.10%
Feb-99	1280	1238	−3.23%
Mar-99	1238	1286	3.88%
Apr-99	1286	1335	3.79%
May-99	1335	1302	−2.50%
Jun-99	1302	1373	5.44%
Jul-99	1373	1329	−3.20%
Aug-99	1329	1320	−0.63%
Sep-99	1320	1283	−2.86%
Oct-99	1283	1363	6.25%
Nov-99	1363	1389	1.92%
Dec-99	1389	1469	5.78%
Jan-00	1469	1394	−5.09%
Feb-00	1394	1366	−2.01%
Mar-00	1366	1499	9.67%
Apr-00	1499	1452	−3.08%
May-00	1452	1421	−2.19%
Jun-00	1421	1455	2.39%
Jul-00	1455	1431	−1.63%
Aug-00	1431	1518	6.07%
Sep-00	1518	1437	−5.35%
Oct-00	1437	1429	−0.50%
Nov-00	1429	1315	−8.01%
Dec-00	1315	1320	0.41%
Arithmetic Monthly Mean			0.39%
Annualized Arithmetic Mean (or Annualized Average Mean)			4.72%
Annualized HPR (or Annualized Geometric Mean)			3.64%
Monthly Volatility			4.47%
Annualized Monthly Volatility			15.49%

As an example, in a strong economic environment with high corporate earnings, we might expect to earn a strong return over the next year on our S&P 500 investment. In contrast, if there is an economic decline or recession, investors might expect to lose money on that investment over the next year. Finally, in a normal growth economic environment, investors might expect a more historically average return over the next year.

Investors might estimate probabilities or likelihood for each of these three economic scenarios based on past experience and the current economic environment as follows.

Economic Scenarios	Probability or Likelihood	Expected Rate of Return of S&P 500
Boom or Strong Economy	25%	25%
Normal Growth Economy	60%	15%
Recession or Weak Economy	15%	−10%

Then we can calculate the expected return, $E(r)$, on the S&P 500 investment by multiplying each scenario's probability by its corresponding expected rate of return, and then adding up the three values[4]:

$$E(r) = 25\% * 25\% + 60\% * 15\% + 15\% * (-10\%) = 14\%$$

Throughout this book we characterize probability distribution of returns in terms of their expected return and their standard deviation or volatility, which will be discussed in the next section.

Risk Measurement of Expected and Historical Return

Again, risk means uncertainty about future rates of return. Volatility or standard deviation (these two terms and the term "risk" will be used interchangeably in this book unless specified otherwise) is a popular risk measurement that quantifies how much a series of investment returns varies around its mean or average. With this risk measurement,

---

[4] Formally, the expected return can be calculated as follows:

$$Expected\ Return = E(r) = \sum_{s} p(s)\,r(s)$$

where $p(s)$ = the probability of each scenario s
   $r(s)$ = HPR in each scenario s.

investors can judge the range of returns that our investment is likely to generate in the future.

Consider an investment that gained 2 percent each month over a period of a few years. It would have a volatility of zero since its monthly return did not change from one month to the next. In contrast, an investment that gained 10 percent one month, lost 30 percent the next, and gained 20 percent the next would have a much higher volatility.

The standard deviation of the rate of return (σ) is defined as the square root of the variance (σ^2), which in turn is defined as the expected value of the deviation of the mean return. The higher the volatility in the future, the higher will be the average value of these deviations. That is, the more an investment's returns fluctuate from period to period, the greater its volatility.[5] In the prior example of three economic scenarios, variance would be calculated as:

$$\sigma^2 = 25\% \times (25\% - 14\%)^2 + 60\% \times (15\% - 14\%)^2 + 15\% \times (-10\% - 14\%)^2 = 1.17\%$$

Volatility (standard deviation) would therefore be the square root of 1.17 percent.

$$\sigma = 10.83\%$$

This is a hypothetical example. In the real world, it is almost impossible to accurately forecast future scenarios and compute an expected return. Although historical returns do not represent future performance, they are still good indicators for what the future might hold in terms of returns. Many practitioners at major Wall Street firms as well as researchers at academic institutions have used various historical means as an estimate of expected mean return.

Standard deviation, or volatility, is a way of qualifying an investment's performance. For most investments, future returns will fall within one standard deviation of its mean of return 68 percent of the

---

[5] Symbolically:

$$\sigma^2 = \sum_s p(s)[r(s) - E(r)]^2$$

where $p(s)$ = the probability of each scenario s
      $r(s)$ = HPR in each scenario s
      $E(r)$ = expected return.

time, and within two standard deviations of its mean of return 95 percent of the time.

Consider the prior example again. This investment has an expected return of 14 percent and volatility of 10.83 percent. Most of the time (or, more precisely, 68 percent of the time), the investment's future returns can be expected to range between 3.17 percent and 24.83 percent. This constitutes one standard deviation, or the investment's 14 percent average expected return plus or minus its 10.83 percent volatility. Almost all of the time (or, more precisely, 95 percent of the time), the investment's returns can be expected to range between −7.66 percent and 35.66 percent, or within two standard deviations (i.e., the investment's 14 percent average expected return plus or minus 2 times its 10.83 percent volatility). Per Figure 1.1, the mean or average return is represented, as we might expect it to be, in the middle of a normal distribution. One standard deviation is represented by the middle-most portion of the distribution (i.e., the range created by the fields to the immediate right and left of the mean). Two standard deviations is represented by the middle-most portion of the distribution plus the next field to either side.

To measure the risk for a series of historical rates of returns, we can use the same measure as we did for expected returns, except that we use the historical holding period returns. In Table 1.1, the monthly

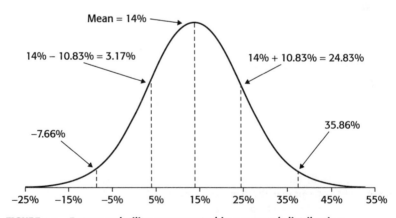

FIGURE 1.1 Return volatility, represented in a normal distribution.

volatility is 4.47 percent. The monthly volatility times the square root of 12 (the number of months in a year) will result in an annualized monthly volatility.

$$4.47\% \times \sqrt{12} = 15.49\%$$

The interested reader might want to check the detailed formulas in the footnote.[6]

One drawback of standard deviation or volatility is that it is not intuitive. A volatility of 15 percent is obviously higher than a volatility of 12 percent, but are these high or low figures? What exactly do they mean relative to one another? Since an investment's volatility is not a relative measurement, and not comparable to a benchmark, to another investment, or to an asset class, it is not very useful to investors without some context.

In the next section, we discuss return and volatility for major asset classes, which should provide appropriate context for volatilities. We suggest you start by considering two important asset classes: U.S. large cap equities and U.S. government bonds. At the end of December 2000, for example, the U.S. large cap index (S&P 500) had a volatility of 14.96 percent, while the U.S. government bond index had a volatility of 5.29 percent.

------

[6] The volatility or standard deviation for a series of historical rates of returns can be calculated as

$$\sigma = \sqrt{\sum_{i=1}^{n} [HPR_i - E(HPR)]^2 / n}$$

where
σ = the standard deviation of the series
HPR = the holding period return for period i
$E(HPR)$ = the arithmetic mean of the historical return series
n = the number of returns.

The annualized standard deviation can be computed as follows:

$$Annualized\ Standard\ Deviation = \sigma \times \sqrt{m}$$

where m = the number of periods per year.

For example, in Table 1.1, we have calculated a monthly standard deviation or volatility of 4.47% and $m = 12$ (12 months per year). The annualized volatility will be

$$4.47\% \times \sqrt{12} = 15.49\%$$

Return and Risk for Major Asset Classes

We laid the groundwork for a solid understanding of return and risk (return volatility). Now, we extend that understanding to include the return and risk characteristics of major asset classes. Presumably, no investor would want to commit a sizable chunk of a fortune to any investment without a good idea of its expected return and risk, but as we know, it is difficult, if not impossible, to reliably predict the future rate of return on any individual asset. Knowledge of the return and risk characteristics of major asset classes provides investors with a useful means of framing their expectations. Studies have shown that given a sufficiently long period of historical returns data (typically 20 to 30 years of monthly data), investors can estimate the long-term expected return and risk for an asset class. While investors cannot simply assign an expected return and risk to an individual stock or fund based upon the asset class under which it is classified, they at least know how assets in that class, on average, have behaved over time. In this section, we take a close look at the return and risk behavior of several popular asset classes over a 20-year period, 1981 to 2000. Table 1.2 presents the historical arithmetic mean of return and annualized volatility (risk) for six major asset classes.

Among the asset classes presented in Table 1.2, the U.S. Treasury bill is the safest investment as its volatility, or risk, of 0.77 percent is by

TABLE 1.2 The Return and Risk of Major Asset Classes
(20 Years: 1981–2000)

Major Asset Classes	Average Returns (Arithmetic Mean)	Annualized Volatility (Risk)
U.S. Government 3-Month T-Bills	6.43%	0.77%
U.S. Government Bonds	9.87%	5.29%
U.S. Large Cap Stocks (S&P 500 Index)	15.78%	14.96%
U.S. Small Cap Stocks (Russell 2000 Index)	13.17%	18.95%
International Stocks (MSCI Index)	10.58%	17.32%
U.S. Real Estate	9.65%	13.77%

Data Sources: DataStream, Morgan Stanley Capital International and Wilshire.

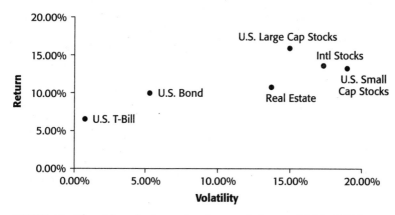

FIGURE 1.2   The risk and return of major asset classes (1981–2000).

far the lowest. The second safest is U.S. Treasury or government bonds, with a volatility of 5.29 percent. Both U.S. small cap stocks and international stocks are the two riskiest asset classes in terms of volatility.

We've all heard clichés like "No guts, no glory" and "High risk, high reward," and to a large extent, Figure 1.2 supports the idea of a risk–return tradeoff in the securities market. U.S. large cap and small cap and international common stocks, which are represented by the S&P 500 Index, Russell 2000 Index, and the MSCI EAFE Index, respectively, have shown greater volatility of returns than bonds, but have offered higher average returns to investor. However, the maxims do not always hold true. As is shown in the table and figure, the U.S. large cap stock asset class has the highest return of 15.78 percent, but its risk (14.96 percent) is lower than that of either small cap stocks or international stocks. Does this mean that the risk investors take on is not always paid off by corresponding return? This is one of the most interesting questions in empirical finance, and certainly worth thinking about. Much research has been done, but unfortunately, the evidence is still inconclusive.

Risk and Return for the Long Run

From Table 1.2, we can see that stocks generally offer higher return over bonds but with higher risk. The results come from a 20-year period, but just how reliable is past performance as a guide to what will

TABLE 1.3 Performance of Global Stock Index: 1921–1996

Index	Real Returns (Adjusted for Inflation)		Nominal Returns (Not Adjusted for Inflation)	
	Arithmetic Return	Risk	Arithmetic Return	Risk
U.S. Index	5.48%	15.83%	8.04%	16.19%
Non-U.S. Index (Survived Markets)	4.52%	10.02%	7.53%	12.17%

Source: Selected from Tables VI and VII in: Philippe Jorion and William Goetzmann, "Global Stock Markets in the Twentieth Century," *Journal of Finance*, June 1999, pp. 953–980, with permission.

happen in future? Do the international stock markets offer similar results over the long run? William Goetzmann, a financial economist at Yale, and Philippe Jorion, an economist at University of California, conducted extensive research that investigated the risk and returns of worldwide stock markets over a 76-year time period (1921 to 1996).[7] The summary of some of their research results is given in Table 1.3, and shows that over those 76 years, the U.S. stock market earned an arithmetic return of 5.48 percent (in real terms) and 8.04 percent (in nominal terms), respectively. For the same period, non-U.S. stock markets in aggregate earned an arithmetic return of 4.52 percent (in real terms) and 7.53 percent (in nominal terms), respectively. Since, in that time, many stock markets went out of business entirely, due to revolution, nationalization, or financial collapse, the study included only those that were in business for the entire 76-year study period. The results are significant in showing that even over a very long time period, U.S. stocks have offered a premium, in terms of return, over non-U.S. stocks. Again, consistent with the concept of a risk–return tradeoff, the return premium associated with U.S. stocks does not come without additional risk. The volatility of the U.S. stock market is 15.83 percent (in real terms) and 16.19 percent (in nominal terms), compared with the non-U.S. markets with volatility of 10.02 percent (in real terms) and 12.17 percent (in nominal terms), respectively. The

---

[7] See Philippe Jorion and William Goetzmann, "Global Stock Markets in the Twentieth Century," *Journal of Finance*, June 1999, pp. 953–980.

lower volatility of the non-U.S. index reflects the fact that the portfolio is spread over a greater number of markets and benefits from imperfect correlations across markets.

So far, we focused on "average" volatility over a given period of time. However, in considering the volatility of an asset class or an individual asset, it is important to understand how volatility has evolved over time. Another interesting research study by John Campbell and colleagues examined extensively the history of U.S. stocks from 1962 to 1997, at the level of firm, the industry, and the broad market.[8] They found that over this time period (1) firm-level volatility was on average much higher than that of the relevant industry or the broader market; and (2) while firm-level or stock-level volatility has trended upward, aggregate stock market and industry-level volatility have remained quite stable. This confirms what many of us have suspected: That the stock market has indeed become more volatile over the years. However, it is important to distinguish that this increased volatility has occurred at the firm level rather than the market or industry level. All the more reason to have an understanding of expected return and risk at the asset class level and asset level.

Alternative Risk and Return Measures

As we mentioned earlier, using volatility or standard deviation as a measure of risk can have its drawbacks. One drawback of volatility is that it is an absolute measure and cannot be compared to other investments or to a benchmark or to other asset classes. Therefore it is not very intuitive.

Beta, meanwhile, is a relative risk measurement, because it depicts an investment's volatility against a benchmark. For example, many institutions calculate betas for stock investments using the S&P 500 Index (market proxy) as the benchmark, which is set at 1.0. Beta is fairly easy to interpret: the higher an investment's beta, the more volatile it is relative to the benchmark. A beta that is greater than 1.0 means that

---

[8] See John Campbell, Martin Lettau, Burton Malkiel and Yexiao Xu, "Have Individual Stocks become More Volatile? An Empirical Exploration of Idiosyncratic Risk," *Journal of Finance,* February 2001.

the investment is more volatile than the benchmark index, and therefore the overall market. A beta of less than 1.0 means that the investment is less volatile than the index, and likewise the overall market.

To illustrate how beta works, an investment with a beta of 1.2 will move up 12 percent when the market (or S&P 500 Index) rises 10 percent. In good times, high betas imply high returns, since a beta above 1.0 amplifies the market's movements. Conversely, an investment with a beta of 0.9 should return 9 percent when the market or index rises 10 percent, but it should lose only 9 percent when the market drops by 10 percent. Therefore, a beta below 1.0 is desirable in down market conditions, since investors would not want a portfolio to magnify downward movements. Ideally, investors want an investment with a low beta and high returns, which is hard to get.

Beta, too, has its drawbacks. The biggest one is that it is really only useful when calculated against a relevant benchmark. If we compare our investment to an inappropriate benchmark, the beta will be meaningless. When considering the beta of any investment, investors should examine another statistic: R-squared. The lower the R-squared, the less reliable beta will be as a measurement of the investment's volatility. The closer to 100 the R-squared, the more meaningful the beta will be.

Drawdown is another interesting risk measurement and is defined as the largest percentage loss within an investment period, from the highest point to subsequent lowest point. Therefore, it is a measure of an asset's historical worst loss.

Consider the example in the Table 1.1 again. For the 2-year period, the drawdown happened in between September and November 2000, where the S&P 500 Index lost 13.38 percent, dropping from 1518 to 1315.

As investors, we can define our own risk tolerance level in terms of the percentage loss we are willing to bear. Once investors match their personal risk tolerance level to a maximum acceptable drawdown, they can establish a stop loss based on it. The drawdown is also one of most important criteria when evaluating and choosing an investment advisor. Many investment advisors provide such risk measurements in their performance table.

The *Sharpe ratio* is an important risk measurement because it enables investors to consider risk in the context of return. Volatility, beta, and drawdown focus on risk alone, but alas, this is just one side of the risk–return equation. The Sharpe ratio is a measure of the risk-adjusted return of an investment, and gives investors a means of measuring how well an investment rewards risk. Consider that we have two alternative investments to choose from. Investment 1 has a return of 20 percent and a volatility (risk) of 10 percent. Investment 2 has a return of 25 percent and volatility of 20 percent. The Sharpe ratio helps us to understand the return per unit of risk that investors can expect with each investment. Whichever has the higher Sharpe ratio can be construed as the better investment.

The Sharpe ratio was derived by Prof. William Sharpe, now of Stanford University, who was one of three economists who received the Nobel Prize in Economics in 1990 for their contributions to what is now called modern portfolio theory. The calculation is pretty straightforward. The ratio is calculated using standard deviation and excess return to determine reward per unit of risk. Basically, the ratio can be computed as follows:

Sharpe Ratio = (Annualized return − Risk-free return)/
Annualized volatility

Let's take the investment in Table 1.1 as an example. First, we subtract the annualized average monthly return of the risk free rate or 3-month Treasury bill (over a 24-month period) from the investment's annualized average monthly return. Let's assume that 3-month Treasury bill rate barely changed for the period, with a rate of 4.5 percent. This resulting excess return is then divided by the standard deviation of the investment's returns. That is

$$\textit{Sharpe Ratio} = \frac{4.72\% - 4.5\%}{15.49\%} = 0.014$$

In general, the higher the Sharpe ratio, the better the investment's risk-adjusted performance. For the two investments we mentioned at the beginning of this section, we can also compute the Sharpe ratios (assuming the risk free rate of 4.5 percent):

$$\textit{Sharpe Ratio for Investment 1} = \frac{20\% - 4.5\%}{10\%} = 1.55$$

$$\textit{Sharpe Ratio for Investment 2} = \frac{25\% - 4.5\%}{20\%} = 1.03$$

As we can see, Investment 1 offers higher Sharpe ratio or risk–reward ratio. Despite the fact that Investment 1 offers a lower return than Investment 2, it can be argued that it is a better investment because of its superior Sharpe ratio.

Value-at-Risk

Value-at-risk (VaR) is one of the most important risk analysis concepts to emerge in recent years. In the final section of this chapter, we introduce the concept of VaR by answering the following questions:

- Why do investors and financial institutions need VaR?
- What is VaR?
- How can we calculate VaR and what are its limitations?

Modern portfolio theory (MPT) tells investors that portfolio risk can be proxied by portfolio standard deviation. However, when investors attempt to apply standard deviation to their real-life financial situations, it tends to lose some of its meaning and appeal. First, investors think of risk intuitively in terms of dollars of loss, whereas standard deviation defines risk in terms of deviations either above or below expected return, which is hardly intuitive. Second, real-life portfolio deviations of a given amount below expected return do not occur with the same likelihood as deviations of the same amount above expected return—a result of positions in options and option-like instruments. In risk management, however, standard deviation assumes symmetry above and below expected return. In addition to demands from individual investors, financial institutions and corporate treasuries require a method for reporting their risk that is readily understandable by non-financial executives, regulators, and the investment public. They also require that this mechanism be scientifically rigorous. The answer to this problem is value-at-risk (VaR) analysis.

VaR is a number that expresses the maximum expected loss for a given time horizon, for a given confidence interval, and for a given position or portfolio of instruments, under normal market conditions, attributable to changes in the market price of financial instruments. To be more concrete, VaR is an amount, say $1,000, where the chance of losing more than $1,000 has some probability, say 5 in 100, over some future time interval, say 1 day. This is a probabilistic statement and, therefore, VaR is a statistical measure of risk exposure.

Sound complicated? Consider the following example. Suppose you are an investor with positions in stocks, mutual funds, and fixed income. You need an assessment of what you can expect to be the worst-case loss for the position overnight, with a 95 percent degree of confidence. The VaR number gives you this measurement. For example, your portfolio might have a value of $100,000 and a daily 95 percent confidence interval VaR of $2,000. This means that 19 times out of 20 your biggest loss should be less than $2,000. You can also express VaR as a percentage of assets, in this case, 2 percent.

VaR is also useful when comparing the riskiness of different portfolios. Let us now consider portfolios that are managed by two investors, Janet and Kevin. Each of them starts the year with $100,000. Janet makes a return of 20 percent, easily beating her return target of 15 percent. Kevin makes a return of 15 percent, which just meets his return target. Who is the better investor? It really depends. To make an accurate judgment, we have to compare the risk involved in these two portfolios. Let's say that Janet's average daily 95 percent VaR was $10,000 and Kevin's portfolio's average daily 95 percent VaR was $5,000. Since VaR is a measure of potential loss from market changes, it is convenient to denote the VaR as a risk capital. One way of calculating the return on risk capital for these two portfolios is as follows.

$$Janet's\ portfolio\ return\ on\ risk\ capital = \frac{\$100,000}{\$10,000} = 1,000\%$$

$$Kevin's\ portfolio\ return\ on\ risk\ capital = \frac{\$100,000}{\$5,000} = 2,000\%$$

From this example, we can easily see that Kevin is a better investor because he has used his risk capital more efficiently. Many people have invested their money with mutual funds or hedge funds. But just a few people know about the risk these money managers take. Most hedge fund and mutual funds simply do not report this kind of risk-adjusted number.

This is especially important when evaluating how closely a portfolio manager conformed to the stated risk tolerance of his or her fund. If the fund is advertising itself as a very low-risk investment vehicle suitable for retired workers, the average daily VaR as a percentage of assets is an important number to watch. On the institutional side, many financial institutions and corporate treasuries have used VaR for the same purpose. They need to have an idea of how their market exposures behave under normal market conditions. There are three popular approaches to calculate VaR.[9]

- Variance/covariance matrix (VCV), or parametric method.
- Monte Carlo (MC) simulation method
- Historical simulation method

The VCV method assumes that the portfolio's profitability is normally distributed and depends linearly upon applicable risk factors. The VCV's VaR is most closely tied to MPT, as the VaR is computed directly from the variance and covariance of applicable risk factors and is expressed as a multiple of the standard deviation of the portfolio's return. The advantage of using VCV is that the VaR result can be computed very quickly. However, the quality of the VaR estimate degrades with portfolios of complex financial instruments such as exotic options. Departures from normality in the portfolio return distribution also represent a problem for the VCV approach.

Monte Carlo simulation is a methodology for complex, nonlinear portfolios. It constructs a histogram of possible portfolio returns over a specific period. The returns are obtained from a given distribution of price and rate changes estimated with historical data. Monte Carlo VaR simulation is not limited by price changes observed in the sample period; therefore, it eliminates many of modeling constraints of other approach such as VCV. However, it usually involves many revaluations of the portfolio and is a very expensive and time-consuming approach.

To some extent, historical simulation is a simplification of the MC simulation method, where instead of randomly generating return paths or scenarios, paths are drawn directly from historical data. It expresses the distribution of portfolio returns as a bar chart or histogram of historical hypothetical returns. Each historical hypothetical return is calculated as that which would be earned on today's portfolio

---

[9] The discussion of three approaches to VaR calculations is adapted from http://www.gloriamundi.org.

if a day in the history of market prices were to repeat itself. Historical simulation is free from distributional assumptions, but requires the portfolio to be revalued daily in the historical sample period. Because the number of scenarios used is limited by the availability of historical data, the methodology may have greater convergence error than Monte Carlo VAR.

Many investors' portfolios consist of relatively simple financial instruments, such as stocks and mutual funds, so in general, the VCV methodology, which is characterized by both simplicity and calculation speed, is suitable for most investors. As such, we turn now to a detailed discussion on how to apply VCV methodology to calculate the VaR for a portfolio.

Let's assume that VaR is calculated on a daily basis (such VaR is called daily VaR or DVaR). If investors report VaR as the daily maximum loss of a portfolio P that can occur within a 95 percent confidence interval (or 95 days out of 100 days), the VaR can be calculated as follows.

$$VaR = 1.65\sigma_p W_p$$

where W_p = the portfolio value and σ_p = the standard deviation or volatility of the portfolio P. Please refer to the footnote below for a formula of calculating the portfolio standard deviation σ_p and further reference material.[10]

Now let's turn to a real life example. Assume that we are invested in the U.S. equity market (e.g., an S&P 500 Index fund) for 3 years from 1998 to 2000. The initial investment is $100,000. Based on daily market changes, we can easily compute daily profit and loss (P&L) for every trading day. Then we can use the S&P 500 trailing 3-month daily level

---

[10] Assume that there are N assets in the portfolio P, σ_i is the estimate for the standard deviation of asset i, w_i is the weight of the asset i and $\rho_{i,j}$ is the correlation between assets i and j, the portfolio deviation σ_p can be computed as follows:

$$\sigma_p = \sqrt{\sum_i w_i^2 \sigma_i^2 + 2 \sum_{i<j} \sum w_i w_j \sigma_i \sigma_j \rho_{i,j}}$$

where $i,j = 1, \ldots, N$

A complete technical discussion can be found from the following document, *RiskMetrics Technical Document*, 4th ed. by J.P. Morgan, 1996.

returns to compute the volatility of the portfolio, as given earlier in this chapter.

For example, for the trading day of April 1, 1998, we can use trailing 3-month daily S&P 500 returns data (from January 2, 1998, to March 31, 1998) to calculate a daily VaR, which is about $1,672. It shows that the portfolio's maximum expected loss of that trading day is about $1,672. Table 1.4 shows selected results for daily P&Ls and VaRs of the S&P 500 portfolio. From the calculation, we know that for most of trading days (644 out of 675), realized daily loss is less than corresponding VaR on same day. The percent of trading days with daily loss less than VaR is about 95.41 percent (this is consistent with predefined 95 percent confidence interval). In another words, the percent of trading days with a

TABLE 1.4   Sample Daily P&L and VaR for S&P 500 Portfolio and Statistics Summary

Sample Daily P&Ls and VaRs			
Trading Date	**Daily Profit & Loss**	**Daily VaR (95%)**	**Daily Loss Less Than VaR?**
Apr 1, 1998	$ 580	−$1,672	Yes
Apr 2, 1998	$1,656	−$1,687	Yes
Apr 3, 1998	$ 240	−$1,719	Yes
. . .			
Aug 30, 1998	−$1,473	−$2,240	Yes
Aug 31, 1998	−$6,763	−$2,176	No
. . .			
Apr 14, 2000	−$5,883	−$3,799	No
Apr 17, 2000	$3,164	−$4,098	Yes
. . .			
Dec 27, 2000	$1,042	−$3,390	Yes
Dec 28, 2000	$ 399	−$3,428	Yes
Dec 29, 2000	−$1,054	−$3,460	Yes

Summary:
  Number of trading days: 675
  Number of trading days when daily P&L is less than daily VaR: 644
  Percent of trading days when daily P&L is less than daily VaR: 95.41%

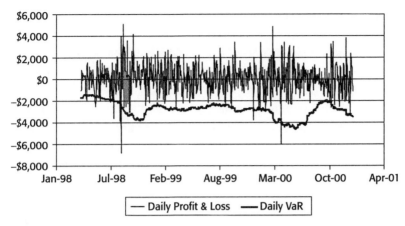

FIGURE 1.3 VaR backtest: S&P 500 portfolio daily realized profit and loss versus daily VaR. Daily VaR is calculated based on 3-month trailing daily S&P 500 level returns. Initial investment $100,000.

daily loss exceeding same day's VaR is less than 5 percent. This can also be seen in Figure 1.3, which draws the daily P&Ls and VaRs for all trading days of the period. The daily VaR is marked by a dark line and the daily P&L marked by a light line. In short, daily VaR is an appropriate risk measure of maximum expected loss under normal market conditions.

The VaR is only good for calculating an expected maximum loss under normal market conditions. Let's consider the previous example again. When a giant hedge fund, Long-Term Capital Management, collapsed in summer 1998 during the Russian debt crisis, the realized daily loss of our portfolio largely exceeded the expected VaR on August 31, 1998 (daily loss of $6,763 versus daily VaR of $2,176). This shows that VaR analysis is not necessarily a good risk analysis tool for abnormal market conditions. Stress testing or scenario analysis is a good complement to VaR. Stress testing is a measure of potential loss as a result of a plausible event in an abnormal market environment. In stress testing, investors will simulate various hypothetical evolutions of events in order to determine their effect on the value of a portfolio. There are two popular types of stress testing. The first is "matrix" based, in which someone can change several assumptions about variances and correlations of assets and see what happens to a portfolio value. The second is based on economic scenarios, in which an investor can simulate a portfolio's behavior during a known historical market event, such as the early 1970s oil crisis or 1987 stock market crash, and see the potential loss of a portfolio.

Whether in good times or bad, tools exist to help investors understand the risk of loss on a portfolio. By using both VaR and stress testing, investors should have a better idea of the potential loss of a portfolio under both normal and abnormal market conditions.

CHAPTER 2

The Benefits of Diversification

The benefits of diversification have been preached for thousands of years. We have all heard the expression, "Don't put all your eggs in one basket" and for most investors, it is common sense to take steps to protect assets from a single catastrophe. In the analogy of the chicken farmer, diversification is putting eggs in a few different baskets, reducing the chance that he will break all the eggs if the basket falls from his cart on the way to the market. But it is human nature to want more, and protecting ourselves on the downside may conflict with our desire to obtain more on the upside. For the farmer, if putting all the eggs in one basket allows him to get to the market quicker and be the first farmer to meet the demand of the consumers, it is very tempting to take the risk.

In this chapter, we will answer the questions:

- How can investors benefit from diversification without compromising the goal of high returns?

- Is diversification simply holding a reasonable number of different assets? Or is there such a thing as high quality diversification?

Modern portfolio theory quantifies the age-old adage on diversification and provides a framework for making good decisions regarding our overall portfolio. The theory is applicable to all investors, large and small, meaning everyone can reap rewards from diversification.

Asset Class Diversification

Deciding how much to invest in U.S. stocks, bonds, international stocks, cash, real estate, or some other asset class may appear to be a straightforward decision. If we look at the returns of the U.S. stock market for some limited period of time and compare them to the returns of other asset classes, it might seem obvious that we should put 100 percent of our money in U.S. stocks. For example, over the 5-year period 1994 to 1999, U.S. stocks soared in value an average of 22.26 percent (S&P 500, annualized monthly average return) each year. Let's assume we're back in January 2000, trying to decide how to invest the $100,000 we just won in the lottery. Looking at the prior 5 years, a $100,000 investment in the broad U.S. stock market (S&P 500) in January 1994 would have been worth $355,669 ("true" total return over the period) in December 1999. During the same period, U.S. bonds returned a mere 12.58 percent (Lehman Brothers Aggregated Bond Index, annualized monthly average return), and international stocks only 5.80 percent (MSCI EAFE, annualized monthly average return). We know from actual returns over that 5-year period, that in spite of the risk associated with putting all one's eggs in a single basket, investing all one's money in the U.S. stock market back in 1994 would have been a winning bet. Based on what we saw from 1994 to 1999, putting all of our lottery winnings into U.S. stocks might have seemed like a complete no-brainer, right?

Not really. . . . We have all seen the disclaimers: "Past performance is no guarantee of future results." There is a reason why we see a line like this almost every time we read about stock or fund returns— because it's true. We have already seen that in 2000 and 2001, the markets have behaved very differently than they had from 1994 to 1999. Back in January 2000, who could have known?

The fact is, we do not know what the markets are going to do. Just like the chicken farmer, the uncertainty of what may occur should concern us. We want to maximize gains, but not risk losing all we have if the market drops significantly. Divvying up money across asset classes, such as domestic stocks, international stocks, bonds, and cash, can greatly reduce the downside risk while still providing a good return. Why? Because each asset class has a somewhat different expected return and level of risk. A U.S. investor should consider international stocks the most risky asset, followed by domestic stocks, bonds, and then cash or money market securities. Further, asset classes, such as U.S. stocks and U.S. bonds, do not move in lockstep, therefore, it is rare that a disastrous market event will cause both stock and bond holdings to collapse.[1] Similarly, but to a lesser extent, U.S. stocks and international stocks do not rise and fall at the same time.

Research shows that over 90 percent of a portfolio's return variability can be explained by the portfolio's asset allocation.[2] Therefore, the first, and perhaps most important, investment decision for any investor is at the asset class level: How much money will be invested in each asset class? There are several important considerations before making this asset allocation decision. (We talk more about what mix of asset classes should comprise a portfolio in the next chapter.) Diversification does not end there. After determining an appropriate asset class mix, there are still significant benefits to diversifying within each asset class.

Diversifying Your Individual Assets

We have defined risk as the volatility an investment experiences. Low volatility, or small swings in the price of an asset, creates less uncertainty that the price of the asset will fall to zero, but also reduces the likelihood that the asset will multiply many times in value. But what causes these swings in the price of the asset? There are two types of influences on the price of a stock: Firm-specific influences and the market's influence.

Firm-Specific Risk

There are an infinite number of factors that contribute to a firm's ability to compete in the marketplace and earn profits. Management, product innovation, competition, and customer base all influence the

---

[1] An example of an exception is the Long Term Capital Management crisis of September 1998, during which both stock and bond prices fell quickly and dramatically.

[2] See Gary Brinson, Hood Randolph, and Gilbert Beebower, "Determinants of Porfolio Performance," *Financial Analysts Journal*, July/August, 1986. Gary Brinson, Brian Singer, and Gilbert Beebower, "Determinants of Portfolio Performance II: An Update," *Financial Analysts Journal*, May/June, 1991.

daily performance of a company. As any of these factors changes (e.g., the senior management team leaves the company, a competitor develops a "better" product, the firm loses a major client, etc.), the value of the company (the price of the stock) reflects the change. The uncertainty associated with these factors is collectively called firm-specific risk. For investors, it is difficult to monitor and impossible to control the many uncertainties a company faces, but fortunately, it is possible to reduce your exposure to these risks by diversifying.

Assuming, as we did before, that we have $100,000 in lottery winnings to invest, it is fairly intuitive that our portfolio will be riskier (i.e., have a greater degree of volatility) if invested 100 percent in Company ABC than if invested 50 percent in Company ABC and 50 percent in Company XYZ. A firm-specific event, such as the departure of key management personnel from Company ABC to a rival firm, could wipe out the value of our portfolio if we have all our money in just that company's stock. But the same event will impact the value of our portfolio to a lesser extent if we have spread our money equally across the stocks of both Companies ABC and XYZ. By investing in more than one stock, we have diversified away some of this firm-specific risk. In our example, investing in two stocks equally seems to reduce the impact of the firm-specific event on the portfolio. This suggests that if we continue to buy more stocks, we will continue to reduce the risk of our portfolio.

Ok, so how many stocks should an investor own?

Several research studies have been carried out to prove that investors benefit from a reduction in risk when they add stocks to their portfolios. The researchers have quantified the benefit each new stock adds to a portfolio, demonstrating that by adding randomly selected stocks one by one to a portfolio, portfolio risk continues to fall, though there comes a point where the incremental decrease in risk stops becoming meaningful. Professors Edwin Elton and Martin Gruber of New York University indicate that the marginal reduction in portfolio risk diminishes substantially once the investor has about 20 stocks in the portfolio.[3] Given every new stock purchase involves a transaction cost, there comes a point where the cost of including the additional

---

[3] See Edwin J. Elton and Martin J. Gruber, "Risk Reduction and Portfolio Size: An Analytical Solution," *Journal of Business*, Volume 50, Issue 4, October 1977.

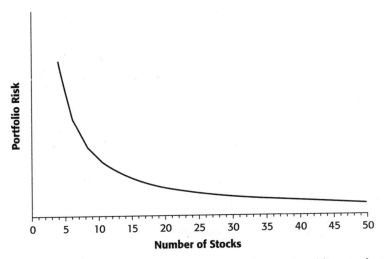

FIGURE 2.1 Firm-specific risk can be diversified away by adding stocks to a portfolio.

stock may outweigh any benefit. From this research, there is a strong argument that individual investors should hold about 15 to 20 stocks to diversify against firm-specific risk. The argument, however, is not universally accepted. Recent research by Professor John Campbell of Harvard suggests that even more assets are required to ensure adequate portfolio diversification.[4] Figure 2.1 shows that as the number of stocks in a portfolio increases, the portfolio's risk level falls. Firm-specific risk is diversified away as more stocks are included in the portfolio.

Market Risk

Every stock is affected to varying degrees by changes in the broad market. This uncertainty of what may or may not transpire in the market is called market risk. Changes in things such as macroeconomic conditions impact every company's ability to make profits and return capital to investors. Therefore, unlike firm-specific risk, market risk cannot be eliminated by owning many stocks. Figure 2.2 includes market risk and firm-specific risk. The graph suggests that regardless of the number of

---

[4] See John Campbell, Martin Lettau, Burton Malkiel, and Yexiao Xu, "Have Individual Stocks become More Volatile? An Empirical Exploration of Idiosyncratic Risk," *Journal of Finance*, February 2001.

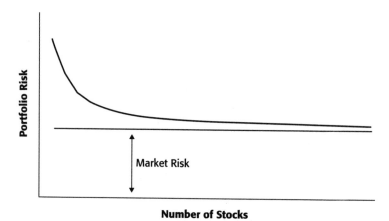

FIGURE 2.2 Market risk cannot be diversified away.

stocks in the portfolio, the impact of market's influence on the portfolio risk remains the same.

For example, during the Gulf War, oil and energy prices soared. Costs increased for businesses in many industries forcing them to raise prices for their products, while at the same time, consumers were faced directly with higher prices at the gas pump. The result: Most companies were impacted by a reduction in consumer demand, and those companies with a high percentage of their input costs tied to energy prices suffered greatly.

Investors could not have done much to protect the stocks in their portfolios from unforeseen events like the Gulf War. Because the reduction in consumer demand affected so many firms across industries around the world, we can hardly call the Gulf War a firm-specific event.

But not all of our stocks will react the same to market events. In many cases, a negative event for most stocks will actually spur a price increase in others. So owning stocks that behave differently under different market conditions will reduce the risk of our portfolio. Understanding the behavior of stocks relative to other stocks (correlation) is, therefore, a valuable bit of information. (As we show in the next chapter, allocating some money to assets other than stocks will provide some insulation against negative events in the stock market.)

No discussion on market risk would be complete without discussion of beta. As we know, the total return and total risk of a stock depends on the influence of the market and the influence of firm-specific events. A stock's sensitivity to the market is measured using beta. Simply put, the influence of the market can be written as:

Return of stock ABC associated with the market
= Beta × Return of the market

Using the example from Chapter 1, if a stock has a beta of 1.2, it is expected to return 12 percent when the market returns 10 percent. Conversely, should the market fall 10 percent, the stock is expected to lose 12 percent of its value.

Adding the second component, the impact of firm-specific events, we get the equation:

Return of stock ABC = Beta × Return of the market
+ Return associated with firm-specific events

This equation concisely describes the return of an individual stock. But as just discussed, firm-specific influences can be eliminated by owning 15 or 20 stocks in a portfolio. Therefore, the return on a portfolio might be more like the first equation.

Return of portfolio of stocks associated with the market
= Beta of the portfolio × Return of the market

With this equation, we can predict a portfolio with a beta of 1.4 to return 14 percent when the market returns 10 percent. But what if the portfolio actually returns 16 percent? In other words, the portfolio returns 2 percent above and beyond the 14 percent we predicted based on the portfolio's beta. This additional return is called alpha.[5] The

---

[5] The actual return of your portfolio less the return predicted by an equilibrium model. Alpha is the extent to which a portfolio's returns exceed or fall short of the market (S&P 500) portfolio returns.

$$\alpha = (\bar{r}_p - \bar{r}_f) - \beta(\bar{r}_M - \bar{r}_f)$$

where $\bar{r}_p$ = the historical average return of the portfolio
  $\bar{r}_f$ = the historical average return of the risk free rate
  $\bar{r}_M$ = the historical average return of the market S&P 500
  σ_p = the standard deviation of the portfolio
  β = the market sensitivity

higher the alpha, the better your portfolio has done in achieving "excess" returns. It is generally considered that the higher the alpha, the higher the "value added" to the portfolio by the portfolio manager. (Alpha is discussed in more detail in Chapter 9.)

Correlation

With a little commonsense, we can predict the relative behavior of certain stocks. Returning to the prior example, when oil prices soared during the Gulf War, alternative energy sources, such as nuclear power, became much more attractive, hence, the value of a firm engaged in generating nuclear power must have increased. With a little thought, we could come up with thousands of similar examples of companies or industries that do well when others suffer. In portfolio management, the relative co-movement of two assets is referred to as correlation.

The quality of the diversified portfolio depends on more than the number of stocks alone. Correlation among the individual stocks is also a key factor. Correlation means simultaneous co-movement of two assets. As the price of Company ABC's stock rises, what happens to the stock of Company XYZ? Assets that move in tandem are correlated; assets that move in opposite directions simultaneously are negatively correlated; and assets that move independently of one other are said to have no correlation. It is common for companies operating in the same industry to be highly correlated because market events tend to affect the companies in the same way; whereas companies in distinctly different businesses may react differently to market events and, therefore, evidence little or negative correlation.

Without any further explanation, we can see the importance of understanding correlation in building a diversified portfolio. If all of the stocks in our portfolio are highly correlated, they are moving together as changes occur in the market. Market influences (not firm-specific influences) that negatively affect one stock will likely affect all others that are highly correlated. In other words, owning a portfolio of highly correlated stocks is like holding one big stock. Figures 2.3, 2.4, and 2.5 show how highly correlated, uncorrelated, and negatively correlated asset pairs might behave, relative to market events.

The correlation coefficient is a statistic that is calculated by observing the price fluctuations of any two securities (or asset classes) over a

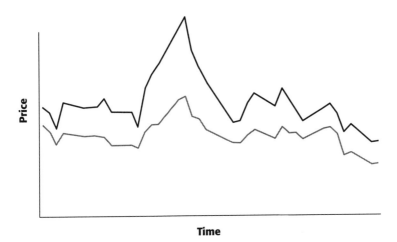

FIGURE 2.3 Behavior of two highly correlated stocks.

given period of time. Let's assume we currently own a single stock, Company ABC (a hi-tech company), and we are considering adding either Company DEF (a diversified consumer services company) or Company XYZ (an oil and gas company) to our portfolio. We have determined an expected return and risk level (standard deviation) for all three assets (Table 2.1). DEF and XYZ are very similar in terms of expected return and standard deviation, so without considering each asset's correlation with ABC, we might just flip a coin to determine which stock to include in our portfolio.

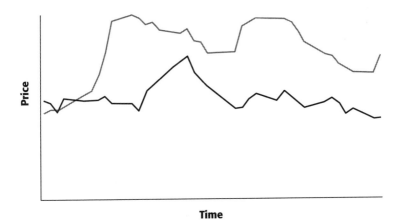

FIGURE 2.4 Behavior of two uncorrelated stocks.

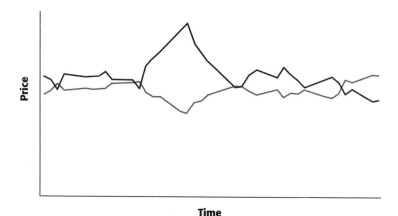

FIGURE 2.5 Behavior of two negatively correlated stocks.

To calculate the correlation coefficient for ABC and XYZ, we start by determining the covariance of ABC and XYZ or the tendency of ABC and XYZ to stray in tandem, either positively or negatively, from their average returns. First, we need to know the deviation from the average return for each security on a daily, weekly, monthly, or annual basis—we use daily returns. We then multiply the deviation of ABC by the deviation of XYZ each day, and sum the products of the deviations for the length of the period in analysis. By taking an average of the product of deviations, we come up with the covariance for ABC and XYZ. Covariance is an absolute number that, if positive, indicates that our two securities tend to move in the same direction at the same time. A negative covariance indicates that the two securities move in opposite directions most of the time.

A covariance statistic result can range from a single digit number (e.g., 5) to infinity (no limit), therefore, it is difficult to compare the covariance for ABC and XYZ with the covariance for ABC and DEF. So

TABLE 2.1 Expected Return and Volatility for Each Stock

	Expected Return (%)	Standard Deviation (%)
Company ABC	24	14
Company DEF	13	7.1
Company XYZ	12	6.8

TABLE 2.2 Portfolio of Companies ABC and DEF: Expected Return

	Weight ABC	Exp Return ABC (%)	+	Weight DEF	Exp Return DEF (%)	=	Exp Return Portfolio (%)
Mix 1	0.5	24.0		0.5	13.0		18.5
Mix 2	0.75	24.0		0.25	13.0		21.25
Mix 3	0.25	24.0		0.75	13.0		15.75

we use the correlation coefficient, which is taken from covariance and provides us with a number between −1 and 1, making it easier for us to compare co-movement between any pairs of assets. In other words, we are normalizing the covariance statistic. By dividing the covariance by the product obtained by multiplication of each standard deviation of each security, we will get a number between −1 and 1. A negative number indicates that the securities tend to move in opposite directions. A positive result indicates that the securities tend to move together. The closer to the extremes of −1 and 1, the stronger the tendency of the returns to move in opposite directions or to move together. A number somewhere in the middle (close to zero) suggests that there is no relationship in the movement of the securities.

So how can we use the correlation coefficient to improve the quality of diversification in our portfolio? In other words, how can we use our knowledge of correlation to increase expected returns without taking on more risk?

Let's examine a portfolio of Companies ABC and DEF in three scenarios, each of which has a different mix (this is called a weighted mix and is based on percent of the total) of the two stocks. The expected rate of return on the portfolio is simply the weighted (percent of the mix) average of the expected returns of the two assets (Table 2.2).

TABLE 2.3 Portfolio of ABC and XYZ: Expected Return

	Weight ABC	Exp Return ABC (%)	+	Weight XYZ	Exp Return XYZ (%)	=	Exp Return Portfolio (%)
Mix 1	0.5	24.0		0.5	12.0		18
Mix 2	0.75	24.0		0.25	12.0		21
Mix 3	0.25	24.0		0.75	12.0		15

TABLE 2.4 Portfolio of Companies ABC and DEF: Simple Weighted Average Risk

	Weight ABC	Std Dev ABC (%)	+	Weight DEF	Std Dev DEF (%)	=	Std Dev Portfolio (%)
Mix 1	0.5	14.0		0.5	7.1		10.55
Mix 2	0.75	14.0		0.25	7.1		12.28
Mix 3	0.25	14.0		0.75	7.1		8.83

Now let's examine a portfolio of Companies ABC and XYZ in three scenarios, each of which has a different weighted mix of the two stocks. Again, the expected rate of return on the portfolio is simply the weighted average of the expected returns of the two assets (see Table 2.3).

Based on the returns we are expecting for each asset, we see that the expected return of a given portfolio mix of ABC and DEF is roughly the same as the expected return of the corresponding portfolio mix of ABC and XYZ.

How about risk? Are the portfolios equally risky? Let's assume we calculate the risk of the portfolio by simply averaging the standard deviations of each asset (see Tables 2.4 and 2.5).

Taking a weighted average of the standard deviation indicates that the portfolio of ABC and DEF is about as risky as the portfolio of ABC and XYZ.

However, the risk of the two-asset portfolio is *not* simply the weighted average of the risk of each asset. The correlation coefficient plays an important role in the equation that determines the risk of the

TABLE 2.5 Portfolio of Companies ABC and XYZ: Simple Weighted Average Risk

	Weight ABC	Std Dev ABC (%)	+	Weight XYZ	Std Dev XYZ (%)	=	Std Dev Portfolio
Mix 1	0.5	14.0		0.5	6.8		10.4
Mix 2	0.75	14.0		0.25	6.8		12.20
Mix 3	0.25	14.0		0.75	6.8		8.60

TABLE 2.6 Portfolio of Companies ABC and DEF: Portfolio Risk

	Weight ABC	Std Deviation ABC (%)	Weight DEF	Std Deviation DEF (%)	Portfolio Correlation	Portfolio Variance (%)	Std Deviation (%)
Mix 1	0.5	14.0	0.5	7.1	0.93	107.82	10.38
Mix 2	0.75	14	0.25	7.1	0.93	148.07	12.17
Mix 3	0.25	14	0.75	7.1	0.93	75.27	8.68

portfolio. Refreshing our memory, Chapter 1 defines variance as the mathematical calculation of how far the returns of any asset, asset class, or portfolio swing from the average return. Standard deviation, the most commonly used expression of risk, is simply the square root of the variance. The calculation for the standard deviation of a portfolio, using Companies ABC and DEF for illustration, is as follows.

Portfolio risk or standard deviation of the portfolio
= Square root of [(Weight ABC × Standard deviation ABC)²
+ (Weight DEF × Standard deviation DEF)² + 2(Weight ABC
× Standard deviation ABC × Weight DEF
      × Standard deviation DEF) (Correlation coefficient)]

Applying this formula to our two-asset portfolios, we see a big impact on the portfolio risk (see Tables 2.6 and 2.7).

Examining mix 1 for each pair of stocks, we see that in the portfolio containing ABC and the highly correlated asset DEF, the total portfolio risk is 10.38 percent; whereas in the case of ABC and XYZ, total portfolio risk is only 7.53 percent, considerably less. The results

TABLE 2.7 Portfolio of Companies ABC and XYZ: Portfolio Risk

	Weight ABC	Std Deviation ABC (%)	Weight XYZ	Std Deviation XYZ	Portfolio Correlation	Portfolio Variance	Std Deviation (%)
Mix 1	0.5	14.0	0.5	6.8	−0.08	56.75	7.53
Mix 2	0.75	14.0	0.25	6.8	−0.08	110.28	10.50
Mix 3	0.25	14.0	0.75	6.8	−0.08	35.40	5.95

Calculating Volatility and Correlation Statistics on Our Own

Let's walk through an example. We will calculate the volatilities of GE and Exxon and then determine how the stocks are correlated. First stop is *Moneycentral.com* to obtain the necessary time-series data. In the "Investing" section of the site, we follow the "Stocks" link to gather information on individual companies. Entering "GE" into the ticker field, clicking "Go" and then clicking "Charts," we get an interactive chart applet. Within the chart applet, there is a menu for various functions. The "Period" option contains a "Custom" feature that allows us to select the beginning and ending dates for the time series we are interested in, as well as the frequency of the data we are looking for (daily, weekly, monthly, or annually). After choosing the appropriate period, we utilize the "Export Data" feature, which is under the "File" option (in our example, we use daily prices for a 1-year period). When we click this, an Excel spreadsheet is automatically opened and a column of data containing the closing price for each market day over the requested time period is displayed. (We can delete the columns indicating high, low, and volume. Also, it is important to sort the data so that the earliest date in the time series is at the top of the column and there are no spaces between each date in the time series).

After saving this column of data to a new spreadsheet, we can repeat the steps to obtain the same time series for another stock (in our example, Exxon: XOM). Then, for each stock, we need to create a return series—that is, the return between each period (in our case each day). A simple Excel formula will do the trick: "=(A23-A22)/A22", where A23 and A22 represent cells for consecutive dates in our time series.

The next step is to calculate the volatility of each stock. In an empty cell below the column of returns for each stock, we enter the formula: "=STDEV(A1:A252)*SQRT(252)", where A1 and A252 represent the first and last return numbers in our series, and SQRT(252) serves to annualize the volatility statistic (refer to Chapter 1 for formulas used to calculate volatility or risk for different periods). For correlation, we choose an empty cell and enter

prove that diversification provides real benefit in terms of reducing portfolio risk whenever the assets in the portfolio are not perfectly correlated, regardless of the relative weights of each asset. Anything less than perfect correlation adds to our quality of diversification, and as we move from positive correlation to negative, the benefits increase further.

The results stress that correlation is the most important element

"CORREL(A1:A252, B1:B252)", where A1:A252 and B1:B252 represent the return series for our two stocks.

See Table 2.8 for the data and resulting statistics. Plugging these volatility and correlation statistics into the following formula, we can determine the riskiness of our portfolio.

Portfolio risk or standard deviation of the portfolio
= Square root of [(Weight GE $\times$ Standard deviation GE)^2
+ (Weight XOM $\times$ Standard deviation XOM)^2 + 2(Weight GE $\times$ Standard deviation GE
$\times$ Weight XOM $\times$ Standard deviation XOM) (Correlation coefficient)]

Assuming a portfolio with equal weights of GE and XOM, we calculate:

Portfolio risk = Square root of [(0.50 $\times$ 0.41)^2 + (0.50 $\times$ 0.24)^2
+ 2(0.50 $\times$ 0.41 $\times$ 0.50 $\times$ 0.24) (0.12)] = 0.25

For a portfolio with N assets, the portfolio risk is a sum of each asset's standard deviation multiplied by its percentage weight in the portfolio, squared, plus, for every possible pair of assets in the portfolio, a term that accounts for the correlation among the asset pair.

Portfolio Risk or Standard Deviation of the Portfolio = Square root of [(Weight A
$\times$ Standard deviation A)^2 + (Weight B $\times$ Standard deviation B)^2 + . . .
(Weight N $\times$ Standard deviation N)^2 + 2(Weight A $\times$ Standard deviation A
$\times$ Weight B $\times$ Standard deviation B) (Correlation coefficient A, B)
+ . . . 2(Weight A $\times$ Standard deviation A $\times$ Weight N
$\times$ Standard deviation N) (Correlation coefficient A, N)] . . .

(You may also wish to refer to the formula provided in footnote 10 of Chapter 1.)

of achieving quality of diversification. Quantity of assets is essential to minimize firm-specific risk, but low correlation leads to quality. Employing this knowledge, we can pull together the information on our current holdings (or the assets we are considering for investment) and generate portfolio risk numbers. All we need is data on each asset's volatility and correlation with other assets in the portfolio. Provided that we have access to historical price data for individual assets, these

TABLE 2.8 Volatility and Correlation for GE and XOM for 9/18/2000–9/17/2001

	General Electric Company (GE)	
Date	**Daily Closing Price**	**Daily Returns (%)**
9/18/2000	57.5	
9/19/2000	57	−0.87
9/20/2000	56.625	−0.66
9/21/2000	56.25	−0.66
9/22/2000	57.313	1.89
9/25/2000	58.063	1.31
. . .	. . .	. . .
8/29/2001	40.61	−1.50
8/30/2001	40.2	−1.01
8/31/2001	40.9	1.74
9/4/2001	40.83	−0.17
9/5/2001	41.7	2.13
9/6/2001	40.5	−2.88
9/7/2001	39.66	−2.07
9/10/2001	39.35	−0.78
9/17/2001	35.15	−10.67
	Annualized Standard Deviation	41.08

(continued)

volatility and correlation statistics can be generated on a computer spreadsheet program. Excel is used in the example in the above box and Table 2.8.

In Chapter 3 and in Chapter 8, we build on the concept of correlation and introduce mean-variance optimization—the process by which an investor can maximize expected returns while minimizing risk.

TABLE 2.8   Volatility and Correlation for GE and XOM for 9/18/2000–9/17/2001 (*Continued*)

Date	EXXON Corporation (XOM)	
	Daily Closing Price	**Daily Returns (%)**
9/18/2000	44.82	
9/19/2000	44	−1.83
9/20/2000	43.25	−1.70
9/21/2000	43.156	−0.22
9/22/2000	43.25	0.22
9/25/2000	42.93	−0.74
. . .	. . .	. . .
8/29/2001	40.38	−0.32
8/30/2001	40.15	−0.57
8/31/2001	40.15	0.00
9/4/2001	40.75	1.49
9/5/2001	41.22	1.15
9/6/2001	40.9	−0.78
9/7/2001	40.9	0.00
9/10/2001	41.24	0.83
9/17/2001	40.15	−2.6
	Annualized Standard Deviation	23.59
	Correlation GE:XOM	0.12

Using Asset Allocation

A sset allocation is the process of dividing a portfolio among asset classes (such as U.S. stocks, foreign stocks, bonds, cash, etc.). It is a high-level plan that is typically developed before any investments are made. We all invest to reach certain financial goals in our life, whether for retirement, children's college education, a dream house, or other things. A properly designed asset allocation plan will significantly increase our chances of investment success, and therefore increase our chances of achieving our goals. This chapter provides answers to the following questions:

- Why is asset allocation important?
- How do we properly design an asset allocation plan?

Risk and Return Revisited

In Chapter 2, we learned that a portfolio's historical total return is not the sole criteria by which to judge its performance. We also need to consider the portfolio's risk over a given period, and one of the easiest and most common ways to measure a portfolio's risk is by calculating the standard deviation, or volatility, of the portfolio's historical returns. Take the two portfolios in Table 3.1 for example. "Conservative Joe's" portfolio consists of fairly conservative allocations, such as

TABLE 3.1   Portfolio Risk/Return Comparison

Portfolio Name	Weight of US Stocks[1]	Weight of US Bonds[2]	Portfolio Return[3]	Portfolio Volatility[3]	Portfolio Sharpe Ratio[4]
Conservative Joe	20%	80%	9.46%	4.84%	1.02
Fast Eddie	80%	20%	15.30%	11.25%	0.96

[1] US Stocks is represented by Wilshire 5000 Index.
[2] US Bonds is represented by Lehman Brothers Aggregated Bond Index.
[3] Portfolio returns and risks are annualized from 1990 to 1999.
[4] A risk free rate of 4.5% annually is used in Sharpe ratio calculation.

20 percent in U.S. stocks and 80 percent in U.S. bonds; "Fast Eddie's" portfolio, on the other hand, is more suitable for an aggressive investor, with 80 percent in U.S. stocks and 20 percent in U.S. bonds.

By looking at total return from the beginning of 1990 to the end of 1999, we see that "Fast Eddie" outperformed "Conservative Joe" by an additional 5.84 percent every year. On the surface, it looks like "Fast Eddie" has a much better allocation than "Conservative Joe"; so one might think that all investors should allocate their assets to match the "Fast Eddie" mix. Right? Not so fast! We have not taken risk into consideration yet.

From 1990 to 1999, "Fast Eddie" had an annualized volatility of 11.25 percent. As we recall from Chapter 2, an annualized volatility of 11.25 percent means there will be a 95 percent chance in the future that "Fast Eddie" will earn an annual return between −7.2 percent (15.30% − 2 ∗ 11.25%), and 37.8 percent (15.30% + 2 ∗ 11.25%). "Conservative Joe," on the other hand, had an annualized volatility of 4.84 percent during the same period—significantly less than that of "Fast Eddie." A more proper measurement of two portfolios' performance is the Sharpe ratio, which takes risk into consideration. From Table 3.1, we see that "Conservative Joe" outperformed "Fast Eddie" in terms of Sharpe ratio, or risk-adjusted return. This means that an investor who held "Conservative Joe" would have gotten more return per every unit of risk than an investor holding "Fast Eddie." A more aggressive investor holding a portfolio with a "Fast Eddie" allocation seeks higher return by taking on higher risk, but needs to be prepared to lose more money in a down market than someone with a "Conservative Joe" allocation. Indeed, with our example, "Fast Eddie" had an annual return

TABLE 3.2   Hypothetical Asset Class Parameters

Asset Class Name	Annual Return	Annual Volatility
Asset Class A	10%	10%
Asset Class B	10%	10%
Asset Class C	10%	10%

Correlation	Asset Class A	Asset Class B	Asset Class C
Asset Class A	1.0	0.5	−0.5
Asset Class B	0.5	1.0	−0.5
Asset Class C	−0.5	−0.5	1.0

of −8.6 percent in year 2000, while "Conservative Joe" had a return of +6.2 percent in the same year.

Importance of Diversification

To control the risk of a portfolio, we learned in Chapter 2 the importance of diversification. Correlation plays a key role in diversification. Referring to Table 3.2, let's assume hypothetically that there exist three asset classes: A, B, and C, all with the same annualized return of 10 percent and annualized volatility of 10 percent. The correlations among these asset classes are also shown in Table 3.2.

In Table 3.3, we compare four portfolios made up of various allocations across these asset classes. If we follow Portfolio 1's allocation of

TABLE 3.3   The Importance of Diversification

	% of A	% of B	% of C	Return	Volatility	Sharpe Ratio[1]
Portfolio #1	100%	—	—	10%	10%	0.55
Portfolio #2	50%	50%	—	10%	8.6%	0.64
Portfolio #3	50%	—	50%	10%	5%	1.10
Portfolio #4	33%	33%	33%	10%	4.7%	1.17

[1] In this hypothetical example, risk free rate is assumed to be 4.5% in Sharpe ratio calculation.

100 percent asset class A, our portfolio will generate an annualized return of 10 percent and the corresponding risk will be 10 percent. However, if we allocate our portfolio with half of A and half of B, as in Portfolio 2, our annualized return will be the same as before, but the risk we take on will be reduced. (For risk calculations with correlation, please refer to Chapter 2.) This means that the Sharpe ratio for Portfolio 2 will be higher, as we generate more return per unit of risk. Even better, if we follow Portfolio 3, which has half of A and half of C, the annualized return for our portfolio will still be 10 percent, but volatility will be significantly reduced to 5 percent. And finally, if we hold each asset classes A, B, and C in equal weight, as in Portfolio 4, we will still achieve the same annualized return, but the resulting volatility will be the lowest among the four portfolio allocations presented in Table 3.3. Clearly, in this hypothetical example, Portfolio 4's allocation is most desirable.

This brings us to the concept of asset allocation—investing simultaneously in multiple asset classes. The purpose of asset allocation, as illustrated in our previous hypothetical example, is to control and reduce the risk of a portfolio through diversification. Returning to an example, if the farmer puts his eggs into different baskets, he knows that he will not lose all of his eggs should one of those baskets fall from his cart on the way to the market. Similarly, by investing in different asset classes such as U.S. equity, international equity, and bonds, we can sleep comfortably knowing that we have reduced our downside risk should the markets turn bad.

Historically, a period of high interest rates is very unfavorable to fixed income investments, yet the stock market is not nearly as sensitive to interest rate movements. We can also diversify our assets abroad. By holding international equity, we can protect ourselves against a down market in the United States and reap the potential benefits of high growth emerging markets overseas. By holding different asset classes at once, we can ensure that our portfolio will be less sensitive to rapidly changing market conditions, reduce the potential for sudden huge losses, and, as a result, sleep well at night.

Of course, it is tempting to ask: Isn't it better to invest all of the money in stocks when the market is favorable to stocks, and then switch all of the money to bonds when the market becomes favorable to bonds? Why do we have to invest in both U.S. equity and international equity when the market currently favors U.S. stocks, for example? The answer is that we cannot consistently predict market movements. U.S. stocks might outperform other asset classes currently, but it is impossible to predict whether or not they will continue to do so. Similarly, it is difficult to predict which other asset classes will perform stronger in the future. Therefore, many uncertainties, or risks, will always exist. By investing in multiple asset classes simultaneously, we forego the potential to generate the huge returns we might achieve by investing in a single asset class, but at the same time, take on less risk. So the question becomes: Is it worthwhile giving up huge potential gains for the sake of reducing risk and avoiding a huge potential loss? For example, are we willing to invest in a risky asset class that can potentially return 50 percent of our investment, but can also result in a 50 percent loss on our investment? If we cannot afford to take on the risk of potentially losing 50 percent of our investment, we should take on less risky investments with less expected returns.

The Impact of the Asset Allocation Decision

In 1986, G. Brinson, L. Hood, and G. Beebower[1] conducted extensive research on 91 large pension funds to see which investment decisions had the biggest impact on funds' returns and volatilities. Three investment decisions were studied: Investment policy, market timing, and security selection. Investment policy is the asset allocation defined to meet a fund's financial objective. For example, allocating a fund's holding to 60 percent U.S. equity, 30 percent U.S. bonds, and 10 percent cash is one investment policy. (We discuss more on how to choose an asset allocation that fits your financial objective later in this chapter and in the next chapter). Market timing is the strategy to overweight or underweight certain asset classes during certain periods in an effort to enhance returns or reduce risks. For example, if a manager believes the stock market might not perform well in the next year or so, he or she can reduce the weight in U.S. equity, and increase the weight in U.S. bonds and cash. The third and final investment decision, security selection, is the individual assets a manager selects in each asset class.

---

[1] Gary P. Brinson, L. Randolph Hood, and Gilbert L. Beebower, "Determinants of Portfolio Performance," *Financial Analyst Journal*, January–February 1995.

For example, a manager might choose Wal-Mart (Ticker: WMT) and Microsoft (Ticker: MSFT) to represent the U.S. equity portion of the asset allocation plan.

By regressing historical returns of these 91 funds from 1974 to 1984 against corresponding investment decision return series, Brinson, Hood, and Beebower found that, on average, 93.6 percent of the return variability of these portfolios can be explained by asset allocation. Market timing only adds 4.2 percent to the total explanation power. Security selection adds 1.7 percent to the total explanation power. This means the return and volatility behavior of a portfolio can be almost entirely explained by the asset allocation plan on which it is based. Therefore, asset allocation is critical in our investment decisions and should not be taken lightly.

So how effective is market timing? Brinson, Hood, and Beebower found that market timing is actually detrimental to overall portfolio returns. These 91 managers, on average, lost about 0.66 percent of return annually due to market timing. Of the pension funds studied, the best manager added 0.25 percent return annually to his fund by timing the market. The worst manager lost 2.68 percent annually trying to time the market. This shows that it is still possible to add value by timing the market, but the odds are against you.

The effect of security selection is slightly better than market timing. The managers, on average, lost about 0.36 percent of return annually due to individual asset selection. The best security selection manager added 3.6 percent return annually to his fund. The worst security selection manager lost 2.9 percent return annually. A similar research study was conducted again in 1991, and the results were consistent. In Chapters 5, 6, and 7, we explain several methods to help you select better stocks and mutual funds.

Creating an Asset Allocation to Fit Our Needs

Now that we understand the importance of asset allocation, let's see how we can draft an asset allocation plan that fits our needs. Before we can determine how much to put in each asset class, we must first define which asset classes to include in our asset allocation plan. There are two important factors to consider when choosing asset classes. First, the asset classes should be as mutually exclusive as possible, meaning that they should have relatively low correlations between each other. For example, asset classes for stocks and bonds are normally included simultaneously in asset allocation policies because the correlation between stocks and bonds is usually very low. The objective with asset allocation is diversification. If two asset classes have a high correlation between them, they should then have very different rates of return and volatility for both to be included in an asset allocation plan. If two asset classes are too similar, it defeats the purpose of diversification and asset allocation. The second important factor in choosing asset classes is that the asset classes chosen should cover as much of the broad capital market as possible. This allows an investor to maximize the benefit of diversification.

For example, a fairly complete asset allocation plan should not only include various types of domestic and international stocks and bonds, but also other asset classes, such as mortgage and real estate. On the other hand, we must also strike a balance between theory and practice. It may not be practical for a portfolio of limited wealth to include so many finely defined asset classes because the cost of analysis and the cost of transactions very likely will not justify the additional potential gains. We demonstrate this later in this chapter. Table 3.4 lists five major asset classes that should satisfy a majority of individual investors.

The asset class set presented in Table 3.4 is a relatively simple pool of asset classes that individual investors can readily have access to without incurring much in the way of research cost or transaction cost. United States large cap stocks are commonly defined as stocks traded in the United States that have a market capitalization above $5 billion. This asset class consists of stocks issued by well-established United States firms. These stocks are relatively less risky, thus the U.S. large cap stock asset class is expected to generate less return than the more volatile asset classes. In this book, U.S. large cap stocks are represented by the Standard & Poor 500 Index. United States small cap stocks are commonly defined as stocks traded in the United States that have a market capitalization under $1 billion. These stocks are commonly issued by younger firms in the rapid growth stage of the business cycle. Among these stocks, there exists the possibility of huge upside potential gains, but at the same time, there is an increased chance of bankruptcy relative to more established firms. Due to the volatile nature of

TABLE 3.4   Financial Structure of The Five Asset Classes

Asset Class Name	Annual Return	Annual Volatility
U.S. Large Cap Stocks[1]	13.97%	15.65%
U.S. Small Cap Stocks[2]	14.75%	19.57%
International Stocks[3]	13.16%	17.09%
U.S. Bonds[4]	9.19%	6.24%
U.S. Cash[5]	6.65%	0.77%

Correlation	U.S. Large Cap Stocks	U.S. Small Cap Stocks	International Stocks	U.S. Bonds	U.S. Cash
U.S. Large Cap Stocks	1.0	0.80	0.51	0.32	−0.08
U.S. Small Cap Stocks	0.80	1.0	0.46	0.20	−0.06
International Stocks	0.51	0.46	1.0	0.19	−0.06
U.S. Bonds	0.32	−0.20	0.19	1.0	0.13
U.S. Cash	−0.08	−0.06	−0.06	0.13	1.0

[1] U.S. Large Cap Stocks uses S&P 500 Index.
[2] U.S. Small Cap Stocks uses Russell 2000 Index.
[3] International Stocks uses MSCI EAFE Index.
[4] U.S. Bonds uses Lehman Brothers Aggregated Bond Index.
[5] U.S. Cash uses the U.S. 30-day Treasury Bill. All data are calculated from 1976 to the end of 2000 except for U.S. Small Cap Stocks, which has the earliest data on January 1979.

these companies, the expected return for this asset class also is relatively high. In this book, U.S. small cap stocks are represented by the Russell 2000 Index. Investors can invest in these two asset classes directly, by purchasing stocks in the equity market, or indirectly, by purchasing shares of equity mutual funds. Chapter 5 discusses in detail how to select mutual funds, and Chapter 6 explains several techniques on how to select individual stocks. The third asset class in our simple asset allocation plan is international equity. This asset class consists of representative stocks that are traded outside of the United States. Foreign stock markets are expected to behave differently from the U.S. stock market because of the economic, political, and regulatory differences. It is commonly perceived that international equities are more volatile than their U.S. counterparts, thus the return expected on them is also higher. In this book, the international equity asset class is represented by the MSCI EAFE Index. It might not be economically feasible for individual investors based in the United States to invest directly in foreign equity markets. However, there are many international equity mutual funds to choose from. There are two nonequity asset classes in our asset allocation plan: U.S. bonds and U.S. cash. United States bonds are debt securities issued by governments or corporations. They are fixed income securities because they yield interest. United States bonds are generally safer than equities issued by the same firm because bondholders have priority claim over assets in the case of bankruptcy. The U.S. bonds asset class in this book is represented by the Lehman Brothers Aggregated Bond Index. Investors can invest in this asset class by either purchasing bonds directly, or purchasing bond mutual funds. The U.S. cash asset class consists of short-term government Treasury notes. Because they are backed by the United States government, short-term treasuries are considered extremely safe, or risk free.

Large cap stocks behave differently from small cap stocks despite their relatively high correlation. Small cap stocks are historically more volatile than large cap stocks, but they also generate higher returns. That notion has been challenged recently however, because small cap stocks have been significantly under-performing large cap stocks as a whole in the 1990s. As shown in Figure 3.1, U.S. small cap stocks significantly outpaced U.S. large cap stocks in the early 1980s. The two asset classes broke even in the early 1990s, and in recent years, large cap stocks have outpaced small cap stocks. In the near future, both small cap stocks and large cap stocks will likely revert to their long-term average. If this happens, small cap stocks will again outperform large cap stocks, and the cycle will continue.

Many investors should also allocate a certain percentage of their portfolio to international stocks. International investments can serve as protections against a U.S. down market. For example, while the S&P 500 Index lost 9 percent in Year 2000, China's Shanghai Composite Index jumped 51.7 percent. Historically, international stocks as a whole have under-performed U.S. stocks. However, due to the low correlation between international stocks and U.S. stocks, international stocks should be included in allocation plans to hedge against the

*Log scale for wealth is used for clearer illustration; U.S. Large Cap Stocks uses
S&P 500 Index; U.S. Small Cap Stocks uses Russell 2000 Index; Data from 1979
(Russell 2000 earliest available data) to 2000.

FIGURE 3.1   Growth of U.S. large cap stocks versus U.S small cap stocks.

U.S. equity market. Figure 3.2 shows the historical performance of
U.S. stocks against international stocks. We use the Wilshire 5000 to
represent the overall U.S. equity market.

Figure 3.2 clearly shows the advantage of owning international
stocks during the U.S. downmarket of 1987. Unfortunately, as studies
have shown, the globalization of economies and capital markets in
recent years has resulted in increasing correlation among world markets. We will talk more about this later in the chapter.

Bond asset class returns, in general, are lower than equity asset
class returns, but they also have much less volatility. Bonds are most
suitable for people who rely on incomes from investments, as opposed
to capital appreciation. For example, retired people or near-retirement
people should allocate a greater portion of their portfolio to bonds
as opposed to stocks, because they cannot afford to take on the high
volatility of the equity market, and need a steady stream of income.
The bond and stock markets also have relatively low correlation historically. Figure 3.3 shows the performance of both U.S. stocks and U.S.
bonds from 1979 to 1999.

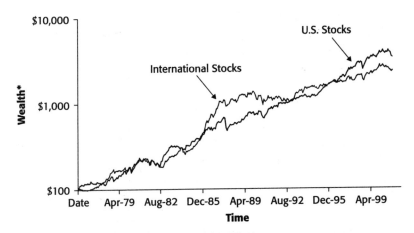

*Log scale for wealth is used for clearer illustration.
U.S. Stocks uses Wilshire 5000 Index. International Stocks uses MSCI EAFE Index.
Data presents 25-year performance from 1976 to 2000.

FIGURE 3.2 Growth of U.S. stocks versus international stocks.

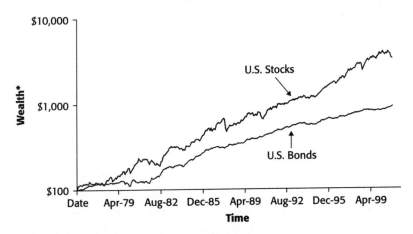

*Log scale for wealth is used for clearer illustration.
U.S. Stocks uses Wilshire 5000 Index. U.S. Bonds uses Lehman Brothers Aggregated
Bond Index. Data presents 25-year performance from 1976 to 2000.

FIGURE 3.3 Growth of U.S. stocks versus U.S. bonds.

If you are a high net-worth individual or a sophisticated investor, you can explore more opportunities by choosing a more detailed breakdown of asset classes than the ones just mentioned. Table 3.5 lists ten asset classes to consider when designing an asset allocation plan. The international equities asset class is broken into two parts: developed markets and emerging markets. (In the five-asset class allocation plan developed previously, the international equities asset class benchmark index is for developed markets.) The U.S. bond asset class is broken into three parts: government and corporate, municipal, and high yield. Two additional asset classes are included: U.S. mortgage and U.S. real estate.

A Few Words on International Diversification

International diversification has been a hotly debated topic of late. The original idea behind investing overseas was that foreign investments could serve as a cushion against declines in the U.S. market. However, research has shown that the correlation between the U.S. stock and international stock markets has risen considerably in recent years. Figure 3.4 shows the changes of correlation between the U.S. stock market and foreign developed market from 1973 to 2000.

As we can see, the correlation figure between the two markets has been very volatile historically. In 1979, the correlation between U.S. stock market and foreign developed market went below 0.2, and it was again close to that level as recently as 1993. Since then, however, the correlation rose steadily to about 0.8 by the end of 2000. This rise in correlation can be partially explained by the globalization of world economies. Emerging markets should be less correlated with the U.S. market than developed markets are with the U.S. market. Figure 3.5 shows the correlation change between the U.S. stock market and foreign emerging stock market between 1991 and 2000.

Again, we can see that the correlation between the U.S. stock market and foreign emerging market has also been rising steadily in recent years. In 1994, correlation between the two markets was approximately 0.2—its lowest level during the 10-year period. Since then, the correlation rose steadily to approximately 0.7 at the end of 2000. While lower than the correlation between the U.S. stock market and foreign developed market, it is still high by historical standards.

So how useful is international diversification? There have been no

TABLE 3.5 Financial Structure of The Ten Asset Classes

Code	Asset Class Name	Annual Return	Annual Volatility
A	U.S. Large Cap Stocks[1]	13.97%	15.65%
B	U.S. Small Cap Stocks[2]	14.75%	19.57%
C	International Developed Market[3]	13.49%	16.49%
D	International Emerging Market[4]	12.15%	23.71%
E	U.S. Government & Corporate Bonds[5]	9.07%	6.19%
F	U.S. Municipal Bonds[6]	8.31%	8.19%
G	U.S. High Yield Bonds[7]	10.07%	7.01%
H	U.S Mortgage[8]	9.42%	7.76%
I	U.S. Real Estate[9]	13.32%	16.23%
J	U.S. Cash[10]	6.65%	0.77%

Correlation	A	B	C	D	E	F	G	H	I	J
A	1.00	0.80	0.52	0.46	0.32	0.32	0.46	0.29	0.60	−0.08
B	0.80	1.00	0.50	0.50	0.20	0.24	0.52	0.19	0.71	−0.06
C	0.52	0.50	1.00	0.46	0.19	0.21	0.30	0.17	0.36	−0.07
D	0.46	0.50	0.46	1.00	−0.07	0.06	0.37	−0.02	0.32	−0.06
E	0.32	0.20	0.19	−0.07	1.00	0.76	0.41	0.92	0.27	0.07
F	0.32	0.24	0.21	0.06	0.76	1.00	0.42	0.78	0.29	−0.01
G	0.46	0.52	0.30	0.37	0.41	0.42	1.00	0.43	0.51	−0.03
H	0.29	0.19	0.17	−0.02	0.92	0.78	0.43	1.00	0.22	0.06
I	0.60	0.71	0.36	0.32	0.27	0.29	0.51	0.22	1.00	0.01
J	−0.08	−0.06	−0.07	−0.06	0.07	−0.01	−0.03	0.06	0.01	1.00

[1] U.S. Large Cap Stocks uses S&P 500 Index.
[2] U.S. Small Cap Stocks uses Russell 2000 Index.
[3] International Developed Markets uses MSCI World Ex. U.S. Index.
[4] International Emerging Markets uses MSCI Emerging Markets Index.
[5] U.S. Government & Corporate Bonds uses Lehman Brothers Gvt/Credit Index.
[6] U.S. Municipal Bonds uses Lehman Brothers Muni Index.
[7] U.S. High Yield Bonds uses Lehman Brothers High Yield Index.
[8] U.S. Mortgage uses Lehman Brothers Mortgage Index.
[9] U.S. Real Estate uses Wilshire Real Estate Index.
[10] U.S. Cash uses US 30-day Treasury Bill. All data are calculated from 1976 to the end of 2000 or from the longest available series.

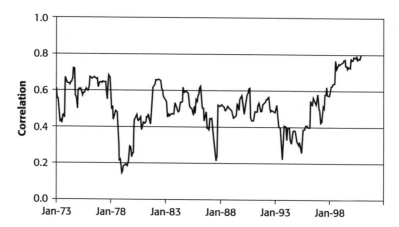

Correlation is based on trailing three-year monthly returns; U.S. stock market is presented using S&P 500 Index; Foreign developed stock market is presented using MSCI EAFE Index.

FIGURE 3.4   Correlation (U.S. versus foreign developed market).

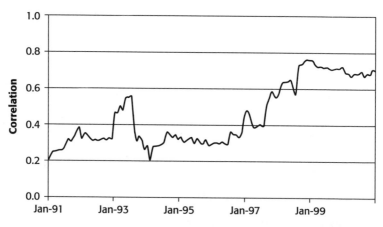

U.S. stock market is presented using S&P 500 Index; Foreign developed stock market is presented using MSCI Global Emerging Market Index; Correlation is based on trailing three-year monthly returns.

FIGURE 3.5   Correlation (U.S. versus foreign emerging market).

conclusive statements yet. Given the volatile nature of the correlations, it is possible they will fall back to historical averages in the future. For completeness, we have included foreign stock markets in our asset allocation analysis. The primary purpose of international equity asset classes is to reduce the overall risk of the portfolio by taking advantage of the relatively low return correlation between U.S. and international securities. However, investors should not expect to significantly increase the portfolio's return by investing in international equity. History shows that over a long period, the international equity market does not necessarily outperform the U.S. equity market.

Simple and Naïve Asset Allocation

Having chosen which asset classes to include in an asset allocation plan, we can now determine exactly how much we should allocate to each asset class in the portfolio. There are several ways to do this. We will illustrate two. The first is called simple asset allocation, and is based on a common rule that an investor should always hold a percentage of stocks that is equal to 100 minus his or her age. So for example, a 55-year investor should hold 45 percent stocks. This rule fails to tell us a great number of things. Looking at our simple asset class set of U.S. large cap, U.S. small cap, international equity, U.S. bond, and cash, for example, how much should be allocated to U.S. bond and cash? Of the 45 percent stocks, how much should be invested in small cap? How about international equity? For lack of better knowledge, we can equally divide the 45 percent stock allocation across U.S. large cap, U.S. small cap, and international equity. Likewise, we can equally divide the remaining 55 percent of the portfolio into U.S. bond and cash. The resulting portfolio asset allocation is shown in Table 3.6.

Of course, as an investor grows older, the asset allocation plan would continually change according to this rule. A second way to determine how much to allocate to asset classes is called naïve asset allocation, which involves allocating to each asset class equally. Table 3.7 shows the portfolio asset allocation according to naïve diversification.

So how would our two asset allocation strategies fare against owning each asset class individually? Figure 3.6 shows the performance of these two asset allocation plans against each individual asset classes in a risk versus return chart.

TABLE 3.6 Simple Asset Allocation

Portfolio Annualized Return	10.64%
Portfolio Annualized Volatility	7.32%
Sharpe Ratio[1]	0.84
ASSET WEIGHTS	
U.S. Large Cap Stocks[2]	15.0%
U.S. Small Cap Stocks[3]	15.0%
International Stocks[4]	15.0%
U.S. Bonds[5]	27.5%
U.S. Cash[6]	27.5%

[1] A risk free rate of 4.5% annually is used in Sharpe ratio calculation.
[2] U.S. Large Cap Stocks uses S&P 500 Index.
[3] U.S. Small Cap Stocks uses Russell 2000 Index.
[4] International Stocks uses MSCI EAFE Index.
[5] U.S. Bonds uses Lehman Brothers Aggregated Bond Index.
[6] U.S. Cash uses U.S. 30-day Treasury Bill. All data are calculated from 1976 to the end of 2000 except for U.S. Small Cap Stocks, which has the earliest data on January 1979.

Looking at the naïve diversification point in Figure 3.6, the obvious question arises: Is it possible to adjust the portfolio's allocation in each asset class to achieve a higher return without changing the volatility? For example, can we have a portfolio with the same level of risk as our naïve asset allocation plan (9.30 percent) but a higher return? As shown graphically in Figure 3.7, is it possible to achieve an allocation X in the real world?

The answer is: Yes! If we change the allocation of the portfolio to 27 percent U.S. large cap, 12 percent U.S. small cap, 17 percent international equity, 44 percent U.S. bond, and 0 percent cash, we could achieve a return of 11.82 percent without changing the volatility! (We will talk about how we arrived at this allocation later in the chapter.)

TABLE 3.7   Naïve Asset Allocation

Portfolio Annualized Return	11.54%
Portfolio Annualized Volatility	9.30%
Sharpe Ratio[1]	0.76
ASSET WEIGHTS	
U.S. Large Cap Stocks[2]	20.0%
U.S. Small Cap Stocks[3]	20.0%
International Stocks[4]	20.0%
U.S. Bonds[5]	20.0%
U.S. Cash[6]	20.0%

[1] A risk free rate of 4.5% annually is used in Sharpe ratio calculation.
[2] U.S. Large Cap Stocks uses S&P 500 Index.
[3] U.S. Small Cap Stocks uses Russell 2000 Index.
[4] International Stocks uses MSCI EAFE Index.
[5] U.S. Bonds uses Lehman Brothers Aggregated Bond Index.
[6] U.S. Cash uses U.S. 30-day Treasury Bill. All data are calculated from 1976 to the end of 2000 except for U.S. Small Cap Stocks, which has the earliest data on January 1979.

Table 3.8 shows we have an increase of 0.28 percent in return without taking on additional risk. That's a free lunch!

To take the example one step further, not only does allocation X generate a higher return than the naïve diversification, but allocation X also generates the highest possible return for the risk level 9.30 percent. It is not possible to have another allocation that can produce a higher return than 11.82 percent without taking additional risk or change asset classes. Similarly, there also exists an allocation that allows us to take the minimal possible risk without sacrificing any of the naïve asset allocation's 11.54 percent return. This point is illustrated in Figure 3.8 as allocation Y.

We call allocation X and allocation Y optimal points. Allocation X

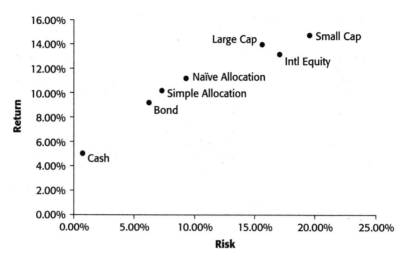

FIGURE 3.6 Portfolio performance.

generates the highest return for the risk level 9.30 percent. Not only that, it also takes on minimal risk of all allocations generating a return of 11.82 percent. Allocation Y has the same properties. It generates the highest return for the risk level 8.69 percent. It also takes on minimal risk of all allocations generating a return of 11.54 percent. In fact, there exist a series of optimal points that maximizes return at a certain range of volatility. The entire series of optimal points for the portfolio consisting of U.S. large cap, U.S. small cap, international equity, U.S. bond, and cash is plotted in Figure 3.9.

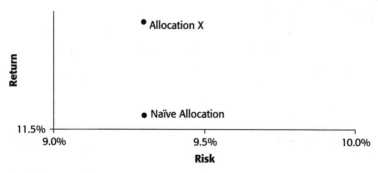

FIGURE 3.7 Risk versus return.

TABLE 3.8   Asset Allocation Comparison

	Naïve Allocation	Allocation X
Portfolio Annualized Return	11.54%	11.82%
Portfolio Annualized Risk	9.30%	9.30%
Sharpe Ratio[1]	0.76	0.78
ASSET WEIGHTS		
U.S. Large Cap Stocks[2]	20%	27%
U.S. Small Cap Stocks[3]	20%	12%
International Stocks[4]	20%	17%
U.S. Bonds[5]	20%	44%
U.S. Cash[6]	20%	0%

[1] A risk free rate of 4.5% annually is used in Sharpe ratio calculation.
[2] U.S. Large Cap Stocks uses S&P 500 Index.
[3] U.S. Small Cap Stocks uses Russell 2000 Index.
[4] International Stocks uses MSCI EAFE Index.
[5] U.S. Bonds uses Lehman Brothers Aggregated Bond Index.
[6] U.S. Cash uses U.S. 30-day Treasury Bill. All data are calculated from 1976 to the end of 2000 except for U.S. Small Cap Stocks, which has the earliest data on January 1979.

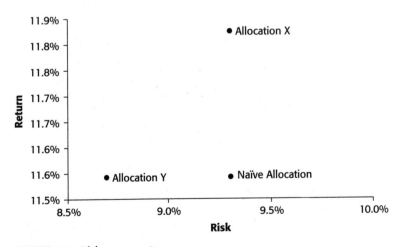

FIGURE 3.8   Risk versus return.

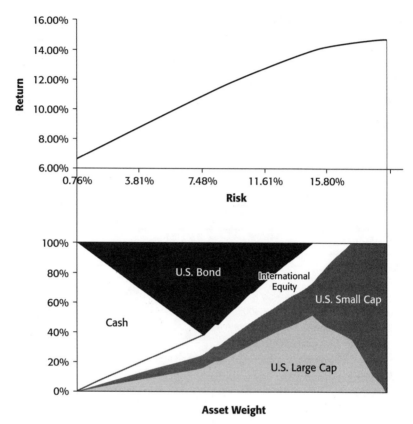

FIGURE 3.9   Optimal portfolios.

Portfolio Optimization and the Efficient Frontier

This brings us to the process of portfolio optimization, a method that enables an investor to find the entire series of optimal points for a portfolio, given the asset classes and their characteristics—return, volatility, and correlation. Essentially, portfolio optimization is a methodology for controlling portfolio risk and return. The particular optimization method used in this book is called mean-variance optimization, or MVO, which was developed by Nobel laureate Harry M. Markowitz. Mean-variance optimization reduces a portfolio's risk by combining various asset classes with specific risk levels that offset each other through low correlations. The series of optimal points, shown in Figure 3.9, is called the efficient frontier of the portfolio. Each point on the efficient frontier represents an allocation that can achieve the highest return for that specific level of risk. This allocation also represents the lowest possible risk for that specific rate of return. To explain, using the optimal portfolios graph in Figure 3.9, it is not possible to have allocation points that are above the efficient frontier. Any portfolio below the efficient frontier would be suboptimal (i.e., an alternate portfolio with a higher return would be possible at the same level of risk). Therefore, when we allocate portfolios, we should try to build a portfolio that is on the efficient frontier instead of below it. There is one important observation we can make about the efficient frontier. It always takes a convex shape and follows the law of diminishing returns. As we move from left (less risky allocations) to right (more risky allocations), the additional increases in return become incrementally smaller.

To illustrate the importance of correlation in portfolio optimization, let's consider a portfolio consisting of two assets classes: asset class A, with an annualized return of 10 percent and volatility of 10 percent; and asset class B, with an annualized return of 18 percent and volatility of 20 percent. Figure 3.10 shows the efficient frontiers for a portfolio containing asset class A and asset class B, assuming correlations between the two are 1.0, 0.5, 0.0, −0.5, and −1.0.

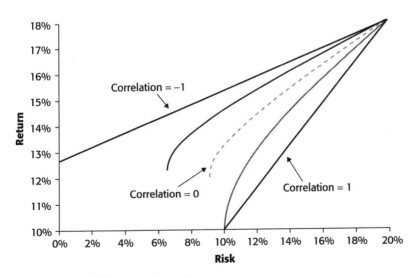

FIGURE 3.10 Efficient frontiers of two assets.

When correlation is equal to 1, the portfolio's return and risk is the weighted average of the return and risk of the individual assets. Thus, the benefit of diversification does not exist in this case. However, when correlation is reduced to 0, the corresponding efficient frontier pushes both up and to the left of the curve (line) created by a correlation of 1. In other words, for each given level of risk, the highest achievable return will always be greater when correlation between asset class A and B is equal to 0 than when the correlation is equal to 1. In the extreme case, when the correlation between asset class A and B is −1, we can not only achieve the highest return possible for any given level of risk, but also eliminate portfolio risk entirely (the left-most point on the −1 correlation efficient frontier is where the portfolio's risk level is 0). This simple hypothetical example demonstrates the importance of choosing low correlation asset classes in asset allocation and portfolio optimization.

Asset Class Selection Impacts the Efficient Frontier

In the real world, unfortunately, we seldom find asset classes with a −1 correlation, as illustrated in the previous example. In fact, it is nearly impossible to find asset class sets with a correlation of 0. However, we can still achieve reasonably good diversification if we choose our asset classes carefully. We have shown the efficient frontier for our five-asset class plan. The efficient frontier for a ten-asset class plan is shown in Figure 3.11.

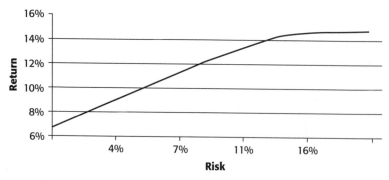

FIGURE 3.11 Optimal portfolios (ten-asset classes).

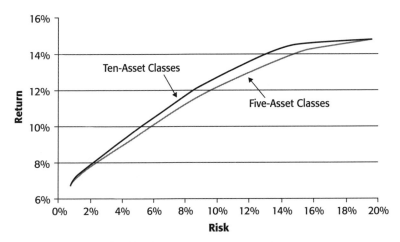

FIGURE 3.12   Efficient frontiers.

When comparing this efficient frontier with the efficient frontier generated by our five-asset class plan, we can see the importance of choosing asset classes that cover as much of the market as possible. As shown in Figure 3.12, every optimal point for the ten-asset class plan is higher than the corresponding point for the five-asset class. By covering the broader market, we give the portfolio optimizer more options to work with to calculate the best return for every risk level.

We Have an Efficient Frontier—Now What?

So how does a portfolio optimizer find the efficient frontier for a group of asset classes? He or she uses quadratic programming and relies on a computer to do the job. There are many implementations of an optimizer, but they are all beyond the scope of this book. Fortunately, investors do not need to write computer programs to find efficient frontiers. There are many computerized portfolio optimizers available both online and offline. A list of online and offline optimizers can be found in the Appendix.

Once an efficient frontier is obtained, the next step is to determine which optimal point along the efficient frontier should be chosen to implement an asset allocation plan. To show how we might do this, we revisit the previously discussed five-asset class plan. Figure 3.13 shows

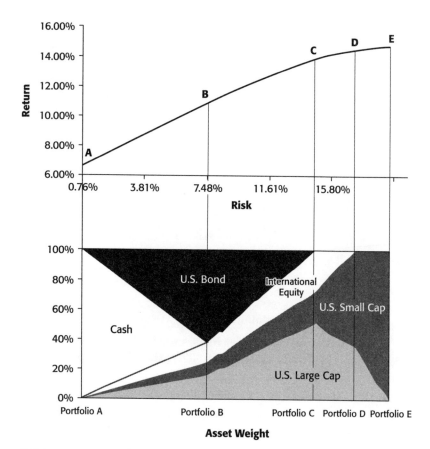

FIGURE 3.13   Optimal portfolios.

the efficient frontier and the asset class breakdown at various levels of risk for the five-asset class plan.

Optimal portfolios A, B, C, D, and E are called corner portfolios. Although they represent only six of perhaps 50 or 100 optimal portfolios along the efficient frontier, they are useful to illustrate the asset allocations associated with various levels of risk and return for the portfolio. These corner portfolios are the boundary portfolios with a number of asset classes that differ from that of the very next optimal portfolio. For example, portfolio A contains only cash, but portfolios to the immediate right of portfolio A (i.e., those that are riskier) also include U.S. bonds. At the other end of the spectrum, portfolio E contains only U.S. small cap, but portfolios to the immediate left of portfolio E (i.e., those that are less risky) also include U.S. large cap. Most investors are likely to have risk tolerance falling somewhere between portfolio B and portfolio E. For those who have a very short investment horizon, or for those who are near retirement and need a steady stream of income, optimal portfolios to the far left (i.e., in the portfolio A and B range) might be satisfactory. Optimal portfolios in the portfolio E range are rarely recommended to anyone because of the high risk associated with them. Ultimately, to determine an appropriate asset allocation (i.e., to choose the appropriate point along the efficient frontier), we need to understand our tolerance for risk. In the next chapter, we talk about how to choose an allocation that is most suitable for achieving individual financial objectives.

Is Portfolio Optimization Too Good to Be True?

By now, portfolio optimization is probably looking pretty good. It might even seem like a sure ticket to financial investment success. Pick a few asset classes and the portfolio optimizer computer program tells us exactly how much to invest in each asset class. What could be simpler? Unfortunately, portfolio optimization has many limitations.

One of the biggest problems in using portfolio optimization to do asset allocation relates to determining input values. A portfolio optimizer requires investors to specify return, risk, and correlation of each asset class to be included in the optimization. In our previous five- and ten-asset class plan examples, we use asset class historical returns from 1976 to 2000; the returns we used as inputs are annualized monthly average returns; the volatilities are annualized monthly return volatilities; and the correlations are also based on monthly returns from the chosen period. Notice how everything is based on history. However, this is not what we really want to know. We want to know what are the optimal asset allocations from now to the future. Therefore, what we should have put into the portfolio optimizer are the long-term returns of each asset class we expect in the future, or expected returns, and expected volatilities. The correlation matrix should also be of what we expect in the future, instead of what has been in the past. So how do we determine expected return, expected volatility, and expected correlation? One of the most common ways is what we have been using in our previous examples—to use past asset class performance to estimate. You must be very cynical of this approach at this point. After all, we have all heard the phrase "Past performance is no guarantee of future results." However, past results are still relatively good indicators of future performance if we choose our period of analysis carefully. In our previous examples, we have always used a historical period of 25 years. What will happen if we use only 10 years of historical data instead of 25 years? Figure 3.14 compares two efficient frontiers of the five-asset classes allocation plan generated from 25 years of historical data and 10 years of historical data.

From Figure 3.14, we can see that by using 10-year historical data, U.S. small cap stocks and international stocks asset classes are virtually nonexistent across the entire efficient frontier. This is due to the recent

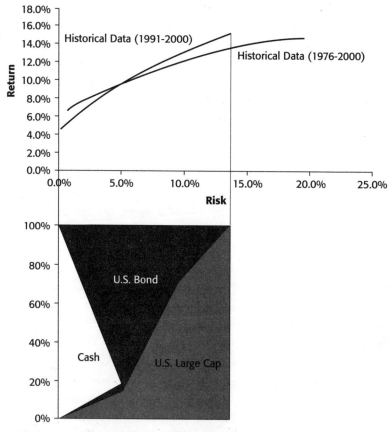

FIGURE 3.14   Efficient frontier comparison.

poor performance of small cap stocks and international stocks. However, an investor should not take short-term performance into consideration when making a long-term asset allocation decision. As a rule, one should always generate input parameters for portfolio optimization using a historical period of at least 20 years to achieve reasonable results.

Because we use historical performance of asset classes to estimate expected performance, there are various levels of uncertainty. While we can be fairly certain that the U.S. 30-day Treasury bill will return roughly 6 percent annually in the future, we are less sure about the international emerging market's annual expected return of 12 percent. The international emerging market has been very volatile, and we face much greater uncertainty when we estimate expected return using past emerging market performance. Portfolio optimization, unfortunately, does not take these various levels of uncertainty into account. Every input parameter is assumed to be certain on equal levels. The results, therefore, will be rather inaccurate. (In Chapter 9, we learn how to use constraints to overcome this portfolio optimization limitation.) For each prediction of expected return, there are sure to be uncertainties. These are the risks investors take. If we were certain about the future, we would not need a portfolio optimizer. We would simply invest everything in the asset class that we knew would yield the highest return. Certainty means there is no risk. All of our input parameters for the portfolio optimizer contain estimation errors. A portfolio optimizer, much to our dismay, maximizes the effect of these estimation errors. It significantly over-weights asset classes with high returns, low volatility, and low correlations. It also significantly under-weights asset classes with low returns, high volatility, and high correlations. Jobson and Korkie[2] quantified the magnitude of "error-maximization" effect in their studies in 1981. In one of their experiments, they estimated the input parameters using simulation and fed the results into a portfolio optimizer. The "optimal" portfolio was then tracked over a 60-month period. A true optimal portfolio was constructed at the end of the 60-month period when market behavior over the period was already known. This true optimal portfolio was tracked in the same

[2] J.D. Jobson, B. Korkie, "Putting Markowitz Theory to Work," *Journal of Portfolio Management*, Summer 1981.

60-month period so its performance could be calculated. The Sharpe ratio for the simulated "optimal" portfolio was 0.08, and it was 0.34 for the true optimal portfolio. An equally weighted portfolio, using naïve diversification, scored a Sharpe ratio of 0.27. This experiment illustrates the seriousness of portfolio optimization's tendency to maximize input estimation errors, which of course can result in significantly biased output. For example, the true level of risk an "optimal" asset allocation has may be much higher than the risk of that optimal point on the efficient frontier suggests.

A portfolio optimizer is also unreasonably sensitive to small changes in the inputs. For example, if expected return, volatility, or correlation changes just a little, the resulting optimal allocation can change significantly. Let's try one example. We change the expected return of U.S. large cap stocks in our five-asset classes plan from 13.97 percent to 14.07 percent. The resulting optimal allocations, in comparison with the original optimal allocations shown in Figure 3.9, are illustrated in Figure 3.15.

By increasing the U.S. large cap stocks average annualized return by a mere 0.1 percent, the resulting optimal allocation shifts widely. Table 3.9 illustrates the breakdown of a single optimal point where risk is fixed at 12 percent.

The allocation of U.S. large cap stocks increases to 54 percent of the entire portfolio while the weight of other asset classes all decreased. A mere 0.1 percent change in expected return caused a 4 percent change

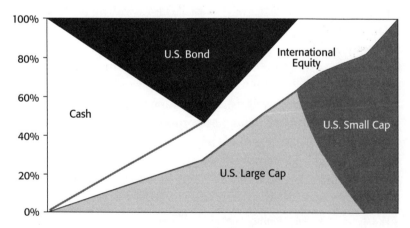

FIGURE 3.15 Large cap return increased by 0.1%.

TABLE 3.9 The Effect of Increasing U.S. Large Cap Annual Return By 0.1%

	Original Allocation	New Allocation
Portfolio Annualized Return	13.33%	13.34%
Portfolio Annualized Risk	12.00%	12.00%
Sharpe Ratio[1]	0.73	0.74
Asset Weights		
U.S. Large Cap Stocks[2]	50%	54%
U.S. Small Cap Stocks[3]	3%	1%
International Stocks[4]	33%	32%
U.S. Bonds[5]	14%	13%
U.S. Cashs[6]	0%	0%

[1] A risk free rate of 4.5% annually is used in Sharpe ratio calculation.
[2] U.S. Large Cap Stocks uses S&P 500 Index.
[3] U.S. Small Cap Stocks uses Russell 2000 Index.
[4] International Stocks uses MSCI EAFE Index.
[5] U.S. Bonds uses Lehman Brothers Aggregated Bond Index.
[6] U.S. Cash uses U.S. 30-day Treasury Bill. All data are calculated from 1976 to the end of 2000 except for U.S. Small Cap Stocks, which has the earliest data on January 1979.

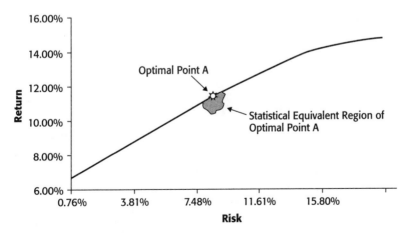

FIGURE 3.16 Optimal portfolios.

in U.S. large cap stock allocation. Is the new U.S. large cap stocks expected return of 14.07 percent more erroneous than our original expected return of 13.97 percent? It's impossible to say. But the resulting optimal portfolios are very different. So which one should we choose?

An optimal portfolio, as defined previously, is a portfolio that can achieve the highest return given a certain level of risk. This portfolio also has the lowest risk of any portfolio with the same return or greater. Statistically, however, this is not true. Because of input estimation errors, the solution is never unique. As Figure 3.16 illustrates, there is a confidence region surrounding any optimal point. Any allocation in that confidence region is a statistically equivalent portfolio to that optimal portfolio. We can call these portfolios optimally equivalent. Optimally equivalent portfolios can have drastically different allocations from that of the optimal portfolio. This phenomenon undermines the significance of an optimal asset allocation.

Portfolio optimization can be a very helpful tool in designing an asset allocation plan. It allows an investor to control the risk of the investment plan, while helping us to maximize expected return at the chosen risk level. However, we learned that applying portfolio optimization techniques is not always straightforward. Given the benefits and shortcomings of portfolio optimization, it should be used with care and caution.

CHAPTER 4

Planning for the Future

For many Americans, mutual fund and stock portfolios have come to represent a major portion of their investments, dedicated to important future goals like retirement, the funding of a child's education, or the purchase of a second home. Yet few investors devote sufficient attention to actually planning those investments.

In this chapter, we focus on the following two questions:

- Why is investment planning so important?

- How can investment planning be effectively incorporated into one's investment process?

We first examine the "drivers" behind investment planning (i.e., those needs that only investment planning can satisfy), then identify the tools and techniques for addressing those needs, and finally present a disciplined process for investment planning, using those tools and techniques.

Uncertainty Drives Investment Planning

At the highest level, investment planning is driven by the need to reduce the uncertainty surrounding both our future goals and the investments we've dedicated to them. For many investors, the following vexing questions probably sound quite familiar:

- Will we be able to live the way we want to in retirement, put our kids through college, afford our dream home?

- Will the value of our investments grow enough to enable us to achieve those goals?

- How do we strike the appropriate balance between our goals and our investments?

We all have goals—things we'd like to do, buy, pay for, or even leave behind. And most of us have set up or intend to set up investments for the purpose of achieving those goals. Yet many of us have little notion of how our goals and investments actually relate to one another—i.e., whether or not we're investing enough and with the right asset allocation to be reasonably sure of achieving our goals. The result is uncertainty.

How Can We Reduce Uncertainty?

To reduce the uncertainty that surrounds our goals and investments, we need to understand the implications of any given goal for future cash needs, have confidence that we are pursuing an appropriate asset allocation, and understand the likely future cash value of our investments. With that understanding and confidence, we can strike the necessary balance between our goals and our investments (see Figure 4.1).

Understanding Our Goals

Most of us know what our goals are. Identifying them is the easy part. To understand the implications of our goals for future cash needs, how-

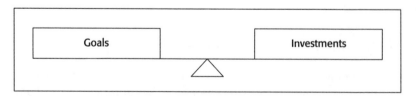

FIGURE 4.1 Striking a balance between our goals and our investments.

ever, we need to be able to quantify those goals, and in order to quantify our goals, we need to know or be able to estimate the following:

- *Time horizon:*   The point in time at which we will need to draw on our investments to satisfy a particular goal.

- *Cost:*   The cost, in today's dollars, of satisfying the goal.

- *Number and schedule of payments:*   The period of time over which we will draw on our investments to satisfy the goal, and the frequency of those payments. To satisfy our goal, will we need to make a single lump-sum payment or a number of regular payments over time?

- *Inflation rate:*   The rate of inflation we expect between now and the time we begin drawing on our investments to satisfy the goal. Estimating this allows us to project the cost of satisfying our goal, which we have stated in today's dollars, at the point of time when we will actually be satisfying it.

Quantifying our goals is essential because it reduces all of our goals (no matter how different they are from one another) to a common denominator: *future cash needs*. The ability to express and measure our goals in common terms enables us to analyze them holistically, which is important for realistic investment planning. Table 4.1 compares a retirement goal as many of us would express it with a retirement goal that has been quantified for planning purposes.

The ability to express and measure our goals in terms of future cash *needs* puts us one step closer to analyzing (and understanding) our goals relative to our investments, which we will express in terms of future cash *available* (i.e., the value to which we expect our investments

TABLE 4.1   A Quantified Retirement Goal

A Typically Expressed Retirement Goal	A Quantified Retirement Goal
I would like to be able to retire comfortably.	I would like to be able to retire at age 60 with a 30-year retirement income of $50K/year, beginning at age 60.

to grow). However, before we turn our attention to actual investments, we need to determine how we ought to be investing at a macro level, across broad asset classes, given our tolerance for risk and the understanding of our goals that we now have.

Determining an Appropriate Asset Allocation

Proper alignment of our goals and our investments begins with a technique called *asset allocation*. As discussed in Chapter 3, asset allocation is the process by which we spread our investments across multiple asset classes in order to maximize expected return, given our tolerance for risk, our financial "big picture," our investment time horizon, and our cash needs over time.

Asset allocation is typically determined by gathering investor information through a questionnaire, using that information to create an investor profile, and matching that profile to one of several asset class mixes. Each recommended asset class mix would be appropriate for a certain type of investor, categorized in terms of investing traits and behavior. Typical categories, representing the full range of risk aversion, might include highly conservative, conservative, moderate, aggressive, and highly aggressive.

Today, thanks in large part to the Internet, investors have access to a large variety of asset allocation tools. In fact, there are almost as many different questionnaires as there are financial service institutions. While asset allocation questionnaires vary in length and in the depth of their questions, most seek to gather information on an investor's investment time horizon, financial "big picture," prior investing experience and behavior, and tolerance for risk, in order to determine a profile of that investor. Table 4.2 is an example of a simple asset allocation questionnaire.

Based on the combination of responses and the investor profile that emerges, an asset allocation that is appropriate for the investor is recommended. Table 4.3 is an example of the range of possible asset allocations, ranging from highly conservative to highly aggressive, that could be recommended for an investor who has completed a questionnaire like the one in Table 4.2. Beside each asset allocation, we describe in very general terms the type of investor for which it might be appropriate. In considering the information presented in Table 4.3, it is important to understand that there will always be variations in the

TABLE 4.2 A General Asset Allocation Questionnaire

---

1. What is the current value of your investment portfolio? (Including stocks, bonds, mutual funds, CDs, money market investments, savings)
   a. Under $25,000
   b. $25,000–50,000
   c. $50,000–$200,000
   d. Above $200,000

---

2. In how many years do you plan to withdraw your investments?
   a. Less than 2 years
   b. 2–4 years
   c. 5–10 years
   d. More than 10 years

---

3. Are you likely to draw on your investments in advance to satisfy cash needs in the future?
   a. Yes, and the amount will likely be significant.
   b. Yes, but the amount can vary widely.
   c. Likely, but the amount will not be significant.
   d. Not likely.

---

4. Which of the following statements best describes your expected future earnings over the next 10 years? (Assuming annual inflation of 3%)
   a. I expect that my future earnings will easily outpace inflation.
   b. I expect that my future earnings will slightly outpace inflation.
   c. I expect that my future earnings will fail to keep pace with inflation.
   d. I expect that my future earnings will decline.

---

5. Have you invested before?
   a. I have never invested before.
   b. I have recently started investing and I have basic knowledge of investing.
   c. I have been investing for several years and I am comfortable with my investments.
   d. I have been investing for a long time and my financial knowledge is well above average.

---

6. If your investments lost a sizable amount of money in a short period of time?
   a. I would panic and get out of the investments quickly.
   b. I would feel very uncomfortable and might gradually sell my investments.
   c. I would monitor the investments carefully before making any changes.
   d. I invest for the long term, so I'd stay invested for at least a while.

TABLE 4.3   Five Asset Allocations with Associated Investor Profiles

Highly Conservative U.S. Equity: 10% U.S. Bond: 10% Int'l Equity: 5% Cash (T-Bill): 75%	The investor pursuing this style of asset allocation likely has a short-term investment horizon, and a very low tolerance for risk and market fluctuations. In general, he/she is focused on capital preservation and stability of current income, will likely need to draw on investments to meet cash needs in the near term, and is only minimally concerned with protecting against inflation.
Conservative U.S. Equity: 20% U.S. Bond: 30% Int'l Equity: 10% Cash (T-Bill): 40%	The investor pursuing this style of asset allocation likely has a short-term investment horizon and is willing to take some risk, but will tend to sacrifice higher possible return in favor of increased stability. In general, he/she is focused on capital preservation rather than long-term capital appreciation, may need to draw on investments to meet cash needs in the near-term, and is only moderately concerned with protecting against inflation.
Moderate U.S. Equity: 30% U.S. Bond: 50% Int'l Equity: 20% Cash (T-Bill): 0%	The investor pursuing this style of asset allocation likely has a medium-term investment horizon and the ability to withstand moderate market fluctuations. In general, he/she seeks a combination of long-term capital appreciation and regular income, may need to draw on investments to meet cash needs in the next several years, and is concerned with protecting against inflation.
Aggressive U.S. Equity: 50% U.S. Bond: 25% Int'l Equity: 25% Cash (T-Bill): 0%	The investor pursuing this style of asset allocation likely has both a long-term investment horizon and a fairly high tolerance for risk and market fluctuations. In general, he/she has a preference for long-term capital appreciation over regular income, expects little or no need to draw on investments to meet impending cash needs, and is concerned with protecting against inflation.
Highly Aggressive U.S. Equity: 65% U.S. Bond: 5% Int'l Equity: 30% Cash (T-Bill): 0%	The investor pursuing this style of asset allocation likely has both a long-term investment horizon and a very high tolerance for risk and market fluctuations. In general, he/she is focused on long-term capital appreciation rather than regular income, expects no need to draw on investments to meet impending cash needs, and is concerned with protecting against inflation.

recommended allocation percentages from one institution to the next and from one asset allocation tool to the next, even within the same category, such as "conservative." This might be due to a difference in inputs to the asset allocation model, such as the asset classes, benchmark indices, or time series used, or even to an institution's understanding of such terms as *conservative* and *aggressive*. That highlights a major problem with the results that many asset allocation models produce—they are too static.

ASSET ALLOCATION IN ACTION

Asset allocation plays an important role in both portfolio construction and portfolio management. In the early stages of the investment decision-making process, an asset allocation plan provides us with a logical framework for selecting portfolio assets and diversifying across asset classes. Later in that process, once we've invested in a portfolio of stocks and/or funds, an asset allocation plan serves as a guidepost for monitoring our portfolio over time, and enables us to ensure that we are maintaining the desired level of portfolio diversification across asset classes.

Portfolio Construction: Asset allocation is an important first step in constructing a portfolio because it establishes a foundation upon which to build our portfolio and a framework within which to select individual assets.

By selecting stocks and funds according to the asset classes in our asset allocation, and remaining true to the recommended portfolio weightings of those asset classes, we can greatly increase our confidence level that we will achieve the expected return associated with our recommended asset allocation. Recalling the previously cited work of Brinson, Hood, and Beebower,[1] within a diversified portfolio, more than 90 percent of a portfolio's return variability is attributable to asset allocation, so it pays to take it seriously.

Chapters 5, 6, and 7 explore a variety of issues related to asset selection and explain techniques for selecting assets to fit our desired asset allocation.

Portfolio Management: Once we have constructed an investment portfolio, we need to review our asset allocation periodically to make sure that our portfolio accurately reflects our thinking in terms of investment goals, investment time horizon, and risk tolerance. This is important because over time, as a result of uneven returns on

---

[1] Gary P. Brinson, L. Randolph Hood, and Gilbert L. Beebower, "Determinants of Portfolio Performance," *Financial Analyst Journal,* January–February 1995.

individual portfolio assets, the actual allocation of our portfolio assets across asset classes is likely to stray from our desired asset allocation, and therefore our portfolio will need to be rebalanced.

Chapter 10 explains how we can use style analysis to "audit" our portfolio's current asset allocation and determine how far it has strayed from our desired asset allocation.

CHOOSING AN ASSET ALLOCATION TOOL

Today, there are many asset allocation tools available, both on- and offline. Most use some type of questionnaire to profile the investor and propose an asset allocation based on that profile. Do not, however, assume that all asset allocation tools are the same. The following are some of the key features one should look for in an asset allocation tool:

- *Choice of asset classes:* When we are doing asset allocation, it is important that the analysis be based on the asset classes we want represented in our portfolio. While one investor may be satisfied to do asset allocation across very broad asset classes (such as U.S. equity, U.S. bond, international equity, and cash), another may prefer narrower asset classes (U.S. large cap and U.S. small cap instead of U.S. equity, etc.), and yet another may prefer still narrower asset classes (U.S. large cap value and U.S. large cap growth instead of U.S. large cap, etc.).

- *Constraints:* Many of us have ideas about what we ought (or ought not) to be holding in our portfolios. An asset allocation tool should enable us to set a minimum and/or maximum percentage for each asset class in the model so as to ensure results that reflect our views. If, for example, we wanted to ensure that our asset allocation would always include at least 10 percent international equity, a minimum percentage constraint of 10 percent would enable us to do so. Likewise, if we wanted to limit our international equity weighting in any asset allocation to 20 percent, a maximum percentage constraint of 20 percent would ensure that.

- *Interactive (vs. static) results:* Most asset allocation tools will "map" us to one of five or six asset allocations and show us the expected return and return volatility (risk) associated with that allocation. The good ones allow us to see in real time the incremental changes to the allocation as we increase or lower risk.

- *Projection of wealth:*   Ideally, we would like to know how large our investment might grow over time, given our choice of asset allocation. A good tool will tell us this.

- *Tax scenarios:*   The tax status of our investment account will have a major impact on our projected wealth. Since a tax-deferred account such as an IRA or 401(k) has very different tax implications from a fully taxable investment account one might have with a broker, the ability to define the tax status of our investment account helps us to frame our expectations in terms of the account's projected future value.

- *"What-ifs":*   Beyond the recommended mix of asset classes, the asset allocation tool should allow us to run a variety of "what-if" scenarios—i.e., it should allow us to change certain inputs or assumptions and see the impact of those changes on the recommended allocation, our projected wealth, etc.

Asset allocation is all about determining a mix of asset classes that is appropriate for us. A tool that incorporates these features enables us to take the process one step further and truly personalize our asset allocation.

Understanding Our Investments

Once we have committed to an asset allocation and built an investment portfolio around it, we need to understand the likely contribution of our investments to future cash flows. As with our goals, we need to be able to quantify the projected value of those investments in the future, and to do so we need to know or be able to estimate the following:

- *Current value:*   The total current value of our investments and/or investable assets

- *Periodic contribution:*   The frequency with which we expect to contribute to the investment and the amounts we expect to contribute

- *Time horizon:*   The period of time over which we expect to contribute to the investment

- *Asset allocation:*   How we have allocated our investments (or expect to allocate our investable assets) across asset classes

- *Expected return:*   The return we expect to receive on our investments over our investment time horizon

EXPECTED RETURN AND ASSET ALLOCATION

The most difficult aspect of quantifying our investments is determining an appropriate expected return. Reliably projecting long-term future returns on individual assets is virtually impossible, but somehow we need to be able to estimate the expected return on our investment portfolio if we are to have any idea of what that portfolio might be worth years down the road when we will need to draw on it to fund certain goals.

An understanding of our actual asset allocation can help us to estimate the long-term expected return on our aggregate investments. Of course, if we've been disciplined about implementing and maintaining a recommended asset allocation, then estimating our long-term expected return should be as simple as consulting the software or tool that we originally used to determine our asset allocation. As we stated earlier, the better asset allocation tools and software will provide the expected return and return volatility associated with any recommended asset allocation.

Assuming that you've completed the investment profile survey in Table 4.2, have chosen to implement a recommended portfolio from Table 4.3, and have been successful in maintaining that asset allocation over the years, then the expected annual return on that recommended portfolio (at the time you adopted it) is a reasonable number to start with in your investment planning.

If your actual holdings have strayed from your target asset allocation, you can still use your actual asset allocation to "back into" an expected return for your investment portfolio. Here's how:

- *Step 1:*   Use a style analysis tool to determine how your investments are actually allocated across asset classes. This involves categorizing your portfolio assets into asset classes and determining the relative weighting of each asset class in your portfolio.

- *Step 2:*   Use asset allocation software or an online financial analytics service to determine what the long-term expected

TABLE 4.4   Calculating a Portfolio's Expected Return

Asset Class	Weight in Portfolio (A)	Asset Class Expected Return (B)	Weighted Return (A × B)
U.S. Equity (S&P 500)	.50	14.67%	7.34%
U.S. Bond (U.S. Govt. Bond)	.30	9.87%	2.96%
International Equity (MSCI Index)	.20	10.58%	2.11%
	Portfolio Expected Return		12.41%

return is for each of the asset classes in your portfolio. There are many ways of calculating expected return for an asset class; we use average historical return, assuming the calculation is based on twenty-five or more years of return history.

- *Step 3:*   Use your asset class weightings and the expected return for each asset class to calculate the expected return on your portfolio. Table 4.4 presents a simple example of how that can be done.

Knowing the expected return and return volatility of both your actual asset allocation (i.e., your current holdings) and your original target asset allocation will help you to decide whether or not it is wise to rebalance your portfolio back to the target asset allocation.

The Cash Flow Model—Determining if Our Goals and Investments Are Aligned

Quantifying our goals and investments in the way we've just described allows us to create a simple cash flow model, which we can use to determine how well our goals and investments are aligned and to better understand the likelihood of achieving our goals, given the investments we've dedicated to them.

In the most basic terms, a cash flow model is a means of measuring cash inflows and outflows. Of course, depending on the nature of those inflows and outflows, a cash flow model can range from simple (like a piggy bank) to complex (like an investment account). In the context

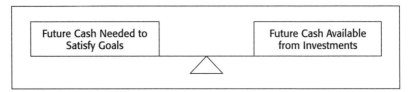

FIGURE 4.2 Striking a balance between our goals and our investments (cash flow perspective).

of our goals and investments, the money we contribute to and gain on our investments over time are the model's inflows; the cash that we draw from those investments in the future are the model's outflows. Figure 4.2 provides a cash flow perspective on the balance that needs to be struck between our goals and our investments.

The following is an example of how a simple cash flow model (i.e., one with a single goal and a single portfolio) would be used for an educational goal and the investment portfolio that has been set up to help achieve it.

Mike and Jane have set up an investment portfolio to help fund their son Billy's college education. Billy is 10 years old, and his parents expect that he will begin college when he is 18. Mike and Jane can afford to invest $50,000 right now and another $7500 per year until Billy is through with college. Since Mike and Jane know that it would cost approximately $40,000 to fund one year of private school education for Billy were he to enroll today, and they feel pretty comfortable assuming that the cost of education will increase approximately 3 percent per year over the next several years, they are able to project a total cost of approximately $212,000 for Billy's four years of college. They expect their portfolio to return about 8 percent per year.

As Figure 4.3 shows, if everything goes according to Mike and Jane's expectations, they should achieve their goal with a little money to spare. In this case, Mike and Jane's goal and investments appear to be fairly well aligned.

Single-Goal vs. Multiple-Goal Cash Flow Modeling

Depending on our planning orientation (i.e., targeted vs. holistic), we may choose to build either simple single-goal models or a highly complex multiple-goal model. Either approach, by itself or in combination with the other, may be appropriate.

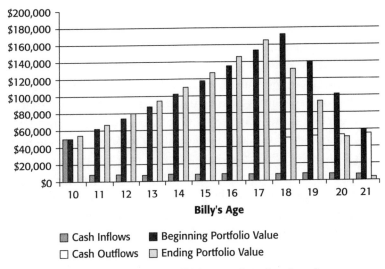

FIGURE 4.3 Simple cash flow model for an educational goal.

- *Single-goal cash flow modeling:*   Single-goal cash flow modeling involves quantifying a single goal and dedicating a single
  investment portfolio to that goal; it is ideal for targeted planning. Since single-goal modeling implies setting up and managing as many investment portfolios as you have goals, not to
  mention creating an equal number of goal-specific cash flow
  models, it can be time-consuming and administratively intensive—that's the downside. The upside, however, is that a goal-
  specific cash flow model will reflect the inputs and assumptions
  that are specific to that goal and the investment portfolio dedicated to it. Returning to Mike and Jane's educational goal, this is
  a high-priority goal for them that they want to be very sure of
  achieving. Therefore, they've set up a fairly low-risk investment
  portfolio (in terms of asset class mix) that they think can earn
  the 8 percent annual return needed to achieve their goal. If their
  goal were a speedboat (which they could definitely live without)
  instead of their son's education, would they dedicate the same
  type of investment portfolio to it? Would their risk tolerance be
  higher? Single-goal cash flow modeling enables Mike and Jane
  to account for any differences that might exist in how they
  approach these and other goals.

- *Multiple-goal cash flow modeling:*   For some of us, single-goal cash flow modeling just doesn't make sense. We look at our life goals and finances holistically, and we need a means of determining whether or not our investments, in aggregate, will enable us to meet all of our future goals. A multiple-goal cash flow model enables us to do that. Since multiple-goal cash flow modeling involves inputting all of our goals and investments into a single model, that model is likely to appear quite complex graphically. While that may be true, creating the model will actually be less complex than creating many single-goal models, because we will be applying uniform assumptions of risk tolerance, asset allocation, and expected return across all goals. However, while a multiple-goal cash flow model has the obvious benefit of a holistic view, our inability to differentiate our goals in terms of risk tolerance and allocate investments accordingly is a definite drawback.

In the end, most of us will probably settle on some combination of the two approaches, perhaps creating a multiple-goal cash flow model for high-priority goals like our children's education and our retirement and single-goal cash flow models for lower-priority goals like a major trip or a second home.

My Cash Flow Model Looks Great, but What If . . . ?

Creating a cash flow model for goals and investments is essential for investment planning, but like any model, the cash flow model is built on assumptions. In our prior example, Mike and Jane's cash flow model assumed an average annual return on investment of 8 percent and a 3 percent annual increase in the cost of a college education. Based on historical averages, both of these are reasonable assumptions, but subject to limitations. Since actual return is sure to vary from year to year, how do we factor in that variability of returns? How do we factor in the possibility of above-average returns in the early years of our investment time horizon and below-average returns in the later years, or vice versa? How do we factor in variability in the rate of inflation? Does it really matter? Consider the following simple example.

We invest $100 today, and in three years we hope to use the proceeds from that investment to buy a watch that currently retails for

$120. Assuming a constant 3 percent annual increase in the cost of the watch and a constant 10 percent average annual return on our investment (both of which seem quite reasonable), our goal seems attainable. In three years, the watch would cost $131.13, and if we were to earn exactly 10 percent on our investment in each of the three years, our investment would grow to $110 after one year, $121 after two years, and $133.10 after three years. We'd even have a few dollars to spare!

Now let's see how variability of returns might affect our investment. (To keep our example simple, we'll assume that the cost of the watch increases at a constant rate of 3 percent annually.) If we earned −3 percent in year one, 10 percent in year two, and 23 percent in year three, our average (arithmetic) annual return would still be 10 percent, but our investment would be worth $97 after one year, $106.70 after two years, and $131.24 after three years. We would attain our goal, but just barely. Assuming an opposite though similar scenario, if we earned 24 percent in year one, 10 percent in year two, and −4 percent in year three, our average annual return would again be 10 percent, but our investment would be worth $124 after one year, $136.40 after two years, and $130.94 after three years. In this case, we would fall shy of our goal. Likewise, if we earned −10 percent in year one, 30 percent in year two, and 10 percent in year three, our average annual return would again be 10 percent, but our investment would be worth $90 after one year, $117 after two years, and $128.70 after three years. Again, we would fall short of our goal.

Because of the simplicity of this example, it only hints at the impact that variability of returns can have on the value of our investment over time. If we factor in as well a longer investment time horizon and variable economic factors such as inflation and interest rates, the future isn't quite so clear as our tidy cash flow model might suggest. Indeed, asset market returns, inflation rates, and interest rates do vary in real life. Therefore we need to recognize that, while over our investment time horizon such rates may ultimately average out to what we expect, the volatility of our portfolio returns and the timing of periods with below-average or negative returns can have a tremendous negative impact on our ability to achieve some goal or goals with an investment.

So the question remains, How do we factor this kind of variability into our cash flow model? The answer is Monte Carlo simulation.

Monte Carlo Simulation

Monte Carlo simulation is a complex mathematical technique that involves using statistical trials to get an approximate solution to a problem. In the context of financial planning, Monte Carlo simulation helps us to understand our likelihood of successfully achieving our goals, given the investments we have set up specifically for those goals.

Monte Carlo simulation is able to estimate the likelihood of our achieving our goals by accounting for variability in the economic factors that contribute to our financial plan's ultimate success (such as the return rates on asset markets, the inflation rate, and the interest rate in any given year) and by running hundreds or even thousands of "trials" on our financial plan. Each trial is an independent projection of our financial plan, where each of the contributing factors noted above can take on a range of possible values in any given year.

When the simulation is complete, in some trials our financial plan will have succeeded in achieving our goals, and in others it will not have succeeded. The large number of trials allows us to know the statistical probability that our financial plan will enable us to achieve our goals. For example, if the simulation runs 1000 trials, and in 650 of those trials we achieve our goals with our investments, then the probability of our successfully achieving our goals is 65 percent. At that point, we need to decide if we are comfortable with a 65 percent likelihood of achieving our goals. If not, then we need to consider how we might adjust our goals and/or our investments to improve our plan's likelihood of success.

With Monte Carlo simulators, determining a plan's likelihood of success is the easy part. Typically, all you need to do is push a button and the simulator does the rest. The hard part is figuring out how to improve a plan's forecast likelihood of success if you are not satisfied with the simulation's results.

Let's return to our previous case of Mike and Jane. The following is an example of how a Monte Carlo simulation could be used to determine the likelihood of their achieving their educational goal with the investment portfolio they have set up for that purpose.

As before, Mike and Jane have set up an investment portfolio to help fund their son Billy's college education. Billy is 10 years old, and his parents expect that he will begin college when he is 18. Mike and Jane can afford to invest $50,000 right now and another $7500 per year

Monte Carlo Simulation and Financial Planning

What is Monte Carlo simulation?   Monte Carlo simulation is a technique for calculating and accounting for uncertainty in a forecast of future events. To better understand the meaning of Monte Carlo simulation, it helps to break up the term into its two parts: *Monte Carlo* and *simulation*. *Monte Carlo* refers to Monte Carlo, Monaco, which is world-famous for its casinos and their many games of chance. Games like roulette and craps (dice) are games of chance because they involve random behavior—i.e., for any given spin of the wheel or roll of a die, any number is just as likely to come up as any other, regardless of what came up the time before. *Simulation* is a process by which a real-life system or process is imitated (typically using mathematical modeling) for the purpose of analyzing and understanding it. Putting the two together, Monte Carlo simulation is a means of accounting for the random behavior of inputs to a system or process, which in turn helps us to predict how that system or process will behave in the future.

Why is Monte Carlo simulation so well suited to financial planning?   At the core of any financial plan is a system or model of *future cash needs* (our goals) and *future cash available* (the fruits of our savings and investments). Since so many of the inputs to the future cash available side of this model are likely to vary (such as the rate of return on our investments, interest rates, and inflation), it's important to be able to factor such variability into our analysis of that model. Monte Carlo simulation enables us to do that, and thereby improves our ability to predict the likelihood that our future cash available will be sufficient to support our future cash needs.

Where can one find planning tools that include Monte Carlo simulation?   There are a number of Web-based and desktop solutions available on the market today that enable one to apply Monte Carlo simulation to financial and investment decision making. Notable online solutions include Financeware.com, FinancialEngines.com, FinPortfolio.com, and TRowePrice.com. Some of the better-known desktop solutions include @Risk, AASim, Crystal Ball 2000, and Silver Financial Planner. Please see the appendix to learn more about these Web-based and desktop solutions, as well as some useful online resources devoted to Monte Carlo simulation.

---

until Billy is through with college. Mike and Jane know that it would cost approximately $40,000 to fund one year of private school education for Billy were he to enroll today. While Monte Carlo simulation allows us to factor in variability of multiple factors, for the sake of simplicity, we will assume that the cost of a college education will increase at a constant rate of 3 percent per year over the next several years. For annual expected return, however, instead of assuming a constant annual rate of return, we will factor in the volatility that comes along with that return.

Figure 4.4 shows the results of a Monte Carlo simulation that assumes 8 percent expected annual return and 4.5 percent volatility, with each line representing a simulated trial. Based on those inputs, the simulation forecasts an 86.10 percent likelihood that Mike and Jane will be able to achieve their educational goal, given the portfolio they have set up and will contribute to over the next twelve years. In other words, in 86.10 percent of the trials, Mike and Jane succeeded in fully funding Billy's college education through the proceeds of their investment. This is reasonably consistent with the results of their cash flow model, but understandably so given the low assumed volatility of the portfolio.

To illustrate the impact that our assumptions can have on forecast results and the advantage of Monte Carlo simulation over standard cash flow modeling, we ran a second simulation, this time assuming a 14 percent expected annual return and a 16 percent volatility. As we can see in Figure 4.5, based on these inputs, the simulation suggests a significantly wider range of possible outcomes and forecasts a 58.70 percent likelihood that Mike and Jane will be able to achieve their

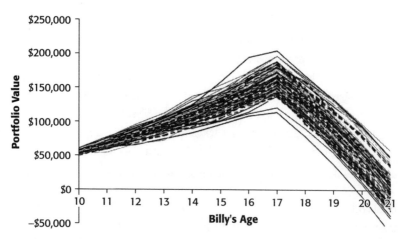

FIGURE 4.4 Monte Carlo simulation for an educational goal (8 percent return, 4.5 percent volatility).

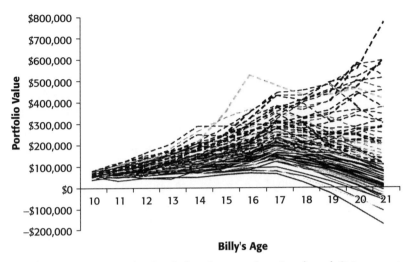

FIGURE 4.5 Monte Carlo simulation for an educational goal (14 percent return, 16 percent volatility).

educational goal, given the portfolio they have set up and will contribute to over the next twelve years.

While the 58.70 percent likelihood of success is telling in and of itself, it is perhaps even more important to consider the fact that a cash flow model based on an average expected annual return of 14 percent would have left Mike and Jane believing that not only would they be able to fully fund Billy's education, but they would have lots to spare as well. By not accounting for the volatility associated with a 14 percent annual expected return, a cash flow model would have lulled them into a dangerously false sense of security.

In either scenario, if Mike and Jane are not happy with their forecast and want to try to improve the likelihood of their reaching their goal, they can adjust a variety of inputs. These include risk level (i.e., they can adopt a riskier mix of asset classes), inputs related to the investment portfolio dedicated to their goal (such as the amount they initially invest in the portfolio and the amount of periodic contributions and/or additional one-time contributions to the portfolio), and finally inputs related to the educational goal itself, such as the time span of the goal (i.e., they could delay Billy's enrollment) and the expected cost of achieving the goal (perhaps Billy could go to a state school instead). Once they've made these adjustments, they can run the forecast over again and see the impact of the adjustments on the likelihood of their reaching their goals. Obviously, adjusting inputs to a Monte Carlo simulation model is an iterative process—it might take Mike and Jane a number of trials and various combinations of goal and investment inputs to arrive at a forecast they can live with.

Always remember, too, that with Monte Carlo simulation, the forecast results are only as reliable as the inputs to the model. It makes no sense to fill a model with unreasonable goal or investment inputs simply for the sake of producing a satisfactory forecast. Used properly, however, Monte Carlo simulation can be a powerful tool in goal-based investment planning.

CHAPTER 5

Selecting Funds

Once an asset allocation strategy is outlined, selecting individual assets for the equity portion of a portfolio can be one of the most interesting parts of the investment process. Selecting assets is a test of both knowledge and skill. For stocks, it tests the investor's knowledge of a company, its economic sector and industry, and its earning potential; for mutual funds, it tests the investor's knowledge of a fund's management and the broad asset class or economic sector it represents. Whether selecting stocks, funds or some combination therein, an investor's skill is tested by the need for quality diversification in the portfolio of assets ultimately assembled.

Research has shown that to achieve quality diversification in a stock portfolio, it should contain 15 to 20 stocks. Of course, if equity index funds or equity mutual funds are part of the portfolio, high quality diversification ought to be achievable with fewer assets since each fund contains a number of individual stocks. To perform asset selection properly, investors need to do homework. Despite many good and inexpensive resources (research, charts, analytical tools, etc.) available to individual investors on the Internet and offline, building a portfolio asset by asset is a time-intensive and challenging process.

As we turn our attention to asset selection, it is important to keep in mind that there is a full spectrum of ways to implement an asset allocation strategy, ranging from a complete hand-offs approach that uses

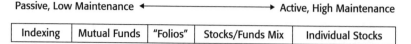

Passive, Low Maintenance ◄─────────────► Active, High Maintenance

Indexing	Mutual Funds	"Folios"	Stocks/Funds Mix	Individual Stocks

FIGURE 5.1   The range of asset allocation strategy implementation options.

index funds, to an intensive security-by-security selection process. Figure 5.1 illustrates the range of options investors have in implementing an asset allocation strategy.

In this chapter, we answer the questions:

- What are the benefits and downsides of mutual fund investing?

- What are the "must know" essentials of selecting mutual funds?

- What criteria should we use in the selection of traditionally "actively managed" funds?

- How can alternatives to traditional "actively managed" funds, such as index funds and "folios" (personal funds), be used to implement an asset allocation strategy, and when are they advantageous?

Mutual Funds

Mutual funds enable investors to pool their money in the hands of a professional investor or fund manager. Investors pay a fee for the fund manager to carry out research on individual assets, execute trades, build a portfolio, and make ongoing changes as he or she sees fit. The fund manager is a specialist whose career is devoted to managing portfolios. In most cases, the fund manager invests in a single asset class (stocks, bonds, real estate, etc.) and has a focus on a particular sub-asset class (large cap value stocks, corporate bonds, European equity, etc.). Therefore, investing in a mutual fund is different than turning over all of our cash to an advisor who provides personal care throughout the asset allocation and investment process. Mutual fund managers provide a specific service. They select and manage individual assets within defined parameters (i.e., asset class and sub-class) and provide instant diversification for a group of investors. Most managers "actively manage" their funds, meaning the manager buys and sells stocks as he or she sees fit. The manager states an investment objective and may outline his or her stock selection process, but once the money is in his or her hands, the investor loses all discretion (except of course the right to sell the fund). (Most funds allow investors to withdraw funds at the close of any market day.)

For many mutual fund investors, the service offered by mutual fund managers is very appealing since it saves the time and effort that would otherwise be expended carrying out asset selection. In addition, the fund manager's experience should enable an investor to achieve higher returns than might be expected from doing it on his or her own. (Although this is arguable, as we discuss later—for now, let it suffice to say that paying a fund manager is attractive, or at least an acceptable cost, to investors who do not have the time or desire to select assets on their own.) Of course, investing in mutual funds does not prohibit anyone from adding a few hand-picked stocks to a portfolio. Combining funds with select stocks can be a very successful investing tactic—as long as investors pay attention to the style of the fund and recognize that the stock picks may already be part of the fund's holdings.

The Benefits of Mutual Funds

For the individual investor, mutual fund investing offers advantages in terms of time, effort, and cost efficiency; reduced transaction costs; and greater liquidity, portfolio diversification, and market or asset class exposure.

Time, Effort, and Cost

For many investors, the total value of time, effort, and actual cost associated with doing investment research exceeds the management fee paid to own a mutual fund. Though it is difficult to quantify the cost of doing research on individual stocks and funds, no one can argue that it does not require significant time and effort. Mutual fund managers take the burden of selecting and managing a group of assets away from investors. They bring experience and a wealth of other resources to security selection and portfolio construction. With the fees investors pay fund managers, an arsenal of research tools is purchased to assist in managing the mutual funds. Despite the rising quality of resources available to individual investors, the professionals (i.e., fund managers) still have a leg-up when it comes to tools that support their research and portfolio management. Given the scale of the operation of many mutual funds companies, these expensive resources can be spread across many investors. For even the most ambitious individual investors, the cost of these resources is usually an obstacle.

Transaction Costs

Fund managers usually pay less per share when buying and selling stocks through institutional brokerage houses. Even the extremely low trading fees individual investors pay through discount online brokers are more expensive than the fee mutual fund managers pay. Why? The size of the average mutual fund trade is many times that of the average individual investor trade, and because the mutual fund manager often manages several funds, each with dozens of assets, the frequency of trades with the broker is high. Brokers, therefore, charge less per share and offer research and other services to attract the mutual fund manager to trade with the brokerage firm.

There is, however, a flip side to the large scale of mutual funds. When funds with large amounts of money attempt to buy (or sell) securities with small trading volumes, the "market impact" of the trade can be large. In other words, fund managers may drive the price of a stock up (or down) as they attempt to acquire (or get rid of) shares. The result is often a higher average purchase price (or lower average sale price). This cost can be more significant than the savings on transaction fees.

Liquidity

Individual investors can buy and sell mutual funds consisting of dozens of stocks or bonds with a single trade. Publicly traded mutual funds allow investors to buy into or sell out of the fund daily. Compared to trying to buy or sell a portfolio of some 40 odd stocks, trading a mutual fund is quick and easy. When necessary, investors can convert the holdings of those 40 stocks into cash immediately.

Diversification with a Small Investment

Let's assume we are starting our investment account with a modest $2500, and we insist on diversifying our portfolio by owning 15 to 20 assets. If we select 15 assets with an average price per asset of $20 per share, we can afford about eight shares of each asset—before transaction costs! If each trade costs $15, we are paying $225 (or 9 percent) just to launch our portfolio! By contrast, many mutual funds provide instant diversification with a minimum investment (as low as $500) and perhaps a small transaction fee to a discount broker. Of course, management fees are charged also, but even at an annual cost 1.5 percent of the investment, the overall cost is lower.

Exposure to Any Market or Asset Class

Mutual funds exist in many shapes and sizes. Most common are stock and bond funds with an array of stated objectives. Many own just stocks, others just bonds, and some both stocks and bonds. Some funds invest only in stocks within in a specific economic sector in the United States. Others invest in dozens of countries globally. Then there are specialty funds such as REITs (real estate investment trusts) that invest indirectly in property.

Access to thousands of mutual funds with hundreds of objectives provides investors with a wide selection of assets to satisfy an optimal asset allocation strategy. As discussed later in the chapter, an investor may keep things simple and choose index funds for each slice of the asset allocation pie. Other investors may prefer to own a combination

---

Advantages of Bond Funds for Individual Investors

- **Participation with a Small Investment Is Possible.** The minimum investment for an individual bond is often as high as $10,000; piecing together a diversified portfolio is not feasible for an individual investor with less than six figures allocated to the bond portion of his or her portfolio. Bond funds enable investors with small amounts of capital to own multiple issues. The minimum investment in a bond fund is as low as $500 or $1000, and additional fund shares can often be purchased in increments of $100.

- **Bigger Investors Enjoy Benefits in the Bond Market.** Bond investors with large amounts of capital pay smaller commissions and receive volume discounts and invitations to closed auctions that small investors do not enjoy.

- **More Frequent Income Flow.** Bond funds often distribute income to investors monthly, as opposed to the bi-annual distributions of many individual issues. Investors may opt to take the income as cash or automatically reinvest in the fund.

of "actively managed" mutual funds or "folios." In all cases, the investor enjoys the benefits of saving time and effort, lower transaction costs, increased liquidity, and instant diversification. (See the Appendix for a list of top "actively managed" funds in each major asset class.)

The Downside of Mutual Funds

Mutual fund investing, of course, is not without drawbacks. The main disadvantages associated with mutual fund investing are that fees tend to add up and that the mutual fund investor lacks control over taxes.

Fees

The total return on an investment in a mutual fund is the appreciation of the fund's shares plus any dividends less the fund's fees, transaction costs, and taxes. Fees vary from fund to fund, but operating expenses are standard to most.

- The *management fee* is the amount the investor pays the fund manager to provide the service of managing the assets.

- *Administrative fees* are paid to the fund to cover costs of record keeping, customer service, monthly statements, etc.

By summing these operating fees, and dividing that sum by the total value of our shares in the fund, the fund's expense ratio is obtained. For large cap funds, the average expense ratio is about 1.3 to 1.4 percent. It is closer to 1.5 to 1.6 percent for small cap funds. Bond funds charge on average just over 1 percent, and international stock funds, while varying greatly, are usually the most expensive, averaging 1.7 percent.

Additionally, some funds charge transactional fees to cover sales and marketing costs.

- Income from *12b-1 distribution fees* is used for marketing, advertising and distribution of the fund. Why should investors pay a separate fee for the fund manager to promote his or her service? Good question. Nonetheless, many funds charge these fees. Investors should take account of this fee (i.e., feel confident that the manager will more than make up for the charges with strong performance) before purchasing a fund that levies 12b-1 fees.

- A *load fee* is simply a sales charge added to the price of a mutual fund to compensate the financial adviser who sells it to the investor. Some funds charge the fee at the time of purchase, and others when the investor sells the fund. A "front-end load" ranges between 1 percent and 6 percent of the initial mutual fund purchase. A "back-end load," which is a percent of the sales value of the investment, is a disincentive to sell the fund, though a fund manager may reduce this fee the longer an investor stays with the fund. Whether front-end or back-end, loads are painful. Assuming all other factors being constant, it is hard to imagine why any investor would choose a load fund over a no-load fund. With a plethora of no-load funds available to investors, it is quite possible that load funds will eventually go the way of the dinosaur.

Table 5.1 and Figure 5.2 illustrate the impact of fees on a mutual fund investor's actual returns. While the example is purely hypothetical, the results are sobering. The assumptions for annual expense ratio, load fee, and annual return are quite conservative. Based on an initial investment of $10,000, a 1 percent annual expense ratio (i.e., the management and administrative fees), 1 percent front-end load, and a 9.5 percent expected annual return, an investor would give up approximately 20 percent of the investment's return after 1 year. This totals approximately 14 percent after 5 years. Fees really do add up! (Fee information is available from the brokerage firm or directly from the fund management firm, as well as on sites like Morningstar.com.)

TABLE 5.1 Understanding the Impact of Mutual Fund Fees

Initial Investment	$10,000	
Annual Expense Ratio	1.00%	
Load Fee (Front-end)	1.00%	
Annual Return	9.50%	
Where the Returns Go	**After 1 Year**	**After 5 Years**
Load	$100	$ 100
To the Investor	$841	$4821
Expense Fees	$108	$ 641

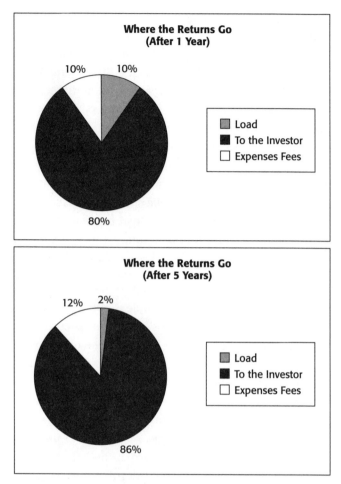

FIGURE 5.2   Understanding the impact of mutual fund fees.

Lack of Control of Taxes

As fund managers sell individual assets, the fund realizes a gain or loss that is directly passed onto to the fund's shareholders. U.S. law requires fund managers to distribute to the fund's shareholders the net of the realized gains minus the realized losses. Fund managers may distribute a net gain to the shareholders at any time during the calendar year. They usually do so at the end of the year. The consequence for the shareholder is a tax liability come April 15th (except, of course, when the funds are held in a tax-advantaged retirement account).

Shareholders must pay taxes regardless of whether they take the cash distributed by the fund or simply reinvest the net gain in the fund. In other words, the fund shareholder has no control over when a capital gain is realized.

Consider, for example, an investor who purchases 1000 shares of fund ABCDE on January 1, 2000, for $12.50 per share. On December 15, 2000, the price per share is only $10.00 and the fund distributes $1.00 per share net gain (the fund sold its holdings in technology company TECHO, originally purchased just 9 months ago). And since the investor had requested automatic reinvestment of all distributions, his holdings increase by 100 shares ($1000 divided by $10 per share). By the end of the year, the value of each share recovers slightly to $10.50/ share. So how did the investor do? The net unrealized loss on the investment is $11,550 (1100 shares × $10.50) minus $12,500 (1000 shares × $12.50), or $950. But despite the fact that the investor has not sold any of the mutual fund shares, the investor still owes Uncle Sam. To be more precise, the investor must pay taxes on a capital gain of $1000. Since the fund owned TECHO for less than 1 year (a short-term gain), the investor must pay his regular tax rate of 33 percent—a burden of $330.

An additional form of taxable income is dividend income from ownership of individual stocks. Investors, whether individual or fund managers, cannot control if or when a company pays a dividend. But investors always have the option to invest in firms that have regularly paid dividends, or firms that prefer to reinvest earnings for future growth. Investors who prefer to avoid taxable income usually avoid dividend-paying stocks.

The best way for investors to control their tax burden when investing in mutual funds is to invest in funds with low turnover and low dividend yields. The average mutual fund has a turnover of 100 percent (i.e., the average portfolio asset is bought and sold once a year).

The Quest of High Returns

Given the fee structure of the mutual fund business, the interests of fund managers and investors are closely aligned. The fund manager provides the investor with a means of gaining instant ownership of a group of stocks. The manager carries out all research and ongoing management of the fund, leaving the investor to decide when to buy, sell, or contribute more to his or her holdings of the fund's shares. In exchange for the service, the manager earns a fee—not a flat dollar amount, but rather a percent of the investor's assets.

The incentive for mutual fund managers is to grow assets under management, therein growing fee revenues. The revenue earned by the fund manager grows in direct proportion to the assets under management, but the fund manager's costs of running his or her business do not. Expenditures on salaries, overhead, audits, research tools, and so forth, do not increase at the same rate as the assets under management. Put simply, it does not take ten times the staff, office space, accountants, or subscriptions to the *Wall Street Journal* to manage ten times the number of assets. The economies of scale are fantastic in the mutual fund business. Table 5.2 provides an example of the increased margins a fund manager might be able to expect in growing a fund's assets under management. Here, the manager's asset under management grew tenfold, while her costs only tripled. The resulting larger margin is tremendous incentive to grow the fund's assets under management.

Fund managers add to their own pockets with every new dollar under management, and often do so with the help of the fund's shareholders. Investors all want to see their investment grow, and typically invest more money into a fund if it is performing well. Therefore,

TABLE 5.2   Increased Assets Under Management Means Increased Margins for the Manager*

	Assets under Management: $100 Million	Assets under Management: $1 Billion
Fees to Manager	1%	1%
Manager's Revenue	$1 Million	$10 Million
Manager's Costs	$600,000	$1,800,000
Manager's Profits	$400,000	$8.2 Million
Margin	40%	82%

*Assuming the manager's costs triple when his assets under management increase tenfold.

TABLE 5.3   The Impact of a Small Difference in Performance Over Time

Investment	Annual Return	Value after 1 year	Value after 10 years
$10,000	10%	$11,000	$25,937
$10,000	11%	$11,100	$28,394

strong performance of the fund is in the obvious interest of both manager and client.

In addition to growing existing assets under management, mutual fund managers constantly strive to bring in new money from new investors. Fund managers advertise, publish books, and give away frequent-flier miles, all in an effort to lure investors to their funds. However, there is no greater attraction to a mutual fund than the prospect of high returns to its investors. Table 5.3 shows how a mere 1 percent difference in a fund's annual return can impact the value of an investment over time.

How can an investor project the performance of a given fund? The most commonly observed factor is the fund's historical performance. Return data for mutual funds is usually available for the previous calendar year, the last 3 years, the last 5 years, as well as an average of the last 3 or 5 years. After a great year, a fund manager will do his or her best to draw attention to only the recent performance, but investors can always obtain the entire track record of the fund through the fund's prospectus, the fund family's own site, or sites like Money-Central.com and Morningstar.com.

Until recently, fund managers were only required to provide the public with audited pre-tax returns. The spotlight on pre-tax returns hides the more important number for many investors: after-tax returns. Since higher returns may come at the cost of higher taxes, some managers ignore the tax consequence and churn (i.e., frequently buy and sell) stocks in their funds. Such high turnover in a rising market inevitably leads to a greater tax burden for each investor. Beginning in 2002, mutual funds must disclose in their prospectus the after-tax returns on their funds. When utilizing mutual funds for taxable accounts, it pays to focus attention on the after-tax performance. Conversely, for a tax-deferred account, like an IRA or 401K, pre-tax returns should be the focus since capital gains are not taxed until retirement. If a manager can succeed in generating higher returns by turning over his or her portfolio frequently, the fund may be a great choice for a 401K or IRA.

Pre-tax or after-tax, investors are drawn to fund managers who have proven they can provide high returns, while investors avoid managers who have underperformed their peers or the market. Dozens of consumer publications identify "winners" and "losers," or funds with the highest and lowest returns. A fund that produces the highest returns in its category (large cap growth, small cap value, corporate bond, etc.) can rapidly increase its assets under management, rewarding the manager with greater margins on his or her business. Managers know the consequence of landing atop these charts and are in constant battle with each other to generate the highest returns.

Returns are not only relative among managers. Skeptics often ask: How good are fund managers? Do they outperform the market? And if they do, can we be confident that a manager's prior success will result in future superior performance? Some studies indicate that the average manager does not outperform his or her benchmark index (after expenses). Given the availability of index funds (discussed later in this chapter), investors may see little reason to invest in "actively managed" mutual funds at all. But a study by Professors Elton and Gruber of New York University indicates that investors can utilize past performance data to select stock funds that will outperform their benchmarks in terms of risk-adjusted returns.[1] The researchers conclude that both 1-year and 3-year returns help predict future performance, though 1-year returns are most useful. The study proves that by applying modern portfolio theory (MPT), investors can combine such funds to build optimal portfolios with higher risk-adjusted returns than portfolios of index funds (we explain this further in Chapter 9). For the individual investor, the conclusion is important. Past performance data can be used to construct an optimal mix of funds using a MPT optimizer. We place high importance on historical returns in our selection of "actively managed" funds.

---

[1] *Journal of Business*, 1996, vol. 69, no. 2. Edwin J. Elton, Martin J. Gruber, of New York University, and Christopher R. Blake, of Fordham University.

In Chapter 8, we explore in depth the concept of risk-adjusted return, commonly measured by the Sharpe ratio.

A Few Thoughts on Past Performance

As much as past performance may be an indicator of a fund manager's stock selection ability, it is important to remember that past performance is no guarantee of future success. Even the best managers may struggle to maintain consistently strong performance. One reason is there is a limit to the new money a fund manager can effectively invest in a short period of time, creating a potential pitfall for investors who chase recent top-performing funds. Take for example the manager of a small fund who diligently researched and selected a portfolio of 25 stocks that returned 10 percent more than the average for small cap growth funds, putting the fund in the top 3 percent of all funds in the category. The financial media touted the fund as a rising star, leading to tens of millions of dollars of new investment at the start of the new year and doubling the total assets under management. The manager, though ecstatic to bring in so many more fee-paying investors, was faced with a huge challenge. "Where do I invest the new money?" The 25 stocks already owned by the fund had appreciated so much in the previous year that their prices were now too high to invest more money. The manager was forced to seek out alternative small cap growth stocks that would provide superior returns. The research effort was daunting and the manager could not invest the new money fast enough to keep up with a rising market. The fund's performance was dragged down by the un-invested cash and the manager's inability to quickly move the fund's money from last year's top performers to this year's hot stocks. The lesson here is that past performance can restrain future performance in the same fund.

But what about a fund manager with a solid long-term track record who decides to launch a new fund in a new category (e.g., she adds a mid cap fund to a family of small cap growth and value funds)? Should we invest in it? There is no historical performance data, but the manager has done well in other funds. Though empirical evidence may not exist, it is popular belief among mutual fund analysts that investing in a new fund of an established, experienced manager is a great bet. An experienced manager working with an empty canvass will often outperform the market in the short-term.

Achieving Optimality with Index Funds

Indexing	Mutual Funds	"Folios"	Stocks/Funds Mix	Individual Stocks

As explained in Chapter 3, determining how much to invest in each asset class is the most important decision an investor makes. Implementing an asset allocation strategy involves purchasing assets that will give the appropriate exposure to each asset class. This might prompt a new investor to ask: Is it possible to just invest directly in each asset class? Can I simply buy an asset that gives me the necessary exposure to U.S. large cap stocks, U.S. small cap stocks, U.S. bonds, international stocks, and/or cash?[2]

The answer, of course, is "yes." Index funds are an exception to actively managed mutual funds and offer a great service to investors. Index funds are designed to give investors direct exposure to the securities in an index. The index fund manager does not select individual assets, but rather ensures that the fund has exposure to individual assets in the same proportion they maintain in the index itself. For indices like the S&P 500 and the Russell 2000, index funds are offered by several fund managers as a means of tracking the actual holdings of each index. The fund owns each stock in the S&P 500 and Russell 2000 in the same percentage as the index.

Index fund managers do not try to outperform other managers or a benchmark index. Instead, they try to match as closely as possible the performance of the given index (i.e., zero tracking error). The downside, of course, is that the investor's upside potential is limited to what the index returns. There is no chance that the manager will strike gold in a few of his or her top picks. The manager spends no time researching or analyzing companies, so he or she earns a much smaller fee than an active manager. Logically, there is a lot less turnover in the holdings of the index fund, which reduces the potential tax liability for the fund shareholder. An index fund only sells a position in a stock if the company is removed from the index. Index funds are often referred to as "passively managed" funds.

The most common index funds track the S&P 500, though index funds exist for some sub-asset classes, including U.S. large and small company stocks; growth (high price relative to earnings) and value (low price relative to earnings) stocks; international large and small company stocks; European, Asian, and emerging market stocks; and others.

---

[2] For U.S. large cap stocks, the common benchmark index is the S&P 500 Index; U.S. small cap stocks are usually represented by the Russell 2000 Index; the MSCI EAFE Index is a proxy for all international stocks; U.S. bonds can be represented by the Lehman Brothers Aggregated Bond Index, and cash is usually substituted by the U.S. 30-day Treasury bill.

Bond index funds are slightly less "passively managed" than their equity counterparts. Given the number of issues that make up an index, such as the Lehman Brothers Aggregate, it is impractical for bond index fund managers to buy issues of all the index's constituents. Instead, they purchase a sample of bonds that have similar characteristics to the bonds in the index (i.e., duration, cash flow distribution, sector, and quality weights, etc.) and utilize bond futures and options. Depending on the manager and the latitude provided in the fund's prospectus, the fund may make "active" bets by over-weighting or under-weighting some of the constituents or by including issues that are not part of the index.

Similar to index funds, ETFs (exchange traded funds) provide investors with instant exposure to a group or stocks or a particular market. ETFs enable an investor to own a basket of index stocks through the purchase of a single share of the ETF. Like index funds, turnover of shares in the ETF is minimal given that the index constituents rarely change. As their name implies, ETFs are traded on an exchange and can be bought and sold throughout the day, unlike most actively mutual and index funds, which can only be purchased at the close. The ability to buy and sell throughout the day is a major attraction for those investors who are "more active" (e.g., speculators can buy and sell an entire index of stocks quickly and efficiently). But because ETFs trade throughout the day, all investors face a pricing risk when buying and selling ETFs. Technically, an ETF will trade at the price the buyers and sellers agree upon. This may or may not be the net asset value (NAV) of the underlying shares. In other words, the ETF may trade at a premium or discount to the actual value of the underlying shares. Arbitrageurs will usually ensure that the premium or discount does not last for long. As the ETF market matures, it is likely that investors will have access to current NAV and price information.

Because ETFs offer broad exposure to an asset class at a low-cost with tax efficiency, they provide the important ingredients for long-term buy-and-hold investors. The pillar of ETF tax efficiency is the lack of distributions (i.e., investors are not impacted by fellow shareholders who choose to sell their shares). This is a clear advantage compared to "actively managed" funds in which the fund manager must make taxable distributions to all shareholders when significant redemptions force the manager to sell stocks for a gain.

ETFs charge a small management fee that is usually a bit less than or equal to a comparable index fund. Transaction fees also apply since an investor executes an order with a broker as he or she would for any other stock. This transaction fee may make ETFs more costly than index funds. It is worth noting that investors can usually buy an index fund directly from the fund manger's firm without a transaction fee, but when purchasing through a broker, a fee is paid.

The most well-known ETF is the SPDR (pronounced "spider," Standard and Poor's Depository Receipt; the symbol is SPY and the fund is traded on the AMEX exchange). Other examples of ETFs are the Nasdaq 100's (symbol is QQQ), the Dow Jones Industrial Average's Diamonds (symbol is DIA), country-specific products such as the World Equity Benchmark Shares (called Webs), and sector specific products offered by Barclay's (iShares), Merrill Lynch (Holders), and Vanguard (Vipers).

With a combination of various index funds and ETFs, it is possible to satisfy an entire asset allocation plan with "passively managed" funds. Table 5.4 shows how we might use index funds and ETFs to invest $150,000 across five major asset classes in an optimally allocated portfolio designed in Chapter 3.

Visiting sites like Indexfunds.com, or simply inquiring with a brokerage firm, investors can quickly obtain a list of available funds and ETFs (see Appendix). The choice of the index fund manager is simple. Choose the no-load index fund with the lowest expense ratio and a low tracking error (i.e., a fund whose returns mimic exactly or very closely

TABLE 5.4 Implementing a Asset Allocation Strategy using Index Funds and ETFs

	Optimal Allocation	Allocation	Index Fund or ETF
U.S. Large Cap Stocks	27%	$40,500	SPY
U.S. Small Cap Stocks	12%	$18,000	NAESX
International Stocks	17%	$25,500	FSIIX
U.S. Bonds	44%	$66,000	BIPFX
U.S. Cash	0%	$0	—

the returns of the index). SPY is an ETF that tracks the S&P 500. The Vanguard Small Cap Index (NASEX) tracks the Russell 2000. The Fidelity Spartan International Index (FSIIX) tracks the most common broad international index, the MSCI EAFE. The SEI Bond Index is a small fund that tracks the Lehman Brothers Aggregate Bond Index. For bits of cash that may remain in an account, most money market funds have a similar risk and return profile as the U.S. 30-day Treasury bill.

Accomplishing the target portfolio mix with passively managed funds is simple and efficient. As discussed in Chapter 10, because index funds replicate the index, their returns-based style is 100 percent that of the benchmark index, which ensures strict compliance with the asset allocation strategy.

Achieving Optimality with "Actively Managed" Funds

Indexing	**Mutual Funds**	"Folios"	Stocks/Funds Mix	Individual Stocks

Opting for "actively managed" funds implies a goal to either outperform the market or to take on lower-than-market risk. Given the low-cost means of achieving neutral market performance via index funds (i.e., achieving the same returns as the benchmark index for each asset class), a rational investor will only choose to pay the higher fees associated with "actively managed" funds if his or her tactical objective is to achieve higher risk-adjusted returns. Given this objective, the investor will likely choose to work with a broad set of asset classes.

To illustrate how to construct a portfolio of actively managed mutual funds, we assume that we are implementing an asset allocation strategy across eight asset classes (the ten asset class set referred to in Chapter 3, less mortgages and cash, since there are few mortgage funds for individuals and since selection of a money market funds is very straightforward). Table 5.5 presents the eight asset classes in our asset allocation strategy and their corresponding indexes.

Selecting the best combination of actively managed funds within each asset class begins with analysis of historical performance. By screening for funds in each asset class with high historical returns but acceptable risk (volatility), we limit the pool of possible funds to those that have a greater likelihood of future success (we are following the

TABLE 5.5   Several Common Asset Classes and Popular Benchmark Indices

Asset Class	Corresponding Index
U.S. Large Cap Stocks	S&P 500 Index
U.S. Small Cap Stocks	Russell 2000 Index
International Developed Markets	MSCI World Ex. U.S. Index
International Emerging Market	MSCI Emerging Markets Index
U.S. Government & Corporate Bonds	Lehman Brothers Gvt/Credit Index
U.S. Municipal Bonds	Lehman Brothers Muni Index
U.S. High Yield Bonds	Lehman Brothers High Yield Index
U.S. Real Estate	Wilshire Real Estate Index

trusted research of Elton and Gruber referred to earlier). Tools, such as Morningstar's Fund Selector, enable investors to search for mutual funds with historically high returns.

In the asset class of U.S. large cap stocks, we uncover a number of different funds, each with good historical returns, but different objectives. They all invest in large U.S. companies but with a focus on a subset of the companies. Some invest in growth companies, while others invest in companies with undervalued stocks. All fit under the umbrella of U.S. large cap stocks, but none seeks to replicate the basket of large companies (the S&P 500), as large cap index funds do. In fact, we usually have no way of being sure of what is actually owned by the fund at any given time. Because the Securities and Exchange Commission requires managers to report their holdings only twice a year, investors who inquire weeks or months after the reporting date cannot rely on the holdings list.

Investors must decide what combination of the funds will give them the exposure to large caps the asset allocation strategy requires, using past performance as an indicator of future performance. The second criteria for selecting funds should always be style consistent with the asset class. If the fund does not invest in the type of securities held in the benchmark index for the asset class, the fund should be eliminated. It is important to observe how closely the fund manager sticks to the style he or she outlines in the fund's prospectus. In

Chapter 10 we look at portfolio style in more detail and offer some useful resources for learning about a fund's style.

Since large cap value and large cap growth are mutually exclusive sub-asset classes (i.e., the holdings in each fund should not overlap), it is logical that we have funds from both categories. Based on what we know about "actively managed" funds, our objective should be to choose two (or more) funds in each sub-asset class. Having screened the large cap fund universe for those with high-risk adjusted returns, and confirmed that the screened funds invest either in large cap growth or large cap value by observing their style, we can focus on our third criterion, which is a reasonable expense ratio and low turnover. A fourth criterion, for investors who choose to research funds in greater depth, is the fund manager's investing experience and tenure with the fund.

Selection Criteria for "Actively Managed" Mutual Funds
   I. Historical Returns and Risk
  II. Style
 III. Low Expense Ratio and Low Turnover
 IV. Manager's Experience

Morningstar.com provides investors with sufficient information on mutual funds listed on U.S. markets.

Similarly, U.S. small cap stocks can be further divided into the sub-asset classes growth and value, and the selection process follows that of large caps. For bonds, we must select funds for four asset classes: government and corporate issued debt, municipal, high-yield, and mortgage. For the international stock portion of our portfolio, selection is a little more challenging. The most popular benchmark index for international developed stocks, the MSCI World ex U.S., however, includes stocks from the major European countries, Australia, New Zealand, Japan, and Hong Kong—all "developed" countries. The MSCI World ex U.S. does not include stocks from the "emerging" markets of South East Asia, Latin America, or Africa, and is exclusive from the MSCI Emerging Markets, our "emerging" markets index. To have exposure to similar investments as each index, we should select a combination of regional or country funds (perhaps a UK fund, a Pan-European fund, a Japanese fund, etc.) in proportion to each region or country's weighting in the MSCI World ex U.S. index, but we would avoid the "emerging" markets. Additionally, we should select a combination of Latin America, Eastern European, or Southeast Asian funds to satisfy the "emerging" market stock asset class.

REITs (real estate investment trusts) are publicly traded securities representing ownership interests in real-estate companies. The Internal Revenue Service has granted REIT investors tax benefits as long as the REIT manager pays out substantially all (95 percent) of the funds income to investors in the form of dividends. Additionally, REITs serve as a valuable diversifier, because REITs respond both to bond and equity markets as well as a to real estate fundamentals.

Following the selection criteria outlined previously, we created a portfolio of actively managed mutual funds, which is presented in Table 5.6. Only time will tell if our portfolio can actually outperform the market.

(For lists of other top mutual funds, see the Appendices.)

Folio Investing

Indexing	Mutual Funds	**"Folios"**	Stocks/Funds Mix	Individual Stocks

Some argue that the benefits of mutual funds are diminished by their weaknesses. Particular damaging is the lack of control of capital gains taxes. Because the turnover of individual assets is up to the manager, the investor has no control over the tax consequences that trade activity generates. A new type of fund gives investors a means of controlling taxes while maintaining the benefit of instant diversification. FolioFn, and a growing number of traditional and discount brokers, offer investors diversified "folios" of stocks or "stock baskets," which can be bought and sold in whole or stock by stock, all at the discretion of the individual investor. The "folios" are designed to give investors exposure to a particular asset class, sector, or other category of stocks; but once the "folio" is constructed, all management of the individual holdings is left to the individual investor.

The primary advantage of "folios" is the control of taxes. Because investors own the stocks directly, they have the benefit of always controlling the exact holdings in the portfolio—no questions over how much the fund manager has changed the holdings since his or her last

TABLE 5.6 Sample Portfolio of "Actively Managed" Mutual Funds (Selection as of 5/2001)

Asset Class	Sub Asset Class	Fund Symbol	Fund Name
U.S. Large Cap	Growth	AGTHX	Growth Fund of America
U.S. Large Cap	Growth	FEXPX	Fidelity Export and Multinational
U.S. Large Cap	Value	CBBYX	Alliance Growth and Income Adv
U.S. Large Cap	Value	ICSLX	ICAP Select Equity
U.S. Small Cap	Growth	BJMIX	Brazos Micro Cap
U.S. Small Cap	Growth	BUFSX	Buffalo Small Cap
U.S. Small Cap	Value	FLPSX	Fidelity Low-Priced Stock
U.S. Small Cap	Value	AMRIX	Armada Small Cap Value
International Developed Markets	Europe	MEURX	Mutual European Z
International Developed Markets	Pacific/Asia	MDPCX	Merrill Lynch Pacific D
International Emerging Markets		ODVCX	Oppenheimer Developing Markets C
U.S. Government & Corporate Bonds		CFICX	Calvert Income A
U.S. Municipal Bonds		EIITX	Executive Investors Insured Tax-Exempt
U.S. High Yield Bonds		TAHYX	Pioneer High Yield A
U.S. Real Estate		CSRSX	Cohen & Steers Realty

report to the Securities and Exchange Commission. Investors decide when capital gains are realized and, therefore, there is no risk that an untimely distribution will stick the investor with a tax bill.

The flip side of control over the holdings is that the investor does not benefit from the fund manager's expertise in managing a portfolio. The investor is on his or her own to make changes to the holdings. For the disciplined investor who is looking to pursue a passive strategy, this management responsibility is not a burden. But those investors who pursue a more active approach using "folios" must be prepared to research stocks, re-balance their portfolios, and manage the tax consequences of their trades. As the market for "folios" matures, brokerage firms will likely offer advice and tools that support an investor in managing the stocks in his or her "folio." Ideally, individual investors will be equipped with the same tools the professionals use to research stocks and optimize portfolios, *plus* tools that help investors minimize their personal tax liability.

Another advantage of "folios" is cost. Investors can acquire an entire basket of stocks in one shot for a small transaction fee, instead of purchasing the stocks one-by-one and paying a transaction fee each time. And as there are no management fees paid to the "folio" constructor, the investor only pays these small trading fees.

In the next chapter we consider building a diversified portfolio via individual stock selection.

CHAPTER 6

Selecting Stocks

A s discussed in the preceding chapter, implementing an asset allocation plan can be achieved with varying degrees of effort, ranging from very passive to very active. For investors who prefer daily personal involvement in the management of their portfolios, selecting individual companies (stocks) may be the way to go. It is a challenging process and it can, of course, be very rewarding. In fact, if it were not possible to select stocks that could reward us with higher returns, we would all stick to index funds or top-performing mutual funds. The decision to actively invest through individual stocks is based on a belief that we can select the stocks that will outperform the market.

In this chapter, we answer the questions:

- How can we predict movement in the price of a stock?

- What are the forces that drive change in the price of stocks?

- How can we organize our stock selection to take advantage of the wealth of information on stocks without being overwhelmed?

In the U.S. market alone, there are thousands of public companies that have issued stock for sale to investors large and small. In the category of large cap stocks, at a minimum, investors can consider the 500 companies listed in the S&P 500. The Russell 2000, the most common small cap stock benchmark, contains 2000 companies; and internationally there are thousands more. Macroeconomic changes affect all companies, but to different extents. The smallest economic change can be great for some companies, disastrous for others, and totally insignificant for the remainder. Appreciating the impact of broad market influences is fundamental to proper evaluation of a stock.

For each company, there is also a wealth of business, financial, and competitive information (microeconomic) available to any investor. Clearly, even for an investor with loads of spare time, it would be impossible to understand all the influences (business, financial, and competitive forces) that drive stocks. But if equipped with an understanding of how these factors impact the price of a stock, the wealth of information available to investors can be leveraged to make decisions on stocks. And by following some simple guidelines, investors can efficiently reduce the research effort and find stocks with high-expected returns.

To understand the business and competitive issues facing any company, an investor has to understand the dynamics of the firm's sector and industry. Keeping up to speed on the factors that affect sectors, ranging from technology to financial services to consumer durables, can be a daunting task in itself. Taking it a step further, appreciating what it takes to be successful in the many industries that make up each sector requires more attention. But each investor can use personal experience and common sense to evaluate stocks in a few self-selected sectors.

When evaluating individual firms, an investor must access the firm's financial statements. The Securities and Exchange Commission requires firms to report their financial status on a quarterly basis in accordance with accepted accounting rules. Income statements, balance sheets, and cash flow statements, collectively referred to as "financials," provide details of a firm's financial status.[1] To assist in the evaluation of a company's financials, as well as a comparison of that firm to others in the same or similar businesses, investors can call on

---

[1] Investors can obtain these reports from companies directly (many firms offer their Annual and Quarterly Reports on their corporate Websites) or via sites like EDGAR online (http://edgar-online.com). Other sites like Marketguide.com summarize each company's financials for the last several quarters.

professional equity research analysts. These employees of brokerage houses and banks spend their days dissecting companies. The analysts produce regular reports on the firms they cover (as well as sector and industry reports) and make buy, sell, or hold recommendations on each stock. These reports are a service to the brokerage's customers (investors) and convey the impact of new developments in a particular industry or at a particular firm. Investors can benefit from the consolidated information in the reports, even if they choose not to follow the recommendation of the analyst. As a customer of the brokerage house or bank, an investor can usually obtain the firm's research for free. Alternatively, investors can purchase reports from many brokerage houses at sites like Multex.com (some reports are also available at no charge).

For timely updates on a company's stock price, its latest earnings, or other news, professionals subscribe to pricey services like Bloomberg or Reuters. For less detailed information that is free, there are a number of financial websites that broadcast information throughout the market day. CNBC.com, motleyfool.com, marketwatch.com, and thestreet.com not only offer the standard fare of business news and financial data, but also call on financial analysts to spin the information.

In this chapter we look at how an investor can take advantage of the limitless information on sectors, industries, and individual companies to make intelligent decisions about the value of a stock. In the absence of a crystal ball, we use common sense to make decisions on the future direction of individual stocks.

The Task at Hand

Since the proportion of equities in most asset allocation plans is more than half, selecting stocks, one-by-one or via funds, is a significant part of the implementation process. Let's look again at the optimal asset allocation (allocation X) in Table 6.1, which we outlined in Chapter 3.

Summing the allocations of U.S. large cap stocks, U.S. small cap stocks, and international stocks, we see that more than half our portfolio consists of investments in shares of corporations around the world. Chapter 2 taught us that to obtain the benefits of diversification, we should own a minimum of 15 to 20 stocks in our portfolio. Though, in this case of three equity asset classes, 15 to 20 in each asset class is

TABLE 6.1 Sample Optimal Allocation
Across Five Asset Classes

	Allocation X
U.S. Large Cap Stocks	27%
U.S. Small Cap Stocks	12%
International Stocks	17%
U.S. Bonds	44%
U.S. Cash	0%

preferable. We want reasonable exposure to each asset class and want to reduce firm-specific risk, and spreading our dollars across a number of firms in each asset class will do just that.

In a dream world, we would have a quick, effective means of sifting through all the data on every stock in each asset class. The analysis would produce crystal clear results: a list of the prices for all stocks as of December 31st of the coming year. Attention to risk and diversification could be thrown out the window, and our only worry would be how quickly we could gather all our money and invest it in the cheapest stock (i.e., the one that is farthest below its anticipated price at the end of the coming year).

So in such a dream scenario, the question remains: If we know the future price, why should we race to invest? Well, if we do not hurry, other investors will uncover the same strategy and buy the cheap stocks. And as they do so, they will push up the prices until the prices are in line with the expected December 31st prices. Thus, a perfect forecasting methodology is only so good as it is a secret one, and the market is efficient enough that good strategies rarely remain a secret. As much as we would like to describe for investors our ultimate stock picking strategy, we must be honest and say no perfect strategy exists.

That said, we can still effectively use simple valuation techniques, attention to the factors that influence stocks prices, and publicly available information to identify stocks that we expect to rise in price. Recalling our discussion of the benefits of diversification, we know that to appreciate the risk of a stock, we have to appreciate the market-specific and firm-specific influences on a stock's price. Under the umbrellas of market-specific and firm-specific influences, there are many factors affecting the returns of a stock. We attempt to understand these factors better so that we may use them to select stocks with high-expected returns. We first look at fundamental valuation and relative valuation and then outline some general rules that all investors should follow.

Fundamental Stock Valuation

Before buying anything, most consumers ask: Is the product worth the price? Investments are no different. So how can an investor tell if a stock is worth its price? Some will argue that a stock, like all investments, is worth what you can sell it for. That helps some—we know what we can sell our stocks for today. But what will the stock be worth tomorrow? That's the ultimate question for investors. We are searching for stocks that are valued less today than they will be down the road. Regardless of their strategies, all investors are looking to take advantage of information they have that leads them to believe a stock will be worth more down the road.

The price of a stock, or share, represents a fraction of the value of the entire company. If a firm has 1 million shares issued to investors, and each share is trading for $20, the firm is valued at $20 million. So when we talk about predicting a rise in a stock's price, we are, of course, really predicting a rise in the value of the company.

As the value of the company rises, each shareholder is rewarded by an increase in the price of the company's stock. Thus it is an investor's job to estimate the impact of firm-specific and market influences on the company's valuation.

In addition to being rewarded by a rising stock price, shareholders earn income from dividends, or cash distributions the company makes to each shareholder. Companies pay dividends from the cash they have on hand, or their profits. Some companies pay regular dividends (annually or even quarterly); others almost never do so. Why? Many firms, especially firms in growing industries, prefer to reinvest the profits they earn to take advantage of new business opportunities. While, larger mature companies feel it is in the shareholder's best interest to distribute the cash and let the shareholder decide how it should be invested. (Many investors, through automatic dividend reinvestment programs, use the cash dividend to purchase additional shares in the firm).

Traditional fundamental valuation of a stock is based on the future cash flow to the investor, and the dividend discount model (DDM) is the basis for all fundamental valuation models.[2] In essence, the model calculates the price of a stock to be the sum of the future cash dividends discounted to their present value. In estimating future dividends, we first examine the current earnings per share (EPS), part of any public company's annual report. We deduct from this EPS the amount of cash the firm will reinvest, and we are left with the dividend payout. A firm that earns $2.00 per share and reinvests $1.50 in the company leaves $0.50 for dividends ($0.50/ $2.00 give us a payout ratio of 25 percent; the retention ratio is just the opposite of the payout ratio; in this case, it is the $1.50 the firm reinvests divided by $2.00 = 75%). We can estimate the future payout ratio by simply averaging the ratio of the past few years. Or to make it even easier, visit Marketguide.com, type in a company's ticker and pull the ratio from the Key Ratios and Statistics table.

Most firms grow their profits each year, but others contract or shrink. To grow, firms have to reinvest money they earn. This growth impacts the earnings per share and thus the dividends that are paid to investors, and therefore growth is an important component in the DDM calculation. A firm's growth rate can be calculated by multiplying the retention ratio by the firm's ROE, or return on equity (net profits divided by the total equity in the firm). The ROE can be found in brokerage analyst reports as well as on Marketguide.com's Key Ratios and Statistics table. Over the long haul, rapid growth rates cannot be maintained and the typical mature company grows at about the same rate as the economy (i.e., gross domestic product growth). Therefore, any valuation model can be broken down to account for multiple stages of growth.[3]

The final component of the DDM calculation is the discount rate, or the factor that accounts for time value of money and the uncertainty of future dividend payments. Investors must be familiar with the con-

---

[2] There are variations of DDM that focus on cash flows instead of dividends. For more details on fundamental valuation using a discounted cash flow methodology, see Gary Gray, Patrick J. Cusatis, and J. Randall Woolridge, *Streetsmart Guide To Valuing a Stock*, McGraw Hill, 1999, and Aswath Damodaran, *Investment Valuation*, John Wiley & Sons, New York, 1996.

[3] Ibid.

cept of present and future value, and know that by dividing a future cash inflow (e.g., a dividend) by the appropriate discount rate, they will determine the value of the cash today. But dividends are not guaranteed. For every company, regardless of size, profitability, or dividend history, there is some uncertainty that future dividends will be paid. Therefore, the discount rate must also account for the risk associated with future dividend payments for any particular firm.

To determine the discount rate for a company, we need to know how risky the company is compared to the market, or all other stocks, and we need to know the risk-free rate, or the interest rate the U.S. government pays on long-term debt. Beta is an estimate of a firm's sensitivity to the market risk, as explained in Chapter 2. Any stock with a beta greater than 1.00 is considered more risky than the market, while those with a beta less than 1.00 are considered less risky.

The risk premium for stocks is the excess return stocks, in general, must earn above and beyond the risk-free rate to compensate for the associated risk. Because the return on stocks carries more uncertainty than government debt, investors must be rewarded with a premium to the risk-free return. By multiplying a company's beta by the risk premium and then adding the risk-free rate, the appropriate discount rate for the firm is calculated. (The risk premium for stocks varies over time; however, it is usually safe to use 5.5 percent.)

Discount rate for a company = Risk-free rate
+ Beta (stock risk premium)

Dividend Discount Model

$$Share\ Price = \frac{EPS * Payout\ Ratio * (1 + g)}{r - g}$$

Stock price today = EPS × payout ratio/$(r - g)$

Where: EPS is the expected earning per share over the next twelve months;

Payout ratio is an estimate of next year's cash dividend/ EPS;

g is the expected percentage increase in earning per share each year (it can be calculated by multiplying the firm's retention ratio by the firm's ROE);

And r is the applicable discount rate for the company, also referred to as the firm's cost of capital.

A little later in this chapter, we take a closer look at one particular company, Southwest Airlines (LUV), and discuss the market and firm-specific influences on its EPS, payout ratio, growth rate, and discount rate.

Relative Valuation

Relative valuation is a technique that compares firms in similar businesses, in an effort to uncover a stock that is relatively cheap compared to others. Would you pay 50 cents for an apple from the neighborhood grocer if you could pay only 40 cents from the deli next store? Of course not. And neither would most investors. Investors can compare stock prices in the same manner as they compare any other good. And just as it is not meaningful to compare apples to oranges, investors usually do not compare companies in different businesses using relative valuation. When comparing stocks in the same industry, we cannot simply compare the absolute values of the companies. Instead, investors look at some set of standardized values. We use the financials that drive the companies' success (e.g., revenue and earnings) and create multiples for comparison. The most commonly used multiples are price to earnings (PE) and price to sales.

The PE and price to sales multiples can be indicators of future performance and are important factors in the evaluation of a stock. As James P. O'Shaugnhessy explains in the book, *What Works on Wall Street,* large capitalization stocks with high PEs relative to all other stocks in the market have performed poorly, while stocks with low price to sales ratios have done very well over time. Investors can find the PE, price to sales, and other ratios for chosen stocks on many sites, though Marketguide.com's "Comparison" link is particularly useful. To search for stocks with low PEs or low prices to sales, screening tools are extremely useful. One of the better screening tools is Money-Central's Stock Screener. It allows investors to perform a custom screen using one or more factors or perform a deluxe search using predefined criteria.

Of course, we can always calculate ratios by looking at the financials of a company. As of December 31, 2000, Southwest Airlines was trading for $22.35. Its EPS was $0.835 for the year 2000. Dividing the price per share ($22.35) by the earnings per share, we get a PE of 26.77.

$$PE\ ratio = Price/EPS$$

$$\text{Southwest Airlines PE} = \$22.35/\$0.835 = 26.77$$

$$\text{Delta Airlines PE} = \$50/\$4.15 = 12$$

Southwest's sales (total revenue) for the year was $5.6 billion. Dividing $5.6 billion by the firm's 761 million shares outstanding, we get $7.36 per share. The price to sales ratio is 3.04 ($22.35/$7.36). Is this high or low? Is Southwest relatively expensive or cheap?

Compared to Delta Airlines, with a PE of 12 and a price to sales ratio of 0.50, Southwest seems extremely expensive. But compared to the airline industry as a whole, which has a PE of 20.0 and a price to sales ratio of 1.31, Southwest does not look quite as bad. But Delta, based on the PE and price to sales ratio alone, appears really cheap compared to Southwest and the industry. Is this all we need to know to purchase Delta and short Southwest? Are we missing something?

The growth rate of each firm cannot be overlooked. Since a stock's value depends greatly on the growth of the EPS, we need to add growth to our relative valuation. The price earnings multiple (PÉ) divided by the expected growth in EPS (g) gives us the PEG ratio, a useful number in comparing the prices of companies that are growing at different rates.

$$PEG = PE/Expected\ growth\ rate\ in\ earnings$$

$$\text{Southwest's Growth Rate} = \text{Retention ratio} * \text{ROE} = 75\% * 25\% = 15\%$$

$$\text{Southwest Airline's PEG} = 26.77/15 = 1.78$$

$$\text{Delta Airline's growth rate} = (97.73\% * 10) = 9.77\%$$

$$PEG = 12/9.77 = 1.23$$

(Source of financial data for this example: Marketguide.com)

Even after factoring in growth, Southwest is relatively more expensive than Delta airlines. Based on relative valuation alone, we may consider buying Delta airlines, or at least avoiding Southwest. But investors should not rely on the PE or price to sales factor alone. Combining an understanding of a stock's relative valuation with an appreciation for the macroeconomic and firm-specific factors that affect the stock's price is a key to successful "active" investing.

Macro Factors that Impact Valuation

When discussing the factors that impact the price of a stock, it is important to remember that risk is a two-sided coin. Without forces that create volatility, a stock is not moving up or down. Anything that increases a stock's volatility (or risk) increases the likelihood that the stock will reach extreme highs or crash to all-time lows. Up to this point, we have referred to market risk as a compilation of all non-firm-specific risks a company faces. We used beta to estimate a company's sensitivity to changes in the broad market. In this section, we break down market risk into a number of factors. Each has a different influence on the performance of the stock. The expected return is a function of the company's reaction (or sensitivity) to the changes in each factor. To make this clearer, we look at the impact of each factor on the components of the DDM equation.

Every company is affected by business cycles, interest rate changes, oil prices, and other factors. Let's continue with our evaluation of Southwest Airlines and forecast the impact of some of the market factors.

Economic Growth

How is Southwest Airlines affected when the economy changes from strong growth to a recession, and personal and corporate budgets are cut as individuals and businesses reduce their spending in response to lower incomes? Let's put a little common sense to work. Airline travel is often a necessity for businesses. To get personnel from the home office to a client's, travel by plane is the most time-efficient. But businesspeople will reduce the number of trips they take during a low point in the business cycle and Southwest will sell fewer tickets to businesspeople during a recession. Similarly, personal travel always falls during a slowing economy. Most people take fewer vacations or use alternative, less expensive transportation when traveling. However, because Southwest sells seats for the lowest price on many routes, it does not feel the pinch as much as other airlines.

Overall, we can confidently say that Southwest Airlines will experience fewer sales during a downturn in the business cycle. Lower revenue will impact the earnings per share and perhaps growth expectations. Plugging the lowered numbers into the DDM equation, it is easy to see that (other inputs remaining constant) the price of the stock will fall.

The Interest Rate Factor

Changes in interest rates impact all companies. The discount rate for every company changes when the risk-free rate changes [Discount rate for a company = Risk-free rate + Beta (stock risk premium)]. A change in the discount rate will inversely impact the price of a stock. Inputting the change into the DDM, we see that lower interest rates increase the value of each future dividend payment and thus increase the value of the stock, whereas as a rise in interests rates does just the opposite. Nevertheless, sensitivity to interest rates can be very different from industry to industry.

Serious investors are closely in tune with the Federal Reserve, the governing body that has a strong influence on interest rate levels in the United States. Particularly during periods of slowing or no economic growth, the Federal Reserve may hold the key to a quick recovery in a stock that has been beaten down by a lower expected EPS and a lower expected growth rate. Lower interest rates stimulate investment and consumer spending. It is cheaper for consumers to buy homes when mortgage rates fall, and an increase in retail purchases inevitably leads to a lot more waste.

The value of Southwest Airlines, like all firms, benefits from interest rate cuts because its discount rate falls. The company also benefits from increased consumer and business spending that follows interest rate cuts.

Oil Prices

Most people probably do not recognize how dependent day-to-day living is on energy sources, such as oil. Although they notice the changes in prices at the gas pump and in the electric bill each month, it is hard to really quantify the importance of energy. The stock market shows the significance of oil to the overall economy whenever there is a rise or fall in the price of oil.

One of the largest costs for all airlines is fuel. A change in the price of oil directly impacts the cost of doing business for all firms in the sector.

When oil prices soar, the EPS of Southwest Airlines will fall, unless, of course, the firm is able to raise seat prices in proportion to the increase in the rise of the price of oil. Therefore, generally speaking, an oil price increase will reduce the value of Southwest Airlines stock. But firms in the oil and gas exploration business will do well. At higher prices, any new energy sources they find will be worth more—the EPS will increase.

Economic growth, interest rates, and oil prices are three macroeconomic factors that investors must observe when investing in stocks. Each factor contributes to the overall movement in price (or risk) of all stocks. As each factor changes, the price of each stock will react almost instantaneously. Savvy investors predict changes in each factor, sum them together, and predict a return on each stock. Quantifying this approach is the process of building a multiple-factor model. There are a handful of well-known multifactor models. To learn more, try Fama and French's three-factor model, and Chen, Roll, and Ross' "Economic Forces of the Stock Market."[4]

Firm-Specific Risk

Continuing the discussion of firm-specific risk from Chapter 2, we can estimate the impact of events that do not affect the broad market, but directly affect a particular firm. There are an infinite number of firm-specific risks, but the impact of most of them on the value of a stock is easy to explain. In Chapter 2, we used the example of an unexpected management team departure. The sudden lack of leadership can cause operational problems leading to higher costs. At the same time, clients of the company become uneasy about doing business with the firm. The result, lower EPS and likely a lower growth rate. In the case of Southwest Airlines, much of the success of the airline is attributed to the leadership of long-time CEO Herb Kelleher. Investors are nervous about his departure and its impact on future growth.

How about a small, growing firm that inks a new contract with a major client? For example, what if a fledgling airline, similar to Southwest in its early years, is contracted by the State of California to be the

---

[4] Fama, Eugene F. and Kenneth R. French, "Size and Book-to-Market Factors in Earnings and Returns," *Journal of Finance*, March 1995, and N. Chen, R. Roll, and S. Ross "Economic Forces and the Stock Market," *Journal of Business*, September 1986.

preferred airline for state employees? Clearly, the impact of the contract itself on the revenue of the firm will be favorable, and will likely lead to an increased EPS. But a change in the growth rate may have an even greater affect on the price of the stock. Investors see a greater likelihood that the firm will be able to grow faster on the back of new business with the new client.

Another example of a firm-specific event is a decision to establish a new division or enter a new line of business. For example, what is the impact on the price of Southwest if the firm decides to pursue online hotel bookings? Investors may ask, does Southwest really know anything about the Internet and the lodging industry? Granted the firm has an outstanding record in the travel business, but can it make money at selling hotel rooms on the Internet? Investors will look to Southwest for an understanding of how much money (EPS) the new business will bring in. Investors will factor the risk of the new venture into the beta of the firm; adding a higher risk business will increase the discount rate for the firm, offsetting to some extent any increase in EPS or increase in the growth rate.

Firm-specific factors can be the most influential in a change in the price of a stock. But they are often the most difficult to monitor. Tracking a company's every move requires constant monitoring. Investors should take advantage of news alerts and other automated services offered by their brokerage firm or online portfolio trackers.

Recommendations

Stock selection strategies vary widely. No approach can guarantee success, though many can ensure failure. Armed with an understanding of the factors that affect stocks and how stocks are priced, investors can devise their own strategies. But more important than an investor's stock selection methodology is the investor's commitment to building a high-quality, diversified portfolio. Bets on a few well-researched stocks may enhance the short-term performance of a portfolio, but failure to diversify across asset classes and individual securities can spell long-term doom. As we entrench ourselves in the research of individual stocks, we must keep things in perspective. It is the performance of the overall portfolio that really matters. The following sections give a few guidelines suggested for all investors:

- **Stick to Your Asset Allocation Plan.**   Have confidence in your asset allocation strategy. Chapter 3 explained how investors can reduce the risk of their portfolio and achieve strong long-term returns if they properly allocate investments across asset classes. Stocks have historically been outstanding long-term investments—in general, they will experience ups and downs, but on average, they are likely to produce high returns over time. Haphazard allocation reduces the benefits of diversification. Owning a mix of Large Cap, Small Cap, and International Stocks in the right combination is the key. Constructing a portfolio in line with the asset allocation strategy requires selection for each asset class. As tempting as it might be to overload in large caps and ignore international stocks, it is important to keep in mind the long-term plan.

- **Limit Your Universe.**   Given the quantity of stocks in each asset class, reducing the list of potential candidates for a portfolio reduces the research effort. We can use a number of criteria to eliminate stocks. One way is to use a top-down investing approach to narrow the universe of stocks further. For example, break down the large cap allocation into the sectors represented in the S&P 500. Then, pick a stock or two in each sector and invest in each in proportion to their weight in the index. The result: you have gained exposure to the asset class consistent with the index.

  Recent returns in the market provide additional support for this top-down approach. In recent years, the correlations among industries have weakened. Therefore, diversification across industries provides greater risk reduction than in previous periods.

- **Don't Undertake More Than You Can Handle.**   Be humble. Just because you decide to use individual stocks in your portfolio does not mean you must ignore mutual funds or folios. The research effort required to select 45 to 60 stocks across three asset classes is huge. Make it smaller by focusing on the types of companies or businesses you know best. For example, if you are comfortable with large U.S. blue chip technology companies, but have never traded a French stock, buy index or mutual funds to satisfy the international equity segment of your portfolio. Investing should never be about ego, or how much responsibility you can take on. Always remember the goal: maximize returns and control risk.

In the next two chapters, we look further at balancing risk and return in a portfolio. We build on the concept of asset allocation, but focus on individual securities instead of asset classes.

CHAPTER 7

Quantitative Asset Selection

There are many ways to choose stocks and mutual funds. In Chapter 5, we discussed how to choose great performing mutual funds, and in Chapter 6, we discussed how to select individual stocks that are likely to earn the best returns. So will every high-return stock or mutual fund be a good fit for our portfolio? The answer, of course, is "no," and because of that, our objective in selecting assets should not be to choose the best performing stocks or mutual funds, but to choose assets that best fit into our portfolio. In this chapter, we provide answers to the following questions.

- Are best performing stocks and mutual funds always good for my portfolio?

- How can I select assets that will best fit my portfolio and investment strategy?

The Importance of the Sharpe Ratio

There are many ways to measure a portfolio's performance. Thus far, we discussed absolute return, the Sharpe ratio, beta, and alpha. In this chapter, we focus our attention on one of the most commonly used performance measurement ratios—the Sharpe ratio, which is:

$$Sharpe\ ratio = \frac{r_p - r_f}{\sigma_p}$$

where r_p = the historical average return of the portfolio,

$\quad\quad\quad r_f$ = the historical average return of the risk-free rate, and

$\quad\quad\quad \sigma_p$ = the standard deviation of the portfolio's historical return.

To explain the equation in simple terms, the Sharpe ratio measures how much return an investor receives from the investment per a given unit risk. The higher an investment's Sharpe ratio, the more the investor is rewarded for the risk he or she is taking. The Sharpe ratio is preferred over absolute returns as a measurement of an asset's performance because it takes risk into consideration. Table 7.1 ranks five mutual funds in terms of absolute returns, and then shows how the order changes if ranked in terms of the Sharpe ratio (i.e., risk-adjusted return). After adjusting each fund's performance for the risk taken, the resulting Sharpe ratio ranking is completely different.

We discussed the importance of taking risk into consideration when investing, and how to identify high performing stocks and mutual funds using the risk-adjusted return, or Sharpe ratio. In constructing a portfolio, the investor should also concentrate on selecting assets that will maximize the portfolio's Sharpe ratio, and give the best return for the risks taken. To construct a portfolio with a high Sharpe ratio, we can choose assets that will increase the return of the portfolio, or reduce the risk of the portfolio, or both.

TABLE 7.1   Mutual Fund Return and Sharpe Ratio Comparison

Return Rank	Name	Return[1]	Sharpe Ratio[2]	Sharpe Ratio Rank
1	Pillar Mid Cap	20.03%	0.23	4
2	ProFunds UltraOTC	17.18%	0.14	5
3	Legg Mason Value	12.25%	0.27	3
4	PIMCO Short-Term	6.23%	0.91	1
5	CUFund Short-Term	5.99%	0.79	2

[1] Arithmetic average annualized daily return from 1999–2000.
[2] A risk free rate of 4.5% annually is used in the Sharpe ratio calculation.

Selecting Assets to Increase Portfolio Return

Selecting individual assets to increase the overall return of the portfolio is fairly straightforward. Portfolio return, as discussed in Chapter 1, is the weighted average of each individual holding's return. Therefore, we can select assets with high-expected returns to increase the expected return of the overall portfolio. Chapters 5 and 6 also discuss in detail how to select stocks and mutual funds with high-expected returns. Suppose we already have a portfolio that is worth $100,000, and has generated an annualized average return of 12 percent. Now let us assume that we have an additional $100,000 cash to invest, and there are three hypothetical assets we are considering as investments. The first asset, Asset A "High Flier," generates a high return of 20 percent annually. Asset B "Moderate Growth" has a moderate return of 12 percent annually. And the third asset, Asset C "Slow and Steady," has an annualized return of 7 percent. Table 7.2 summarizes the returns of the portfolio and each of the three assets.

It seems obvious that we should choose to invest the additional $100,000 cash in Asset A "High Flier." The combination of our portfolio and Asset A should give us the highest return possible. Table 7.3 shows three potential portfolios we can make by adding either Asset A, B, or C to our original portfolio. Keep in mind that we now have $200,000 total, with $100,000 in our original portfolio and an additional $100,000 invested in one of the above three assets.

Figure 7.1 compares the expected return of Portfolios A, B, and C, each composed of the original portfolio, and Asset A, B, or C respectively.

TABLE 7.2   Portfolio Return and Asset Returns

Name	Average Annualized Return
Portfolio (Total Value: $100,000)	12.0%
Invest an additional $100,000 in one of the following assets:	
Asset A—"High Flier"	20.0%
Asset B—"Moderate Growth"	12.0%
Asset C—"Slow and Steady"	7.0%

TABLE 7.3   Possible New Portfolio Compositions

	Original Portfolio Weight	Asset A Weight	Asset B Weight	Asset C Weight
Portfolio A	50%	50%	—	—
Portfolio B	50%	—	50%	—
Portfolio C	50%	—	—	50%

As expected, by investing the additional $100,000 all in Asset A, the resulting portfolio's annualized return is 16 percent. On the other hand, by investing the additional money all in Asset B or Asset C, the resulting portfolio's annualized return will be significantly lower: 12 percent and 9.5 percent respectively. (Please read Chapter 1 for how to calculate expected return of a portfolio.)

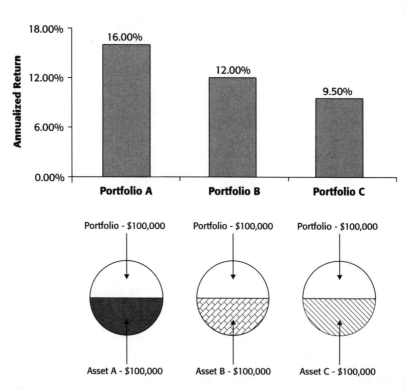

FIGURE 7.1   Portfolio return and composition.

Without additional information about the behavior of these three assets, it's an easy decision to make thus far. Now, we need to examine other factors in the decision. As mentioned previously, another way to increase the Sharpe ratio of a portfolio is to reduce the total risk of the portfolio. Let us take our hypothetical example one step further and consider the risk of the assets. Let us assume that the original portfolio has the annualized risk of 14 percent. Let us also assume that Assets A, B, and C have annualized risks of 25 percent, 13 percent, and 3.5 percent, respectively. Table 7.4 lists the risk of the portfolio and each of the three assets. But, as discussed in Chapter 2, an individual asset's risk is not enough to determine the risk of the portfolio, we also need to know how each of these assets move against each other, or the correlation among them. Table 7.4 also lists the hypothetical correlation figures of the original portfolio and these assets.

Selecting Assets to Reduce Portfolio Risk

Reducing the risk of a portfolio is not as straightforward as increasing the return of the portfolio, shown previously. Risk cannot be calculated using weighted average. Therefore, choosing the least risky asset, "Slow & Steady," in our example, does not guarantee that we will

TABLE 7.4 Portfolio Risk, Asset Risks, and Correlation

Name	Average Annualized Risk
Portfolio (Total Value: $100,000)	14.0%
Asset A—"High Flier"	25.0%
Asset B—"Moderate Growth"	13.0%
Asset C—"Slow and Steady"	3.5%

Correlation	Portfolio	Asset A	Asset B	Asset C
Portfolio	1.0	0.4	−0.2	0.9
Asset A	0.4	1.0	0.1	0.3
Asset B	−0.2	0.1	1.0	0.5
Asset C	0.9	0.3	0.5	1.0

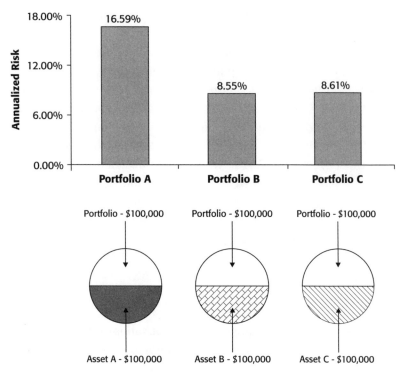

FIGURE 7.2   Portfolio risk and composition.

minimize the risk in the new portfolio. Figure 7.2 compares the overall risk of Portfolios A, B, and C, each composed of the original portfolio, and Asset A, B, or C, respectively. Portfolio B, which consists of the original portfolio plus the additional $100,000 invested in Asset B "Moderate Growth," has the lowest risk at 8.55 percent, among the three portfolios. (Please read Chapters 1 and 2 on how to calculate the risk of a portfolio.)

Surprise, surprise! We can attain the lowest possible portfolio risk not by investing in the asset with the lowest risk, "Slow and Steady," but by investing in "Moderate Growth." This is because overall risk calculation involves two factors: The two assets' individual risks, and correlation between them. In Table 7.4, we see that "Moderate Growth" has a significantly lower correlation with the original portfolio than "Slow and Steady." Despite the fact that "Moderate Growth" has a higher individual risk than "Slow and Steady," the correlation factor is dominant in this example.

Selecting Assets to Increase Portfolio Return and Reduce Portfolio Risk

The third way to increase the Sharpe ratio of the portfolio is to simultaneously increase portfolio return and reduce portfolio risk. "High Flier" increases the portfolio return, but also increases the risk. "Moderate Growth" reduces the portfolio risk, but it does not impact the return for better or worse. "Slow and Steady" reduces the portfolio return, but also reduces the risk at the same time. Table 7.5 shows the Sharpe ratios for the original portfolio and the Assets A, B, and C. As we can see, "Slow and Steady," which on the surface appears to be the most conservative of the three assets, has the highest Sharpe ratio of the three assets we are considering to buy with our $100,000 cash.

So which of these assets will give us the highest possible Sharpe ratio overall in the new portfolio? Based on their respective Sharpe ratios, we might expect it to be "Slow and Steady," which has the highest. However, it is not. The winner in our example is actually "Moderate Growth." Figure 7.3 compares the Sharpe ratios of Portfolios A, B, and C, each composed of the original portfolio, and Asset A, B, or C respectively. Portfolio B's Sharpe ratio of 0.88 is clearly superior to the Sharpe ratios of Portfolios A and C. This illustrates that choosing the asset with the highest Sharpe ratio does not guarantee that the resulting portfolio will also have the highest Sharpe ratio. Sharpe ratio is influenced simultaneously by return and risk. In choosing assets for a portfolio, we cannot simply look at the risk and return behavior of the potential assets on the surface. We must compute the effect it has on the portfolio's Sharpe ratio by incorporating the asset into the portfolio as we have just illustrated.

TABLE 7.5   Portfolio Sharpe Ratio and Asset Sharpe Ratios

Name	Sharpe Ratio[1]
Portfolio (Total Value: $100,000)	0.54
Asset A—"High Flier"	0.62
Asset B—"Moderate Growth"	0.58
Asset C—"Slow and Steady"	0.71

[1] A risk free rate of 4.5% annually is used in the Sharpe ratio calculation.

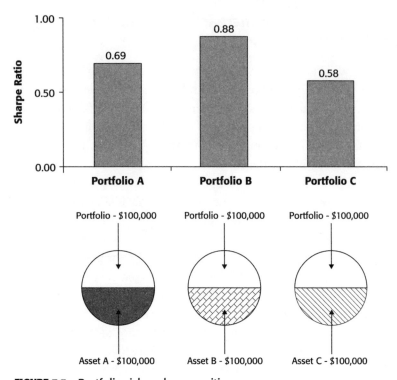

FIGURE 7.3 Portfolio risk and composition.

This extremely simplified example demonstrates that asset selection is not about selecting best performing assets, but about selecting the best fitting assets for the portfolio. "High Flier" generates the highest return, but it is not the best choice for the portfolio. "Slow and Steady" has the highest Sharpe ratio, but it is not the best choice for the portfolio either. To summarize what we learned so far in the chapter, we must consider the following factors *together* when selecting assets for a portfolio.

- Stocks or mutual funds with high returns can increase the portfolio return.

- Stocks or mutual funds with low risks can reduce the portfolio risk.

- Stocks or mutual funds with low correlation to the existing portfolio can reduce the portfolio risk.

In reality, however, asset selection is not as simple as it seems. Stocks and mutual funds that have high returns often are accompanied with high risks. In addition, if your portfolio is already fairly diversified, you will often have difficulty finding new stocks and mutual funds that have very low correlation with the portfolio. Nevertheless, an investor should keep the three rules in mind when selecting new assets for a portfolio. Another important factor to consider is that the return, risk, and correlation statistics we calculate are estimates of future performance of the assets. Often, these estimates are calculated from asset's historical return data. (Please refer to Chapter 2 for how to calculate historical return, risk, and correlation.) Since, as we know, past performance does not guarantee future returns, quantitative asset selection methods are best used in combination with fundamental asset selection methods such as those discussed in Chapters 5 and 6.

The simple hypothetical example is based on many assumptions. For example, we assumed that we could only select one of the three assets A, B, or C in which to invest. However, if we are equally comfortable with all three assets, how can we allocate the additional $100,000 across all three of these assets to achieve the highest possible Sharpe ratio? Another assumption is that we are not willing to change the existing portfolio. If we are willing to sell a certain portion of the existing $100,000 portfolio without changing its return behavior, can we achieve an even higher Sharpe ratio? Table 7.6 and Figure 7.4 show one

TABLE 7.6 Return Behavior of Portfolio B and New Portfolio

	Portfolio B	New Portfolio
Annualized Return	12.00%	12.40%
Annualized Risk	8.55%	8.55%
Sharpe Ratio1	0.88	0.92
Original Portfolio Weight	50%	34%
Asset A Weight	—	11%
Asset B Weight	50%	45%
Asset C Weight	—	10%

[1] A risk free rate of 4.5% annually is used in the Sharpe ratio calculation.

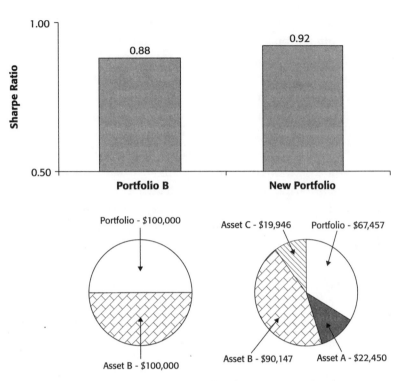

FIGURE 7.4   Portfolio B and new portfolio Sharpe ratio and composition.

possibility of a combination that can achieve a higher Sharpe ratio than Portfolio B. By selling roughly one-third of the original portfolio (the remaining original portfolio value is $67,457), we can allocate the additional money among all three of the assets in the following way: $22,450 in Asset A, $90,147 in Asset B, and $19,946 in Asset C. This new portfolio shares the same risk level as Portfolio B, at 8.55 percent annual risk. However, its expected annualized return is 12.40 percent, 40 basis points higher than that of Portfolio B. (Please refer to Chapters 1 and 2 on how to calculate portfolio return and risk.) Same risk level, but higher expected return allows this new portfolio to generate a Sharpe ratio of 0.92, higher than Portfolio B's Sharpe ratio of 0.88.

So how did we find this new portfolio's allocation in the first place? How can we determine which portfolio allocation will achieve the highest Sharpe ratio for us? Are we doomed to try every single combination? Fortunately, that is not necessary, thanks to a technique called

TABLE 7.7   Return and Risk Behavior of a Five-Stock Sample

Ticker	Name	Return[1]	Risk[2]	Sharpe Ratio[3]
MSFT	Microsoft Corp.	20.22%	45.40%	0.35
WMT	Wal-Mart Stores Inc.	43.31%	43.84%	0.89
GE	General Electric Company	29.11%	31.82%	0.77
XOM	Exxon Mobil Corp.	18.15%	28.82%	0.47
C	Citigroup Inc.	31.99%	43.92%	0.63

Correlation[4]	MSFT	WMT	GE	XOM	C
MSFT	1.0	0.22	0.32	0.15	0.29
WMT	0.22	1.0	0.40	0.18	0.38
GE	0.32	0.40	1.0	0.14	0.46
XOM	0.15	0.18	0.14	1.0	0.23
C	0.29	0.38	0.46	0.23	1.0

[1] Arithmetic average annualized daily return from 1998–2000.
[2] Annualized daily volatility from 1998–2000.
[3] A risk free rate of 4.5% annually is used in the Sharpe ratio calculation.
[4] Daily correlation from 1998–2000.

portfolio optimization, which was first introduced in Chapter 3 and is wdiscussed in detail in Chapter 8.

Before moving on to Chapter 8, we selected a sample group of stocks based on the criterion discussed in this chapter. They have relatively high returns, low risks, and just as importantly, low correlations among them. Table 7.7 shows the characteristics of these five stocks. We use this group of stocks extensively in our discussion in the next chapter.

Tactical Asset Allocation

n Chapter 3, we cited research by Brinson, Hood, and Beebower[1] that found that 93.6 percent of the variability in a portfolio's return can be explained by asset allocation, and that another 1.7 percent can be explained by security selection. Although the average managers in the study lost 0.36 percent return annually due to security selection, the best manager was able to generate an additional 3.6 percent return annually. This shows that active portfolio management, while difficult, can still add value.

This chapter answers the following questions.

- How can investors best use security selection to generate additional return for their portfolios?

- What is asset allocation on a tactical level?

The answer to the first question is actually twofold: First we need to select appropriate individual assets, and then we need to allocate appropriately across those assets. In Chapters 5, 6, and 7, we discussed a variety of fundamental and quantitative techniques for selecting individual stocks and mutual funds. Now we turn our attention to

---

[1] Gary P. Brinson, L. Randolph Hood, and Gilbert L. Beebower, "Determinants of Portfolio Performance," *Financial Analyst Journal,* January–February 1995.

tactical asset allocation—the process of determining just how the individual assets we select ought to be allocated within a portfolio.

Allocating Individual Assets within an Asset Class

Strategic asset allocation helps investors to determine how they ought to be investing across major asset classes. Depending on, of course, the asset classes included in a strategic asset allocation analysis, and the tolerance for risk, investors might determine that some part of the portfolio should be invested in U.S. large cap stocks. For the sake of example, we assume that to be the case. Table 8.1 lists a hypothetical group of stocks selected for the U.S. large cap stocks portion of an asset allocation model, and their respective return behavior. This set of stocks is used throughout this chapter.

TABLE 8.1 Return and Risk Behavior of a Five-Stock Sample Portfolio

Ticker	Name	Return[1]	Risk[2]	Sharpe Ratio[3]
MSFT	Microsoft Corp.	20.22%	45.40%	0.35
WMT	Wal-Mart Stores Inc.	43.31%	43.84%	0.89
GE	General Electric Company	29.11%	31.82%	0.77
XOM	Exxon Mobil Corp.	18.15%	28.82%	0.47
C	Citigroup Inc.	31.99%	43.92%	0.63

Correlation[4]	MSFT	WMT	GE	XOM	C
MSFT	1.0	0.22	0.32	0.15	0.29
WMT	0.22	1.0	0.40	0.18	0.38
GE	0.32	0.40	1.0	0.14	0.46
XOM	0.15	0.18	0.14	1.0	0.23
C	0.29	0.38	0.46	0.23	1.0

[1] Arithmetic average annualized daily return from 1998–2000.
[2] Annualized daily volatility from 1998–2000.
[3] A risk free rate of 4.5% annually is used in Sharpe ratio calculation.
[4] Daily correlation from 1998–2000.

Let's assume that we have $1,000,000 to invest, and we have chosen an optimal asset allocation (please see Chapter 3 on how to select optimal asset allocations) that contains 50 percent U.S. large cap stocks. That means that $500,000 needs to be spread across the five stocks we have selected.

Naïve Diversification

There are several ways to allocate $500,000 to these five stocks. One very easy way is by naïve diversification (e.g., to naïvely allocate the $500,000 evenly across the five assets, $100,000 in each stock). The resulting expected return and volatility of the portfolio is shown in Table 8.2.

Naïve diversification is a passive approach to tactical asset allocation. The advantage of naïve diversification is that it is very simple to implement because investors do not have to form any view on the performance of any individual asset in the portfolio. In our five-stock example, by adopting this methodology we concede that we have no preference for any of these stocks, and are equally unsure about each stock's future performance. Therefore, we have no choice but to invest

TABLE 8.2   Naïve Diversification across Five Stocks

Portfolio Annualized Return	28.56%
Portfolio Annualized Volatility	25.51%
Sharpe Ratio[1]	0.94
ASSET WEIGHTS	
MSFT	20.0%
WMT	20.0%
GE	20.0%
XOM	20.0%
C	20.0%

[1] A risk free rate of 4.5% annually is used in Sharpe ratio calculation.
Arithmetic average annualized daily return from 1998–2000.
Annualized daily volatility from 1998–2000.

equally among the five stocks. In reality, however, investors always have some opinions about a stock's future behavior. Exxon Mobil Corp. (Ticker: XOM), for example, is a defensive stock. The company has a stable stream of income, and investors can expect, to a reasonable degree, that its stock will have low volatility in the near term, given no major corporate changes. Investors can also expect a relatively low return on the stock due to the slow growth of the industry. Microsoft Corp. (Ticker: MFST), on the other hand, is exactly the opposite. Because it's in a high-growth industry, investors can expect the stock to have high returns. The stock, however, can also be very risky because of already high valuations within the high-tech sector, making the stock price extremely sensitive to forecasted earning.

We all have our own opinions about how given stocks will perform in the future. Naïve diversification fails to take into account any additional information or opinions investors might have. Is it beneficial to take our own opinions into consideration? That depends on how accurate our intuitions are. Historically speaking, the odds are stacked against intuitions. Returning to the research conducted by Brinson, Hood, and Beebower, they found that on average, active managers under-perform the benchmark index by 0.36 percent return annually, with the worst manager in the study under-performing the benchmark index by 2.9 percent return annually. But the study also showed that some managers were able to generate additional value by actively selecting securities.

So how did the successful managers in the Brinson, Hood, and Beebower study generate additional value through asset selection? Almost assuredly, they did not achieve that through naïve diversification. One possible approach is a method called tactical asset allocation.

Tactical Asset Allocation

Tactical asset allocation is a method by which a Markowitz mean variance optimizer is used to determine the optimal mix of a set of individual assets at any given level of portfolio risk. As might be expected, tactical asset allocation is very similar to the strategic asset allocation approach discussed in Chapter 3. The tool used, a portfolio optimizer, is the same. However, the inputs for tactical asset allocation are return behaviors of individual assets; whereas those for strategic asset allocation are return behaviors of different asset classes. In the case of our five-stock sample portfolio, if we can fairly accurately forecast the return, volatility, and correlation of the five stocks, we can input these parameters into a portfolio optimizer and generate an efficient frontier with similar shape to that generated in Chapter 3. Of course, in our five-stock example, the optimizer will be allocating across individual assets, such as Microsoft and General Electric, as opposed to asset classes, such as U.S. stocks and U.S. bonds. Figure 8.1 shows the efficient frontier for our five-stock sample portfolio and their weight allocations.

Although similar in mathematics, there are a number of fundamental differences between strategic asset allocation and tactical asset allocation. As with strategic asset allocation, tactical asset allocation

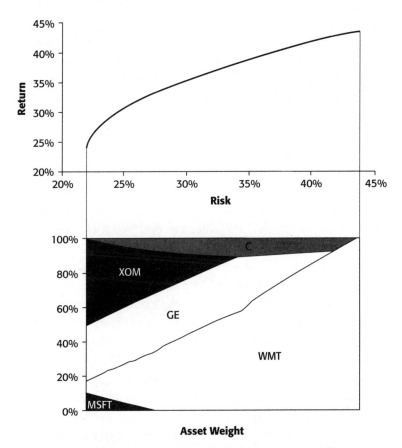

FIGURE 8.1 Efficient frontier for the five-stock sample portfolio.

uses historical returns to forecast future performance. A key difference, however, is that tactical asset allocation typically uses a short returns history for individual stocks (a range from 1 month to 3 years of historical returns are commonly used to forecast return behaviors; we use a 1-year history in our example). This differs from the 25-year returns history on asset classes used in strategic asset allocation. Strategic asset allocation is an investment policy that is carried out over the long term, and should not change very often. Tactical asset allocation, on the other hand, is designed to exploit potential short-term gains. By allocating individual securities to the optimal allocation of choice, investors hope to achieve maximum return for a certain risk level over a short period. Therefore, unlike strategic asset allocation, individual stocks are rebalanced frequently in a portfolio. Rebalancing can mean adjusting the weight of each asset in the portfolio, introducing new assets to the portfolio, or dropping certain assets from the portfolio. Very often, investors rebalance their equity portfolios on a monthly basis, quarterly basis, or semi-annual basis. The rebalance frequency really depends on the nature of the investments, the transaction costs associated with rebalancing, and personal preference.

So how would tactical asset allocation on our five-stock sample portfolio fare against naïve allocation across the same five stocks? Let's examine the 3-year period from 1998 to 2000. On January 2, 1998 (January 1, 1998 was New Year's Day, and the market was closed), we have $500,000 to invest in U.S. large cap stocks. By using 1 year of return history, from 1997, we generate the efficient frontier in Figure 8.2. The equally weighted naïve diversification portfolio is also shown in the figure.

To compare tactical asset allocation with naïve diversification, we need to look at portfolios that carry the same level of risk. Therefore, we choose Optimal Portfolio A, which is the optimal allocation of the five stocks with the same level of risk as the naïve diversification portfolio. Table 8.3 lists the weight and shares of each stock we purchased on January 2, 1998.

We rebalance each portfolio on a quarterly basis. For the naïve diversification portfolio, we adjust the shares at the end of every quarter so all of the stocks return to equal weighting in the portfolio. For our tactical asset allocation portfolio, Optimal Portfolio A, we also adjust the shares at the end of each quarter, but by re-allocating the portfolio

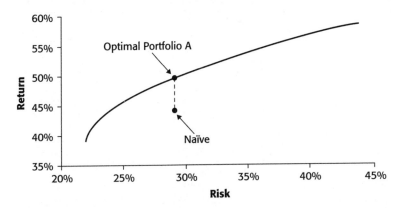

FIGURE 8.2   Optimal portfolio generated on 1/2/1998.

to the optimal allocation that carries the same risk level as the portfolio's risk on that day. For example, at the beginning of the second quarter, April 2, 1998, the risk level of existing Optimal Portfolio A was 23.05 percent, based on a rolling 1-year history. We rebalance the portfolio by running portfolio optimization (using the rolling 1-year history from April 2, 1997 to April 2, 1998) and choosing the optimal allocation that has the same risk level at the time of the optimization, or 23.05 percent. Table 8.4 lists the overall performance, as well as quarterly

TABLE 8.3   Transaction Comparison on 1/2/1998

Ticker	Price[1]	Naïve Portfolio		Optimal Portfolio A	
		# of Shares[2]	Sub Total	# of Shares[2]	Sub Total
MSFT	$32.78	3050.53	$100,000	3541.16	$116,079
WMT	$19.69	5079.37	$100,000	11,790.53	$232,155
GE	$24.42	4095.00	$100,000	2549.95	$ 62,269
XOM	$61.88	1616.16	$100,000	486.64	$ 30,113
C	$26.75	3738.32	$100,000	2220.93	$ 59,410
Total			**$500,000**		**$500,000**

[1] Split-adjusted closing price on 1/2/1998
[2] Shares take decimal form for theoretical purposes

TABLE 8.4   Portfolio Performances between 1998 and 2000

	Naïve Portfolio	Optimal Portfolio A
1st Quarter, 1998		
Quarterly Total Return	22.22%	28.54%
Quarterly Risk	8.08%	9.14%
2nd Quarter, 1998		
Quarterly Total Return	7.77%	12.95%
Quarterly Risk	8.99%	10.61%
3rd Quarter, 1998		
Quarterly Total Return	−12.42%	−8.13%
Quarterly Risk	17.38%	20.04%
4th Quarter, 1998		
Quarterly Total Return	30.49%	34.37%
Quarterly Risk	15.04%	16.46%
1st Quarter, 1999		
Quarterly Total Return	12.20%	22.31%
Quarterly Risk	12.69%	14.88%
2nd Quarter, 1999		
Quarterly Total Return	−3.19%	−4.90%
Quarterly Risk	11.80%	16.71%
3rd Quarter, 1999		
Quarterly Total Return	2.93%	4.44%
Quarterly Risk	10.80%	14.05%
4th Quarter, 1999		
Quarterly Total Return	27.33%	29.33%
Quarterly Risk	11.38%	12.42%
1st Quarter, 2000		
Quarterly Total Return	−0.83%	−8.73%
Quarterly Risk	17.44%	19.84%
2nd Quarter, 2000		
Quarterly Total Return	−7.95%	−3.81%
Quarterly Risk	13.40%	17.14%
3rd Quarter, 2000		
Quarterly Total Return	1.27%	13.78%
Quarterly Risk	7.87%	10.15%
4th Quarter, 2000		
Quarterly Total Return	−8.71%	−7.65%
Quarterly Risk	13.47%	17.94%
Total Performance 1998–2000		
Total Annualized Return	**21.83%**	**37.47%**
Total Annualized Risk	**25.53%**	**30.73%**
Sharpe Ratio[1]	**0.68**	**1.07**

[1] A risk free rate of 4.5% annually is used in Sharpe ratio calculation

performance of the naïve diversification portfolio and the Optimal Portfolio A during the period of study, from 1998 to 2000.

In this particular case, tactical asset allocation was able to significantly outperform naïve allocation, in both absolute returns and risk-adjusted returns. The annualized return for Optimal Portfolio A over the 3-year period is 37.47 percent, significantly higher than that of the naïve diversification portfolio, 21.83 percent. But also note the higher risk taken by Optimal Portfolio A, 30.73 percent, compared to the 25.53 percent risk taken by the naïve diversification portfolio. The greater risk taken by Optimal Portfolio A results from our choice of rebalancing method. We rebalanced Optimal Portfolio A every quarter based on the risk level at the beginning of that quarter. Therefore, our risk exposure changes dynamically over time. In this example, the risk level happens to increase over the 3-year period. To fix our risk exposure over the 3 years, we can rebalance Optimal Portfolio A every quarter to the same fixed risk level. Another way of rebalancing the portfolio is to match the risk exposure at every quarter to the risk exposure of the naïve diversification portfolio. Although our Optimal Portfolio A has greater risk over the 3-year period than the naïve diversification portfolio does, the return per unit risk taken, or Sharpe ratio, is much higher for Optimal Portfolio A than for the naïve diversification portfolio.

However, keep in mind that this does not guarantee that any tactical asset allocation through portfolio optimization will beat naïve allocation all the time or on any portfolio. The reality is far from it. Successful use of tactical asset allocation really depends on how accurately investors are able to forecast the return behaviors of chosen stocks and the correlation among them. If we cannot fairly accurately predict the expected return and volatility of a stock, or the correlation among various stock returns, the results from portfolio optimization will obviously not result in true optimal portfolios. This is the "garbage in, garbage out" effect. The effectiveness of tactical asset allocation using portfolio optimization also depends on how frequently the portfolio is rebalanced. As a portfolio of stock exists over time, the weight of each stock in the portfolio changes. For example, while MSFT may have been only 25 percent of the overall portfolio a year ago, it may be 50 percent of the overall portfolio now due to its good performance throughout the year, the bad performance of other stocks in the portfolio throughout the year, or a combination of both.

As time passes, the return behavior of the stocks in the portfolio can also change. This can be caused by broad economic changes, such as inflation, productivity, and interest rate changes; or firm-specific changes, such as product expansion and acquisitions. Therefore, the expected returns and volatilities of individual stocks in the portfolio can all change over time, and the correlation among various stocks can also change. Without portfolio rebalancing, the portfolio's performance can stray away from that of an optimal portfolio significantly to an unacceptable level. However, rebalancing the portfolio too frequently may not be economically feasible because of the transaction fees involved. To illustrate these points, we use a different tactical asset allocation approach on these same five stocks. Instead of using a 1-year return history to forecast return behavior, we use a 3-year return history, and we also rebalance the portfolio more frequently—on a monthly basis. We call the portfolio resulting from this new approach Optimal Portfolio B. Figure 8.3 shows the growth of $500,000 from 1998 to 2000 using the three approaches we have discussed: Naïve diversification, tactical asset allocation using a 1-year history and rebalanced quarterly (labeled Optimal Portfolio A), and tactical asset allocation using a 3-year history and rebalanced monthly (labeled Optimal Port-

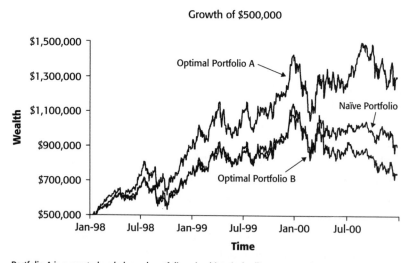

Portfolio A is a quarterly-rebalanced portfolio using historical rolling 1-year as inputs to optimization
Portfolio B is a portfolio started out with equal portions of each stock
Portfolio C is a monthly-rebalanced portfolio using historical rolling 3-year as inputs to optimization

FIGURE 8.3 Comparison of three different investment approaches.

folio B). As shown in the figure, Optimal Portfolio B significantly under-performs Optimal Portfolio A. But more disturbingly, it also under-performs the naïve diversification portfolio.

Can We Rely on Historical Returns in Tactical Asset Allocation?

So far, we have always used historical returns to forecast future performances of assets. In strategic asset allocation, which is for long-term planning, this is reasonable. Long-term historical returns can in fact be a stable indicator of long-term future performance. Using short-term historical returns to forecast near-term performance, however, can lead to inaccurate results in tactical asset allocation. By using historical returns as inputs for tactical asset allocation, we inevitably chase after the near-term best performing assets. That is, we believe high-return stocks will continue to gain high returns, and low-return stocks will continue to generate low returns. Because a portfolio optimizer is extremely sensitive to expected return inputs (as discussed in Chapter 3), it typically over-allocates to assets with high expected return and under-allocates to assets with low expected return. Therefore, tactical asset allocation based on historical returns will always result in a portfolio that is heavy in assets with strong recent performance. This would be a poor investment strategy in a mean-reversion market where high-flying stocks fall to their long-term average return, and low-return stocks rise to approach their long-term average return. Mean-reversion happens often in the stock market. It should not be hard to imagine allocating a big percentage of a portfolio to a high-flyer because of its recent performance only to watch it crash, or selling many shares of an under-performer only to watch it take off.

Another reason why using historical returns can lead to inaccurate results in tactical asset allocation is that a company's structure can change over time, causing a change in its underlying stock price movement. The merger between AOL and Time Warner is an example: If we were to use historical returns to forecast the expected return of the combined company, which company's history would we use? AOL or Time Warner? If a company experienced a sudden large-scale defection of management, would historical returns be a good reflection of the company's performance going forward? Not necessarily. Therefore, we need to have an alternative to historical returns for forecasting expected returns in tactical asset allocation.

The Capital Asset Pricing Model

There are a number of alternative ways to forecast a stock's expected return. We focus on one of the most popular: the capital asset pricing model (CAPM), which builds on the concept of the market portfolio. In theory, the market portfolio consists of all kinds of assets, such as stocks, bonds, mortgages, real estate, and includes virtually every tradable asset in the world. Of course, for the purpose of analyzing a portfolio of U.S. stocks and/or mutual funds (as with our five-stock sample portfolio), a broad market index, such as the S&P 500 or Wilshire 5000, would be appropriate.

In Chapter 1, we briefly touched on the concept of beta, which is an important component of CAPM. Beta measures the variability of an asset's return against that of the market, and the higher an asset's beta, the more volatile that asset's return is relative to the market. The return movement of an asset can be analogous to the swing of a pendulum, and beta can be thought of as a measurement of how far the pendulum swings. The bigger the magnitude of beta is analogous to higher swings of the pendulum. Figure 8.4 uses pendulums to illustrate the return movements of individual stocks relative to the market portfolio. Pendulum A represents the return movement of the market portfolio (i.e., our benchmark pendulum) and Pendulums B, C, D, and E represent the return movements of four stocks, which we compare against this benchmark. Pendulum B has a beta of 1.0, so naturally it swings just as far as Pendulum A (the market portfolio beta is always 1.0). Pendulum C, with a beta of 1.2, swings further than the benchmark Pendulum A. In the investment world, if the market returns 5.0 percent in a month, we can expect an asset with a beta of 1.2 to return 6.0 percent. But let's not get too excited about this asset just yet. If the market returns −2.0 percent in a month, we can expect this asset to return −2.4 percent! Pendulum D, with a beta of 0.8, swings less than Pendulum A. Using the previous example, Asset D can be expected to return 4.0 percent if the market returns 5.0 percent in a month. For the better, though, it can be expected to return −1.6 percent if the market returns −2.0 percent in a month. Pendulum E is an interesting one, with a beta of −1.0.

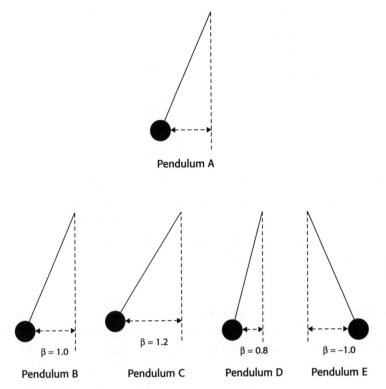

FIGURE 8.4 Beta and the pendulum.

While the magnitude of the swings are identical between Pendulum E and the benchmark Pendulum A, the direction is exactly the opposite, so when Pendulum A swings to the left, Pendulum E swings to the right. And when Pendulum A swings back to the right, Pendulum E swings to the left. In the investment world, Asset E's return variability is exactly opposite to that of the market. Still citing the same example, Asset E can be expected to return −5.0 percent when the market returns 5.0 percent. Likewise, it can be expected to gain 2.0 percent when the market loses 2.0 percent.

Beta is very useful in breaking down an asset's or a portfolio's excess returns into two components: market return and residual return. Excess return is the marginal return received by taking on a certain amount of risk. The equation is as follows:

$$R_P = \beta R_M + \theta$$

Where R_P is the excess return of the portfolio

R_M is the excess return of the market

β is the beta of the portfolio

θ is the residual return of the portfolio

and   Total return $= R_p + r_f$

Where R_P is the excess return of the portfolio

r_f is the risk free rate (4.5 percent in our examples)

The first part of the right-hand side of the equation is the market component of the asset. θ is the residual part of the asset's excess return. Table 8.5 lists the breakdown of total return, excess return, beta, and θ (residual return) of the stocks in our five-stock sample portfolio from earlier in the chapter. Total return for each of the five stocks is obtained from Table 8.1.

So far, we have not talked about CAPM. We have only laid the foundation for the discussion. The capital asset pricing theory is used to forecast expected returns of assets. It states that the expected value of the residual component of a stock's excess return is 0.

$$E(\theta) = 0$$

In other words, the expected excess return of an asset is:

$$E(R_p) = \beta * E(R_M)$$

TABLE 8.5   Breakdown of Stock Returns

Name	Total Return	Excess Return[1] (R_p)	Beta (β)	Residual Return[2] (θ)
MSFT	20.22%	15.72%	1.38	3.37%
WMT	43.31%	38.81%	1.14	28.61%
GE	29.11%	24.61%	1.00	15.66%
XOM	18.15%	13.65%	0.78	6.67%
C	31.99%	27.49%	1.30	15.86%

[1] A risk-free rate of 4.5% annually is used in excess return calculations.

[2] Market excess return over the period is calculated to be 8.95%.

The expected total return of an asset is therefore:

$$E(R_{ptr}) = E(R_p) + r_f = \beta * E(R_M) + r_f$$

Where r_f is the risk free rate (4.5 percent in our examples).

The logic behind CAPM is fairly simple and quite straightforward. The CAPM is based on the assumption that investors all share the same expectation going into the market. Market risk is unavoidable, as discussed in Chapter 2, if we want to invest in the market. However, residual risk is self-imposed. In fact, the game of residual return is a zero-sum game. In order for one person to gain a positive residual return, there is another person having a negative residual return. However, we never *expect* to have negative residual returns. If we do expect to lose money when actively investing, we might as well invest passively in the market index. Therefore, nobody *expects* to have negative residual returns. While all investors hope to achieve positive residual returns, it is impossible for that to happen because then there would not be anybody losing money to other investors. The only logical conclusion for this zero-sum game is that we do not *expect* to have either positive or negative residual gains.

Notice that there are two variables we need to calculate the expected excess return of an asset: Beta and expected market return. When we use CAPM to forecast the expected returns of assets, we are looking forward into the future. The beta we use in the equation is also a forward-looking number, as opposed to the betas listed in Table 8.5, which are calculated from historical return behaviors. It is worth pointing out, though, that historical beta often can predict forward-looking beta with acceptable accuracy. The betas of various stocks and mutual funds can be found in many popular financial portals. Some of these websites can be found in the Appendix.

There are several other ways to estimate a stock's beta, but they are beyond the scope of this book. Expected market return is commonly calculated using historical returns. Historical return, in the case of our five-stock sample portfolio example, can produce reasonably accurate results because we do not have to worry about any firm-specific uncertainties like those discussed previously. Table 8.6 compares each stock's expected return calculated from historical return (also shown in Table 8.1) with its expected return calculated using the CAPM from

TABLE 8.6   A Comparison of Different Expected Return Calculations

Ticker	Expected Return (based on historical return)	Expected Return (based on CAPM)
MSFT	20.22%	16.85%
WMT	43.31%	14.70%
GE	29.11%	13.45%
XOM	18.15%	16.54%
C	31.99%	16.13%

Beta for CAPM can be found in Table 8.5
Excess Market Return is calculated to be 8.95%

1998 to 2000. Notice the expected returns calculated using CAPM are much smaller than those calculated from historical returns. CAPM-based expected returns seem more reasonable, particularly when the market returns to normalcy. For example, expecting Wal-Mart to return 43.31 percent annually is not very realistic. With a 43.31 percent annualized return, an investor can become a billionaire 32 years from now by investing only $10,000 immediately! However, a 14.7 percent annualized return on Wal-Mart is not too much to ask.

The capital asset pricing model is not perfect by any means. It does not work with bonds or any fixed income assets, and how well it works also depends directly on how well investors define the market portfolio. While it is acceptable to use S&P 500 or Wilshire 5000 as the market portfolio for U.S. stocks, it still is uncertain which benchmark or combination of benchmarks ought to be applied when valuing international stocks. The usefulness of beta also depends on how relevant it is to the market portfolio defined. We talk more about the meaningfulness of beta in Chapter 9.

Despite these shortcomings, the CAPM is still one of the best tools available to forecast expected returns of assets. It is very easy to understand and very simple to use. Figure 8.5 shows the efficient frontier generated from CAPM-calculated expected returns.[2] Because of the lower expected returns calculated by CAPM, the whole efficient frontier

---

[2] David Eichorn, Francis Gupta, and Eric Stubbs, "Using Constraints to Improve The Robustness of Asset Allocation," *Journal of Portfolio Management, Spring* 1998.

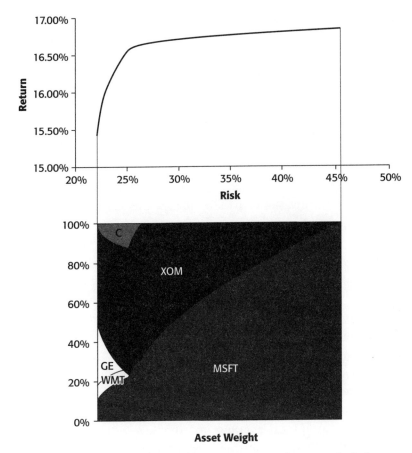

FIGURE 8.5   Optimal portfolio using CAPM expected return calculations.

is lowered as a result, compared to the efficient frontier generated by the historical return calculations shown in Figure 8.1. The risk range of the CAPM efficient frontier does not change much from the historical return efficient frontier. This is because the inputs into the optimizer are changed only for the expected return (from historical returns to CAPM), but volatility inputs and correlation inputs remain unchanged.

Limitations of Portfolio Optimization

In Chapter 3, we discussed various limitations of portfolio optimization. For example, the optimization process is very sensitive to changes in the expected returns of the input assets/asset classes. In the example cited in Chapter 3, a minute addition of 0.1 percent to the expected return of U.S. large cap stocks caused the recommended U.S. large cap stocks allocation to increase from 50 percent of the total portfolio to 54 percent of the total portfolio. The sensitivity problem, in combination with the natural tendency of optimization to maximize errors in inputs, often causes the resulting optimal portfolios to be nonsensical. In our five-stock example shown in Table 8.3, MSFT and WMT seem to be overweighted, while other stocks, like XOM and C, are underweighted in a way that does not make intuitive sense to investors. To implement one of these optimal portfolios actually takes a greater risk tolerance from an investor than the optimal point's suggested risk level. Another shortcoming of portfolio optimization is that it does not differentiate between the differing levels of confidence investors have in their estimations of various assets/asset classes. We are often more certain about some stocks' expected return behaviors than those of other stocks. For example, we are likely less confident in forecasting the expected return of Palm (Ticker: PALM) than we are in forecasting the expected return of General Electric (Ticker: GE). This is because Palm is a new stock that has just made its initial public offering, so there are not enough sample points to make a meaningful statistical estimation. On the other hand, General Electric has been around for decades. We are much more familiar with the company and its behavior.

Another reason for the various uncertainties of different stocks is because of the different industries in which the stocks are categorized. For example, Coca-Cola Company (Ticker: KO), a company in the beverage industry, is much more stable than Cisco Systems (Ticker: CSCO), a company in the networking devices industry. The near-term outlook visibility for the networking devices industry is far less clear than that of the beverage industry. Therefore, while Cisco Systems made 61.87 percent average annualized return in the past 3 years, we are far less certain about whether it will continue to generate that return than we are of Coca-Cola Company's expected return of 4.08 percent. This return is also the average annualized return it generated in the past 3 years. Portfolio optimization, unfortunately, does not take these uncertainties into consideration. It tends to significantly overweight the high-flying stocks about which we are least certain, while underweighting the stocks that generate lower expected returns, but about which we are more certain.

Overcoming Certain Optimization Limitations Using Constraints

One of the common ways to overcome these shortcomings is to use constraints on assets/asset classes. For example, if investors are not confident about Wal-Mart's expected return, they can place a maximum percentage constraint on Wal-Mart that tells the optimizer to generate an efficient frontier in which each optimal portfolio contains at most 40 percent Wal-Mart. On the other hand, if investors believe Microsoft's expected return is too low, and feel confident it will exceed that expected return, they can place a minimum percentage constraint of 20 percent on MSFT. In effect, this tells the optimizer to generate an efficient frontier in which each optimal portfolio will contain at least 20 percent Microsoft. Of course, we can also apply both minimum and maximum percentage constraints at the same time. Please note that not all optimizers allow for constraints. We have been using constraints implicitly throughout our optimization examples. The limits we put on each asset/asset class are a minimum percentage of 0 percent of the overall portfolio and a maximum percentage of 100 percent of the overall portfolio. Without the 0 percent minimum constraint, portfolio optimization could recommend that an assets/asset class have a negative percentage, that is, a recommendation to effectively short the assets/asset class. Without the 100 percent maximum constraint, portfolio optimization could recommend that an assets/asset class be more than 100 percent of the total portfolio, that is, a recommendation to use leverage strategies.

If we put constraints on assets or asset classes, the resulting efficient frontier will be lower than that of an unconstrained efficient frontier. In order words, we will get less return at any given level of risk. This is so because once a constraint is set, the portfolio optimizer has fewer options. For example, if a maximum percentage constraint of 40 percent is set on Wal-Mart, the optimizer will not be able to generate optimal points that contain more than 40 percent of Wal-Mart in the portfolio. As a result, to satisfy the constraints, the optimizer will produce an efficient frontier made up of optimal points with lower expected return at each given level of risk. The benefit of setting constraints is that we usually end up with a less volatile portfolio.[3] When

---

[3] See footnote 2.

applied properly, the benefit of setting constraints to reduce a portfolio's expected risk can outweigh the cost of reduced expected return.

It is important to note that to use constraints properly and effectively, investors need to have a thorough understanding of the fundamentals of the assets in the portfolio, and a sense of accuracy in terms of the forecasts for those assets' expected returns, risks, and correlations to one another. In other words, investors need to do their homework!

Tactical Asset Allocation: Science and Art

Tactical asset allocation, as shown in this chapter, is a very important step in investing. Through the use of portfolio optimization, investors can attempt to construct portfolios that can give them the maximum expected return given a selected risk level, or minimum risk given a selected expected return level. Optimization, in combination with the asset selection techniques described in Chapters 5, 6, and 7, makes introduction of new assets into a portfolio very easy. All an investor needs to do is to input the selected asset(s) into the portfolio optimizer along with all the existing portfolio assets, and let the portfolio optimizer determine the optimal portfolios and how much to purchase in each asset. Portfolio optimization also gives investors the luxury of choosing the portfolio that has the expected return and risk levels with which they are most comfortable from the multiple optimal portfolios. The use of portfolio optimization in tactical asset allocation is very flexible, and it is this flexibility that makes tactical asset allocation just as much an art as a science. Portfolio optimization does not impose any limits on the inputs: stocks' expected returns, volatilities, and correlations. Investors are free to enter any numbers they want into the portfolio optimizer. This can result in a "garbage in, garbage out" effect. The difficult task of predicting asset return behavior is left for investors to deal with. This chapter outlines two simple techniques for predicting an asset's return behavior: estimation based on the asset's historical returns, and based on capital asset pricing model (CAPM). Another choice investors have to make is which optimal allocation to pick on the efficient frontier. To make a proper choice, a good understanding of risk and expected return, as outlined in Chapter 1, is necessary. Investors must also have a good grasp of their risk tolerance and financial situation. Financial planning and simulation methods outlined in Chapter 4 can help in this respect.

Finally, as investors consider a strategy or timetable for portfolio rebalancing, a balance must be struck between maintaining a relatively efficient portfolio over time through frequent portfolio rebalancing, and managing the transaction costs associated with that rebalancing. For most investors, that will mean exercising patience and discipline, and accepting the fact that portfolios simply cannot be optimal at all times.

This concludes the chapter, and also the section on constructing a portfolio. Next, we will discuss various techniques for monitoring an existing portfolio.

Measuring Performance

The objective of investing, of course, is to maximize expected returns. Return is the motivating force in the investment process. It is the reward for undertaking the investment. Yet, as important as return is, it remains only one side of the investment equation. Investors need to take an investment's risk into consideration as well. A 20 percent return, by itself, is a fairly meaningless number. That 20 percent must be compared to the performance, over the same timeframe, of alternative investments bearing a similar level of risk.

Evaluation of portfolio performance, the bottom line of the investing process, is naturally of interest to all investors and money managers. The framework for evaluating portfolio performance consists of measuring both the realized return and the differential risk of the portfolio relative to a benchmark, which enables investors to compare the portfolio's performance with that of other portfolios. Many advances have been made over the past few decades in the measurement and attribution of investment performance. The field began with the simple regression of a managed portfolio return on the return of a single benchmark portfolio (single-index model). It has transformed into one that invokes multiple-style benchmarks (see Chapters 10 and 11) and advanced econometric techniques to determine the statistical significance of a manager's investment ability.

In this chapter, the discussion of performance measurement moves from the very general to the very specific, addressing the following questions:

- How is investment performance measured?
- Why is risk-adjusted performance measurement so important?
- What are the most common risk-adjusted performance evaluation techniques, and how are they used?

In addressing those questions, we present two techniques for measuring performance for a multiperiod investment: dollar-weighted return (DWR) and time-weighted return (TWR). We then introduce the concept of risk-adjusted performance evaluation, and provide a broad and practical coverage of the risk-adjusted performance evaluation techniques that are available today. Throughout the chapter, we provide examples to demonstrate how investors can apply these concepts and techniques to their investments.

Time-Weighted Return versus Dollar-Weighted Return

In Chapter 1, we discussed several basic techniques for calculating the historical returns for both single-period and multiple-period investment horizons. There, for the sake of simplicity, we assumed that there were no cash inflows or outflows for any investment period. However, most real-world investments have both cash inflows and outflows. Even the buy-and-hold investor receives cash inflows, such as stock dividends and fund distributions, every year. Such cash inflows and outflows make return measurement more difficult.

Let's consider a simple example. We purchase one share of stock today for $50. The stock pays a dividend of $1 annually. A year later, we decide to purchase another share of the stock for $60. During the second year, our dividend proceeds are $2 ($1 per share of stock). We hold the shares until the end of year 2 and sell both shares of stock for $65 per share. The investment activity and dividend proceeds are summarized as follows.

Year	Investment Activity	Dividend Proceeds
0	$50 to purchase first share ($50/Share)	—
1	$60 to purchase second share ($60/Share)	$1
2	Sell 2 shares at the end of year ($65/Share)	$2

Dollar-Weighted Return

Traditionally, portfolio measurement consists of calculating the dollar-weighted return (DWR) of an investment, which is equivalent to the internal rate of return (IRR) used in several financial calculations. IRR measures the actual return earned on a beginning portfolio value and on any net contributions made during a given period. Using the discounted cash flow approach, we can determine the average return over a given period of time by equating the present values of the cash inflows and outflows. Generally speaking, the dollar-weighted rate of return can be derived by solving for r in the following equation.

$$MV_0 = \sum_{t=1}^{T} \frac{Inflow_t}{(1+r)^t} - \sum_{t=1}^{T} \frac{Ouflow_t}{(1+r)^t} + \frac{MV_T}{(1+r)^T}$$

where

MV_0 = beginning portfolio value
$Inflow_t$ = the cash inflow at time t
$Outflow_t$ = cash outflow at time t
MV_T = ending portfolio value

Applying that equation to our example, we can solve for the average annual return over two years (r) as follows.

$$\$50 = \frac{\$1}{1+r} - \frac{\$60}{1+r} + \frac{\$132}{(1+r)^2}$$

resulting in $r = 10.28\%$.

This return is "dollar-weighted" because the performance of two shares of stocks in year 2 has a greater influence on the average return r than the performance of a single share of the stock in year 1. It does not tell us whether our portfolio has achieved a superior performance due to our skill or due to the timing of cash inflows and outflows.

Because the DWR is heavily affected by cash flows, it is inappropriate for making comparisons between portfolios or to market indices, a key factor in performance measurement.

Time-Weighted Return

Time-weighted return (TWR) is typically calculated for comparative purposes when cash flows occur between the beginning and the end of a period.

Calculating the TWR requires information about the value of the portfolio's cash inflows and outflows. To compute the TWR, we calculate the return to the portfolio immediately prior to a cash flow occurring. We then calculate the return to the portfolio from that cash flow to the next period, or to the end of the period. Finally, we link these rates of return together by computing the compound rate of return over time. In other words, we calculate the rate of return for each time period defined by a cash inflow or outflow, and then calculate a compound rate of return for the entire period. If frequent cash flows are involved, substantial calculations are necessary. The TWRs are unaffected by any cash flows to the portfolio; therefore, they measure the actual rate of return earned by the portfolio manager.

Returning to our previous simple investment example, the TWR approach ignores the dollar amount of the investment or the number of shares of stock held in each period. We collect a $1 dividend (cash inflow) during year 1. The price of the stock at the end of the first year is $60. Total proceeds from capital gains and dividends is $1 \times (\$60 - \$50) + \$1 = \$11$. Therefore, our first-year investment return is:

$$\frac{\$11}{\$50} = 0.22 = 22\%$$

Total proceeds from capital gains and dividends in year 2 is $2 \times (\$65 - \$60) + \$2 = \$12$. The initial investment for the second year is $2 * \$60 = \$120$. Therefore, our second-year investment return is:

$$\frac{\$12}{\$120} = 0.10 = 10\%$$

Based on our first- and second-year rates of return, we are able to calculate the TWR of the 2-year investment, as well as the annualized TWR.

$$TWR = (1 + 22\%) * (1 + 10\%) - 1 = 34.20\%$$

$$Annualized\ TWR = (1 + 34.20\%)^{\frac{1}{2}} - 1 = 15.84\%$$

Note that the dollar-weighted return (10.28 percent) is less than the time-weighted return (15.84 percent) in this example. The reason is that the stock performed relatively poorly in the second year, when we had more shares. The greater weight that the dollar-weighted return places on the second-year return results in a lower measure of investment performance.

Dollar-weighted return and the time-weighted return can produce different results, and at times these differences can be substantial, so which measure of performance is superior? The answer, actually, is that it depends. Time-weighted return captures the rate of return actually earned by the portfolio manager, while dollar-weighted return captures the rate of return earned by the portfolio owner. Therefore, when evaluating the performance of the portfolio manager, time-weighted return should be used because the manager generally has no control over the deposits and withdrawals made by the clients. Since the objective is to measure the performance of the portfolio manager, independent of the actions of his or her clients, this is better accomplished using the time-weighted return.

Risk-Adjusted Performance Evaluation

While dollar and time-weighted returns are both important means of measuring an investment's performance, unfortunately both techniques ignore the risk side of the investment equation. As discussed in previous chapters, investing is always a two-dimensional process based on return and risk. These two factors must be evaluated together if intelligent decisions are to be made. Therefore, if we know nothing about the risk of an investment, there is little we can say about its performance.

According to the capital asset pricing model (CAPM), which is discussed in Chapter 8, superior return can only be achieved if an investor is prepared to take a higher level of risk. Thus, it is important not only to evaluate a portfolio's return, but also to evaluate that return relative to the risk of the portfolio.

For a stock portfolio, two major types of risk can be determined:

- The portfolio's market or systematic risk, which is measured by its beta (as discussed in Chapters 1 and 8).

- The portfolio's total risk, which is measured by its standard deviation, or volatility (as discussed in Chapter 1).

If an investor's portfolio is fully diversified, then the market risk provides an appropriate measure of the portfolio risk level. Otherwise, the total risk of the portfolio should be the relevant risk measure.

To evaluate portfolio performance properly, investors must determine whether the returns are large enough given the risk involved. To assess performance carefully, investors must evaluate performance on a risk-adjusted basis. Modern portfolio theory (MPT) includes several risk-adjusted performance measurements that enable investors to assess a portfolio's return in the context of the overall risk associated with it.

Treynor Ratio

Jack Treynor developed the first risk-adjusted performance measurement, now called the Treynor ratio (TR). Also known as the reward to volatility ratio, it is the ratio of a fund's average excess return to the fund's beta. It is defined as the excess return of a portfolio divided by the portfolio beta.

$$TR = \frac{r_p - r_f}{\beta_p}$$

where TR = Treynor ratio
   r_p = the average return of the portfolio p
   r_f = risk-free rate
   β_p = the beta of the portfolio p

The Treynor ratio distinguishes between total risk and systematic risk, implicitly assuming that portfolios are well diversified; that is, the ratio ignores any diversifiable risk. If an investor held the market portfolio (e.g., the S&P 500), which has a beta of 1, the ratio would simply be equal to the market risk premium, which defines the slope of the SML (security market line). Therefore, a portfolio with a TR value higher than the market portfolio would plot above the SML, indicating superior risk-adjusted performance.

Treynor Ratio Example

Assume that during the most recent 5 years, the annual average return of the market portfolio (e.g., S&P 500) is 15 percent and the risk-free rate is 5 percent. Assume that during the same period, we have invested our money among three mutual funds, which we call portfolios A, B, and C. Given the results presented in Table 9.1, below, we must now decide whether to continue our investment in all three funds. To make such a decision, we must be able to measure how they have performed on a risk-adjusted basis.

Given this information, we can compute TR values for all three funds and the market portfolio as follows.

$$TR_A = \frac{10\% - 5\%}{0.80} = 0.063$$

$$TR_B = \frac{18\% - 5\%}{1.75} = 0.074$$

$$TR_C = \frac{25\% - 5\%}{1.25} = 0.160$$

$$TR_M = \frac{15\% - 5\%}{1.00} = 0.100$$

TABLE 9.1 Treynor Ratio—Sample Portfolios (Assume Risk-Free Rate of 5%)

Portfolio	Average Annual Return	Beta	Treynor Ratio
A	10%	0.80	0.063
B	18%	1.75	0.074
C	25%	1.25	0.160
Market	15%	1.00	0.100

These results are also listed in the last column in the Table 9.1. They indicate that Portfolio A has not only ranked the lowest among the three funds, but does not perform as well as the market portfolio on a risk-adjusted basis, in spite of its lower beta. Portfolio B has a higher annual return than the market portfolio, however it has a high beta of 1.75. As a result, its risk-adjusted performance, as measured by the Treynor ratio, is still inferior to the market portfolio. In terms of the SML, both Portfolios A and B plot below the line, as shown in Figure 9.1. In contrast, Portfolio C beats the market portfolio in terms of absolute return and risk-adjusted returns, as evidenced by its higher Treynor ratio. As we might expect, it plots above the SML line in Figure 9.1. As a result of our analysis, Portfolio C turns out to be the best investment.

Note that the Treynor ratio focuses on systematic risk (beta), and cannot provide any guidance as to whether a portfolio or a mutual fund portfolio is sufficiently diversified. A portfolio's beta does not necessarily decrease as the number of assets within it increase. A portfolio's Treynor ratio does not necessarily grow larger as the number of assets in the portfolio increase, given the fixed value for the excess return of the portfolio. To assess this particular dimension or performance, the Sharpe ratio offers some additional insights.

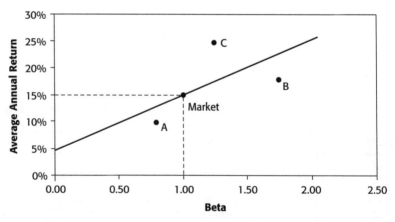

FIGURE 9.1   Treynor ratio: Three sample portfolios and the market portfolio.

Sharpe Ratio

The Sharpe ratio is the best known of risk-adjusted return measurements and is named after Nobel prize-winning economist William Sharpe, creator of the capital-asset pricing model (CAPM). The Sharpe ratio measures the extra return investors receive for each unit of risk they take on, and is defined as the excess return of a portfolio divided by its standard deviation.

$$SR = \frac{r_p - r_f}{\sigma_p}$$

where SR = Sharpe ratio
   r_p = the average return of the portfolio p
   r_f = risk-free rate
   σ_p = standard deviation of the portfolio p

The Sharpe ratio and Treynor ratio are similar measurements of risk-adjusted return, however there is a key difference. The Sharpe ratio seeks to measure the *total risk* of the portfolio by including the standard deviation of portfolio returns, whereas the Treynor ratio, in using beta, considers only systematic risk.

SHARPE RATIO EXAMPLE

Let's assume that for the past 5 years, market return is 15 percent, the risk-free rate is 5 percent, and the standard deviation, or volatility, of the market portfolio is 18 percent. Assume that during the same period, we have invested our money among three mutual funds, which we call Portfolios A, B, and C, as shown in Table 9.2. Now, we want to

TABLE 9.2   Sharpe Ratio—Sample Portfolios (Assume Risk-Free Rate of 5%)

Portfolio	Average Annual Return	Volatility	Sharpe Ratio
A	10%	14%	0.36
B	18%	28%	0.46
C	25%	22%	0.91
Market	15%	18%	0.56

examine the performance of these portfolios, using the Sharpe ratio to measure risk-adjusted performance.

The Sharpe ratios for these three funds and the market portfolio are calculated as follows.

$$SR_A = \frac{10\% - 5\%}{14\%} = 0.36$$

$$SR_B = \frac{18\% - 5\%}{28\%} = 0.46$$

$$SR_C = \frac{25\% - 5\%}{22\%} = 0.91$$

$$SR_M = \frac{15\% - 5\%}{18\%} = 0.56$$

Portfolio A has lower volatility than the market portfolio, but does not offer sufficient return to beat the market portfolio in terms of risk-adjusted return. Portfolio B, on the other hand, offers greater return than the market portfolio, but at too great a cost in terms of added risk. It too fails to beat the market portfolio in terms of risk-adjusted return. In contrast, Portfolio C performs better than the market portfolio, both in terms of absolute returns and risk-adjusted return. Given the results of the market portfolio, we can draw a capital market line (CML). Plotting the results of Portfolios A, B, and C on the graph, as shown in Figure 9.2, we see that both Portfolios A and B plot below the CML line, while Portfolio C plots above the line. This indicates that the portfolio C had superior risk-adjusted performance during the period.

The beauty of the Sharpe ratio is that it summarizes the risk and return of a portfolio in a single measurement, and allows for an apples-to-apples comparison of different assets or portfolios. Quite simply, the larger the Sharpe ratio, the better the portfolio has performed.

As we discussed, the Treynor ratio uses only beta (systematic risk) as the measure of risk, whereas the Sharpe ratio uses volatility of returns. Therefore, the Sharpe ratio evaluates portfolio performance on the basis of both return performance and diversification. For a perfectly diversified portfolio, the Treynor ratio and Sharpe ratio should be identical, as the total variance of the perfectly diversified portfolio

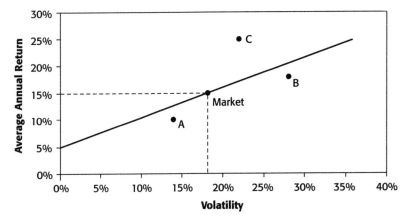

FIGURE 9.2 Sharpe ratio: Three sample portfolios and the market portfolio.

would be equal to its systematic variance. Since most portfolios are not perfectly diversified, these ratios will usually differ. In fact, a poorly diversified portfolio could have a high Treynor ratio value but a very low relative Sharpe ratio value.

Jensen's Alpha

Both the Treynor ratio and Sharpe ratio provide measures for ranking the relative performance of various portfolios on a risk-adjusted basis. Michael Jensen attempted to construct a measure that used the security market line as a benchmark. Jensen's alpha calculates the difference between what the portfolio actually earned and what it was expected to earn given its level of systematic risk.

$$Alpha = (r_p - r_f) - \beta_p(r_m - r_f)$$

where r_p = return of the portfolio p
r_f = risk-free rate
r_m = return of the market portfolio
β_p = the beta of the portfolio p

Basically, it attempts to measure the constant return that the managed portfolio earned above, or below, the return of an unmanaged portfolio with the same market risk. For portfolio managers, this represents the value they add through their investment techniques and stock selection.

JENSEN'S ALPHA EXAMPLE

Assume, as in the Treynor ratio example, that during the most recent 5 years, the annual average return of the market portfolio (e.g., S&P 500) is 15 percent and the risk-free rate is 5 percent. Assume that during the same period, we have invested our money among three mutual funds, which we call Portfolios A, B, and C, as shown in Table 9.3. We want to find out if the managers of these funds added value to our investments, compared to what we would have earned by passively investing in the market portfolio.

Given the information in Table 9.3, we can compute the Jensen's alpha for Portfolios A, B, C and the market portfolio. (Note that the alpha for the market portfolio is always zero.)

$$Alpha_A = (10\% - 5\%) - 0.80 * (15\% - 5\%) = -3.00\%$$

$$Alpha_B = (18\% - 5\%) - 1.75 * (15\% - 5\%) = -4.50\%$$

$$Alpha_C = (25\% - 5\%) - 1.25 * (15\% - 5\%) = 7.50\%$$

$$Alpha_M = (15\% - 5\%) - 1.00 * (15\% - 5\%) = 0.00\%$$

Both Portfolios A and B have a negative alpha, which indicates that the money managers for these two portfolios have added no value to our investments. Portfolio C has an impressive positive alpha of 7.5 percent, suggesting that the manager for the portfolio delivered significant added value to our investment. If the Jensen's alpha is positive, the portfolio plots above the SML line, and this suggests good performance. Likewise, if the Jensen's alpha is negative, the portfolio plots below the SML line, and this suggests poor performance. In Figure 9.3, the negative alpha Portfolios A and B, as expected, plot below the SML

TABLE 9.3 Jensen's Alpha–Sample Portfolios (Assume Risk-Free Rate of 5%)

Portfolio	Average Annual Return	Beta	Jensen's Alpha
A	10%	0.80	−3.00%
B	18%	1.75	−4.50%
C	25%	1.25	7.50%
Market	15%	1.00	0.00%

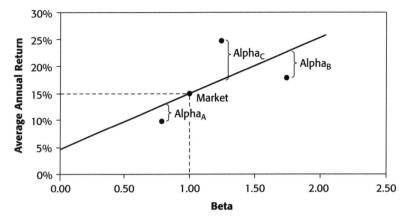

FIGURE 9.3   Jensen's alpha: Three sample portfolios and the market portfolio.

line, whereas the positive alpha Portfolio C plots above the line. Again, as a result of our analysis, Portfolio C has superior risk-adjusted performance.

Like the Treynor ratio, the Jensen's alpha does not evaluate how diversified a portfolio is, because it calculates risk premiums in terms of systematic risk. For a well-diversified portfolio, such as a mutual fund, this is probably a fairly good risk-adjusted performance measure. A superior money manager would have a significant positive alpha value, suggesting that the manager is good at predicting market turns and selecting undervalued assets for the portfolio.

M-*Squared* or M² *Ratio*

The Jensen's alpha and Treynor ratio measure risk-adjusted performance by comparing the excess returns of a managed portfolio with those of a market portfolio with a comparable risk level of the managed portfolio. Both adjust returns for the beta. Leah Modigliani, a U.S. stock strategist at Morgan Stanley, and her grandfather, Nobel Prize winner Franco Modigliani, proposed an alternative measurement of risk-adjusted performance, called *M*-squared or M^2 ratio.[1] This ratio normalizes an investment's risk level to match that of the market portfolio

---

[1] See F. Modigliani and L. Modigliani, "Risk-Adjusted Performance," *Journal of Portfolio Management*, Winter, 1997.

(S&P 500), thereby allowing for a one-to-one return comparison against that benchmark. The M-squared ratio is calculated as follows.

$$M\text{-squared} = (r_p - r_f) * \frac{\sigma_m}{\sigma_p} - (r_m - r_f)$$

where r_p = the average return of the portfolio p
 r_f = risk free rate
 r_m = the return of the market portfolio
 σ_m = standard deviation of the market portfolio
 σ_p = standard deviation of the portfolio p

M-SQUARED RATIO EXAMPLE

Assume, as in the Sharpe ratio example, that for the past 5 years, market return is 15 percent, the risk-free rate is 5 percent, and the standard deviation or volatility of the market portfolio is 18 percent. Assume that during same period, we have invested our money among three mutual funds, which we call Portfolios A, B, and C, as shown in Table 9.4. Now, we want to compare the risk-adjusted performance of these portfolios using the M-squared measure.

The M-squared ratios for these portfolios and the market portfolio are calculated as follows. (Note that the M-squared ratio for market portfolio is always zero.)

$$M\text{-squared}_A = (10\% - 5\%) * \frac{18\%}{14\%} - (15\% - 5\%) = -0.036$$

$$M\text{-squared}_B = (18\% - 5\%) * \frac{18\%}{28\%} - (15\% - 5\%) = -0.016$$

$$M\text{-squared}_C = (25\% - 5\%) * \frac{18\%}{22\%} - (15\% - 5\%) = 0.064$$

$$M\text{-squared}_M = (10\% - 5\%) * \frac{18\%}{18\%} - (15\% - 5\%) = 0$$

The M-squared ratio can be compared with that of the market portfolio over the same period of time. The ratio shows by how much our portfolio or the fund in which we are invested out-performs or under-performs the market on a risk-adjusted basis. The larger the ratio, the

TABLE 9.4   M-Squared—Sample Portfolios (Assume Risk-Free Rate of 5%)

Portfolio	Average Annual Return	Volatility	M-Squared
A	10%	14%	−0.036
B	18%	28%	−0.016
C	25%	22%	0.064
Market	15%	18%	0.000

better the portfolio has performed. In the example, Portfolio C, with the highest ratio of 0.064, has out-performed the market and Portfolios A and B. Portfolios A and B under-performed the market, which resulted in their negative M-squared ratios.

Are Risk-Adjusted Performance Measurements Consistent?

Table 9.5 presents a summary of the various risk-adjusted performance measurements for our Portfolios A, B, and C and the market portfolio. Not surprisingly, a fair amount of consistency is seen across the four. While absolute consistency across the four measurements is not always guaranteed, a fair amount of consistency is common. Such consistency is mainly due to the fact that most of these risk-adjusted measures calculate a ratio by dividing return by the relevant risk measure. Understandably, most of these risk measures are highly correlated, although not necessarily the same.

TABLE 9.5   Summary Example of Risk-Adjusted Performance Measurements

Portfolio	Treynor Ratio	Sharpe Ratio	Jensen's Alpha	M-Squared
A	0.063	0.36	−3.00%	−0.036
B	0.074	0.46	−4.50%	−0.016
C	0.160	0.91	7.50%	0.064
Market	0.100	0.56	0.00%	0.000

An Actual Example

To demonstrate how these various risk-adjusted performance measurements might be used in real life, we have applied them to 15 U.S large cap mutual funds. We use the average return, standard deviation (volatility), and beta for these funds for the 3-year period from June 1998 to May 2001, and assume a risk-free rate of 5 percent. The results are shown in Table 9.6.

The mean of annual average return for all 15 funds is quite close to the market return (6.5 percent versus 6.2 percent). Considering only

TABLE 9.6   Performance Measures for 15 Select Mutual Funds (June 1998–May 2000; Risk-free rate = 5%)

Fund	Average Return	Standard Deviation	Beta	Treynor Ratio	Sharpe Ratio	Jensen's Alpha	M^2 Measure
AIM Blue Chip B	3.7%	22.9%	1.06	−0.012	−0.06	−2.57%	−0.023
AXP Stock A	3.3%	18.2%	0.88	−0.019	−0.09	−2.73%	−0.031
BlackRock Select Equity Inv A	−0.6%	19.2%	0.99	−0.056	−0.29	−6.73%	−0.070
Dreyfus Disciplined Stock	3.6%	20.8%	1.03	−0.014	−0.07	−2.65%	−0.026
Federated Capital Appreciation A	12.8%	25.1%	1.05	0.074	0.31	6.56%	0.051
Fidelity Magellan	8.5%	22.3%	1.06	0.033	0.16	2.27%	0.020
Goldman Sachs Core Equity A	3.6%	21.0%	1.04	−0.013	−0.06	−2.59%	−0.025
INVESCO Equity Income Inv	5.5%	15.3%	0.72	0.007	0.03	−0.33%	−0.005
Janus Twenty	9.8%	38.1%	1.43	0.034	0.13	3.15%	0.014
Kemper Blue Chip A	3.3%	18.6%	0.92	0.036	0.17	2.56%	0.022
Legg Mason Value Trust Primary	15.1%	28.1%	1.16	0.087	0.36	8.69%	0.061
Oppenheimer Total Return A	4.8%	19.0%	0.86	−0.002	−0.01	−1.22%	−0.014
Putnam Research A	8.8%	23.4%	1.09	0.035	0.16	2.51%	0.021
Smith Barney Large Cap Core 1	8.8%	22.8%	1.04	0.036	0.17	2.56%	0.022
Strong Growth & Income Inv	7.1%	23.4%	1.05	0.020	0.09	0.86%	0.006
Mean	6.5%	22.5%	1.03	0.016	0.07	0.7%	0.002
Market	6.2%	20.2%	1.00	0.012	0.06	0.00%	0.000

average return, seven of 15 funds out-performed the market. Among the 15 funds, standard deviation and beta range widely, with standard deviations between 15.3 percent and 38.1 percent, and betas between 0.72 and 1.43. Most of the funds (10 of 15) have larger standard deviations than the market and, again, most funds (10 of 15) have a beta above 1.00.

Risk-adjusted performance measurements rank the individual funds very consistently. Using the Sharpe or the Treynor ratio, eight of the 15 funds have a value better than the market portfolio. Consistent with those results, seven of 15 funds' Jensen's alpha and M-squared values are positive. These results indicate that about half of the 15 mutual funds had risk-adjusted performance better than the market during the time period. The mean values for all four risk-adjusted measurements are close to the market's value. These results indicate that, on average, this sample of mutual funds performed approximately the same as the market during the time period of the analysis.

It is interesting to point out that when adjusted for risk, some of the top performers (in terms of average return) look less attractive. Take the Janus Twenty fund as an example. In terms of average return, it's 9.8 percent ranked third best among the 15 funds. But it has the highest standard deviation and beta among the funds. In terms of risk-adjusted performance, it falls to sixth place in terms of Treynor ratio, and seventh place in terms of both Sharpe ratio and M-squared ratio.

Using Risk-Adjusted Performance Measurements

Regardless of which measurement investors use to assess risk-adjusted performance, the principle is the same. Pay close attention to risk when evaluating performance. To increase the potential investment return, investors generally must accept a higher level of risk. But quantifying return versus the market average, or a relevant benchmark, and factoring in risk gives investors the best understanding of how well the investments are actually performing.

While based on the same principle, the measurements covered here have their differences. The Sharpe and Treynor ratios are relative measures that can be used to both evaluate portfolio performance and to understand how that portfolio performs relative to other portfolios being evaluated. Jensen's measure, on the other hand, is an absolute measure of performance. The M-squared ratio, like the Sharpe ratio, focuses on total variability as a measure of risk. However, it is also like Jensen's alpha, in that its value has the easy interpretation of a differential return relative to the benchmark index.

One warning about published performance is warranted. When investors select money managers, they typically evaluate these managers solely on the basis of their published performance statistics. If the published track record looks good, that is typically enough to convince many investors to invest in a particular mutual fund. However, an investment manager's past performance is no guarantee of his or her future performance, and short-term results in particular may be particularly misleading.

We established the importance of evaluating and comparing investments based on risk-adjusted performance. In doing so, it is also important to choose the appropriate benchmark against which performance will be evaluated. The essence of performance evaluation in investments is to compare the returns obtained on some portfolio with the returns that could have been obtained from a comparable alternative. An equity portfolio consisting of S&P 500 stocks should be evaluated relative to the S&P 500 Index or other equity portfolios that could be constructed from the Index, after adjusting for the risk involved. On the other hand, it would be inappropriate to use the same S&P 500 benchmark to evaluate performance of a portfolio of small capitalization stocks. Obviously, it would be more appropriate to use a small cap index as a benchmark. So what if we need to evaluate an equity fund that holds a majority of S&P stocks, but also includes midcap and small cap stocks? Comparisons for such a widely diversified group of stocks can be quite difficult, and there is no straight answer as to how we might identify the most appropriate benchmark. Many researchers now agree that in the case of mixed portfolios, it may be most appropriate to use some composite of multiple indices or benchmarks when evaluating portfolio returns.

CHAPTER 10

Managing with Style

I t's human nature to categorize and subdivide. We don't just own a car—we own a sedan, a coupe, or an SUV, and beyond that we probably see that car as a luxury, family, or economy model. Depending on how a person behaves, he or she might even be categorized as having a Type A or Type B personality. Such classifications simplify our thinking process and enable us to process information more efficiently.

In this chapter, we take a detailed look at the role of style classification in investing, addressing the following questions:

- What is equity style classification, and why is it important to investors?
- How have the styles indices behaved historically?
- How can investors benefit from style investing?
- What's the most effective way to determine one's investment style?

Equity Style Classification

Ever since the early 1970s, when researchers determined that there were categories of stocks with common characteristics and similar return patterns,[1] style has played a major role in asset classification. Essentially,

---

[1] For example, James Farrell found that stocks could be divided into at least four categories: growth, cyclical, stable, and energy. See James Farrell, Jr., "Homogenous Stock Groupings: Implications for Portfolio Management," *Financial Analysts Journal*, May/June 1975, pp. 50–62.

what that research uncovered was that categories of stock tend to perform differently from one another in terms of return behavior, but that stocks within any given category tend to be highly correlated.

Today, investors broadly classify assets as stocks or bonds (fixed income securities), and stocks are likely to be classified as domestic or international, small or large, growth or value, or perhaps even "old economy" or "new economy." Such groups of assets with similar or common characteristics are often called *asset classes* or *styles*. Understandably, a fund manager who invests in a certain style of assets tends to be labeled that way, giving us growth managers, value managers, large cap managers, small cap managers, etc. Portfolio investment based on selection among styles or asset classes rather than among individual assets is called *style investing*.

Stocks can be classified by style in many ways. The most common way is in terms of "growth" and "value," with a substyle based on company size or market capitalization. The result is a classification scheme that divides stocks into large cap growth, large cap value, small cap growth, and small cap value, as illustrated in Figure 10.1.

There are no universally accepted definitions of *growth* and *value*; they are simply relative descriptions of a manager's style. In general, a growth-oriented manager tends to buy stocks that are experiencing rapid growth in earnings. These stocks are usually associated with price/earnings (P/E) or price-to-book (P/B) ratios that are higher than those of the overall market. The risk in growth investing is that growth in earnings will not materialize and/or that a stock's P/E or P/B ratio will decline.

A value-oriented manager tends to buy stocks that are undervalued compared to the overall market. These stocks tend to carry low P/E and

	Growth	Value
Large Cap	Large Cap Growth	Large Cap Value
Small Cap	Small Cap Growth	Small Cap Value

FIGURE 10.1 A simple equity style classification system.

P/B multiples. The expectation of the value manager is that an under-valued stock's P/E or P/B ratio will return to some more normal level and therefore the price will go up, even if the company's earnings per share or book value per share remains unchanged. High dividend yields are also sometimes used to identify value stocks. The risk in value investing is that the stock's P/E or P/B ratio will not increase.

In the financial world, most institutions, including Russell, Standard & Poor's, and Barra, use the P/B ratio or its inverse, book-to-price, as a key characteristic in classifying growth and value stocks. Like the P/E ratio, the book-to-price ratio has the advantage of being intuitive, mutually exclusive, and suitable for differentiating companies according to growth and value. A key difference, however, is that the book-to-price ratio tends to be more stable over time than alternative measures such as the P/E ratio. As a result, style indices based on the book-to-price ratio tend to have relatively low turnover.

There are some managers who follow both growth and value investing styles, but without sufficient bias in favor of one or the other to be labeled as growth or value managers. Most managers who fall into this category are called *hybrid* or *blend style* managers. These managers tend to own both value and growth stocks. This may represent the manager's ongoing philosophy or simply his or her current portfolio mix.

Now that we have a basic idea of the two main equity style categories, growth and value, and the predominant substyle category of size, let's see how we can classify stocks into these style categories. We will follow a simple style classification system proposed by Frank Fabozzi[2] to show how the stocks in a given universe can be classified according to growth and value. For the sake of illustration, we will use the S&P 500 Index as the universe of stocks.

Step 1: Calculate the total market capitalization of the stock universe. (As of March 31, 2001, the number of stocks is 500 and the total market cap is about $10,399 billion.)

Step 2: Develop a score for each stock based on the price-to-book ratio, with high scores being associated with high growth.

---

[2] Frank J. Fabozzi, "Overview of Equity Style Management," in Frank J. Fabozzi, ed., *Active Equity Portfolio Management* (New Hope, PA: Frank J. Fabozzi Associates, 1998), pp. 57–70.

This involves multiplying each stock's P/B ratio by its market capitalization.

Step 3: Sort the stocks from the highest score to the lowest score.

Step 4: Calculate the capitalization-weighted median of the scores.

Step 5: Classify those stocks with a score above the capitalization-weighted median as growth stocks.

Step 6: Classify those stocks with a score below the capitalization-weighted median as value stocks.

As a result of this exercise, we are able to categorize the stocks in the S&P 500 (or any other universe of stocks) as either growth or value. Standard & Poor's actually used a very similar methodology to that just described to determine the composition of its S&P 500/Barra Growth and S&P 500/Barra Value Indices. The sole criterion for the S&P/Barra Growth/Value split is the price-to-book ratio, the market capitalization of a firm divided by the book value of its common equity. Table 10.1 shows the fundamental characteristics of the S&P 500 index and the S&P 500/Barra Growth and Value Indices.

This simple classification system divides all the selected stocks into growth or value categories, with each group including half of the mar-

TABLE 10.1 Fundamental Characteristics of the S&P 500 Index, the S&P 500/Barra Growth Index and the S&P 500/Barra Value Index (Data as of March 31, 2001)

	S&P 500	S&P 500/ Barra Growth	S&P 500/ Barra Value
Total Cap (*)	10,398,797	4,773,749	5,625,048
Average Price/Earnings	23.48	32.56	18.99
Average Price/Book	3.85	8.09	2.66
Average Dividend Yield (%)	1.66	1.05	2.19
Average Return on Equity (%)	23.26	28.19	19.19

Note: *—in Million U.S.D.
Data Source: http://www.barra.com

ket capitalization of the stock universe. It's important to note, however, that the number of stocks in each group is not necessarily the same. If we want to move further to determine the substyle of a stock universe, we can establish some cutoff based on size or market cap.

But does such an equity style classification make sense? Research suggests that it does. Nobel laureate William F. Sharpe found that the value/growth dimension (as represented by price-to-book ratios), along with the large/small dimension (as represented by market cap), appears to explain many of the differences in returns among U.S. equity mutual funds. Eugene Fama and Kenneth French, two former financial economists at the University of Chicago, also investigated the importance of the distinction between value and growth stocks.[3] They found that the combination of book-to-price ratios and market cap explained much of the cross-sectional variability in average stock returns over the period from 1963 to 1990. Furthermore, they found that book-to-price ratios play an even more important role than market capitalization in capturing this return variability.

How Have the Styles Behaved Historically?

Now we turn our attention to perhaps the most important question associated with style investing: Is it worth the effort and cost? In order to answer this question, we need to examine the relative historical performance of various style categories such as growth and value.

The performance of the different style benchmarks has varied considerably. We will look at the Russell 2000 Small Cap Growth and Value indices. As we can see from Figure 10.2, whether we are looking five, ten, or twenty years into the past, the Small Cap Value index exhibits only three-quarters the volatility of the Small Cap Growth index, while earning a higher average return. We measure volatility by the annualized standard deviation of the monthly total returns for each style index.

These results might prompt us to ask the question: Does the value index (either small cap or large cap) always outperform the growth index? The answer to this question is, no, not always. Returning to the previous example, we compute the historical average return for the

---

[3] See one of their most important papers, Eugene F. Fama and Kenneth R. French, "Common Risk Factors on Stocks and Bonds," *Journal of Financial Economics*, February 1993, pp. 3–56.

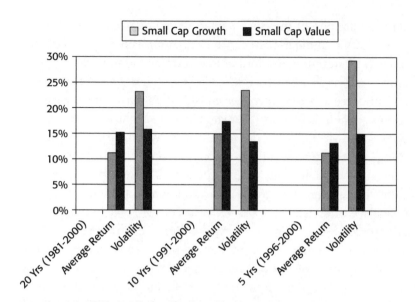

Note: The market index for style benchmark used in the analysis: Russell 2000
Growth Index for Small Cap Growth; Russell 2000 Value Index for Small Cap Value.
Source: Computed from Monthly Returns of the Russell 2000 Growth and Value Indices.

FIGURE 10.2   Risk and return characteristics of small cap growth and value style indices (five, ten, and twenty years).

Small Cap Value and Small Cap Growth indices for each five-year period from January 1981 to December 2000. The results, presented in Figure 10.3, clearly show that the Small Cap Growth index outperformed the Small Cap Value index for the five-year period from January 1986 to December 1990.

We might also be tempted to ask the question: Does this risk and return pattern also apply to the large cap indices? The answer to this question is simply no. Figure 10.4 gives the risk and return characteristics of the large cap growth and value style indices for five-, ten-, and twenty-year periods between 1981 and 2000. The large cap value index has slightly outperformed the growth index with a higher volatility for the twenty years ending December 2000. However, unlike the small cap style index, the returns of the large cap value index for five- and ten-year periods are lower than those of the large cap growth index. The results are not surprising, as large cap growth stocks such as CISCO, Microsoft, and EMC led the U.S. bull market starting in the early 1990s and running through 2000.

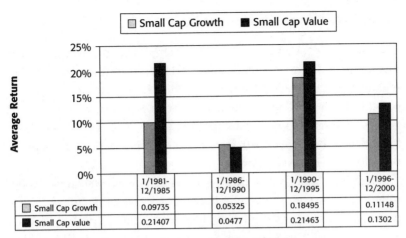

	1/1981–12/1985	1/1986–12/1990	1/1990–12/1995	1/1996–12/2000
Small Cap Growth	0.09735	0.05325	0.18495	0.11148
Small Cap value	0.21407	0.0477	0.21463	0.1302

Five-Year Periods

Note: The market index for style benchmark used in the analysis: Russell 2000 Growth Index for Small Cap Growth; Russell 2000 Value Index for Small Cap Value.

FIGURE 10.3 The historical five-year performance of small cap value and growth (1/1981–12/2000).

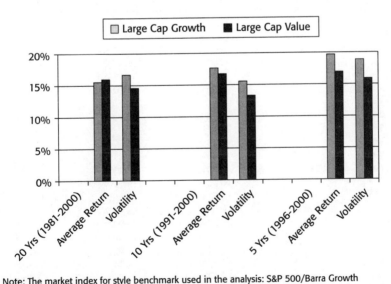

Note: The market index for style benchmark used in the analysis: S&P 500/Barra Growth Index for Large Cap Growth; S&P 500/Barra Value Index for Large Cap Value.

FIGURE 10.4 The risk and return characteristics of large cap growth and value style indices (five, ten, and twenty years).

Style Investing—Style Rotation

The results illustrated in the previous examples are driven by the fact that value and growth stocks have tended to take turns leading the market, and that these "performance cycles" have varied in length and magnitude. Depending on which time period we consider, one style or the other might appear more attractive. While value stocks have tended to outperform growth stocks over long time periods in the past, there have been periods when growth stocks ruled supreme.

So the question is this: Can investors benefit from such cycles by rotating among styles over time? If the answer is yes, then the question becomes, How? Let's see how two types of investors, "perfect timers" and "momentum traders," would have fared shifting their portfolio style among the four major stock style indices—Small Cap Value, Small Cap Growth, Large Cap Value, and Large Cap Growth—between 1981 and 2000. The endnotes to this chapter give the details of the annual return histories for these indices.[4]

---

[4] The twenty-year performance history of four major U.S. stock style indices is as follows:

Year	Large Cap Growth	Large Cap Value	Small Cap Growth	Small Cap Value
1980	39.40%	23.59%	52.26%	25.39%
1981	−9.81%	0.02%	−9.24%	14.85%
1982	22.03%	21.04%	20.98%	28.52%
1983	16.24%	28.89%	20.13%	38.64%
1984	2.33%	10.52%	−15.83%	2.27%
1985	33.31%	29.68%	30.97%	31.01%
1986	14.50%	21.67%	3.58%	7.41%
1987	6.50%	3.68%	−10.48%	−7.11%
1988	11.95%	21.67%	20.37%	29.47%
1989	36.40%	26.13%	20.17%	12.43%
1990	0.20%	−6.85%	−17.41%	−21.77%
1991	38.37%	22.56%	51.19%	41.70%
1992	5.06%	10.52%	7.77%	29.14%
1993	1.68%	18.61%	13.36%	23.84%
1994	3.13%	−0.64%	−2.43%	−1.55%
1995	38.13%	36.99%	31.04%	25.75%
1996	23.97%	22.00%	11.26%	21.37%
1997	36.52%	29.98%	12.95%	31.78%
1998	42.16%	14.67%	1.23%	−6.45%
1999	28.25%	12.72%	43.09%	−1.49%
2000	−22.08%	6.08%	−22.43%	22.83%

Data source: www.barra.com and DataStream. The market index benchmark for each style used in the analysis is as follows: S&P 500/Barra Growth Index for Large Cap Growth; S&P 500/Barra Value Index for Large Cap Value; Russell 2000 Growth Index for Small Cap Growth; Russell 2000 Value Index for Small Cap Value.

Our definition of a "perfect timer" is someone who chooses the right style every year, knowing with certainty at the beginning of each year which style portfolio or benchmark will perform best.[5] A "momentum trader" is someone who always allocates his or her money to the style with the best past performance (relative to other styles) in the previous year.[6] Table 10.2 shows how each type of investor would have fared over the period 1981 to 2000.

Obviously, we can't expect to have perfect style timing, so we won't even dissect these results. It is, however, interesting to look at what happened to our momentum trader. This investor always allocated his money to the style with the best performance (relative to other styles) in the previous year. For example, our momentum trader invested in Small Cap Growth in 1981 because in 1980 its return of 52.26 percent was highest relative to other indices (see the details of twenty years of performance history in footnote 4, above). In 1982, the trader switched to Small Cap Value because it had performed better than the other three indices in the prior year. And so on, and so on. While this is a very mechanical investment strategy, its investment performance is not necessarily bad: In fact, over the twenty-year period it beat all four style indices! Invested through this style of momentum strategy, $1 in 1981 would have grown to $20.98 in 2000, compared with Large Cap Value's $19.18 (the highest among these four indices), Large Cap Growth's $16.48, Small Cap Value's $15.82, and Small Cap Growth's $5.37. Given these findings, it's understandable that the persistence of some types of investments, such as mutual funds, has been a hot topic among finance academics.[7] Figure 10.5 shows the investment growth charts for the four major style indices and our two style investment strategies.

Table 10.3 summarizes the risk and return characteristics of the two style rotation investment strategies and the four major U.S. equity

---

[5] Practically speaking, the idea of a "perfect timer" is implausible. However, it is a perfect example for demonstrating why style rotation is important to investors.

[6] There are different kinds of momentum trading or investing involving length of relative strength. The most common relative strengths are one month, three months, six months, and one year. We use one-year relative strength to illustrate how investors can benefits from style rotation.

[7] See, for example, Edwin J. Elton, Martin J. Gruber, and Chris R. Blake, "The Persistence of Risk-Adjusted Mutual Fund Performance," *Journal of Business*, Vol. 69, No. 2, 1996, pp. 133–157.

TABLE 10.2 Style Rotation—Investment and Return for Perfect Timer and Style Momentum Trader (January 1981–December 2000)

| Year | Perfect Timer | | Momentum Trader | |
	Style Index Invested	Return	Style Index Invested	Return
1981	Small Cap Value	14.85%	Small Cap Growth	−9.24%
1982	Small Cap Value	28.52%	Small Cap Value	28.52%
1983	Small Cap Value	38.64%	Small Cap Value	38.64%
1984	Large Cap Value	10.52%	Small Cap Value	2.27%
1985	Large Cap Growth	33.31%	Large Cap Value	29.68%
1986	Large Cap Value	21.67%	Large Cap Growth	14.50%
1987	Large Cap Growth	6.50%	Large Cap Value	3.68%
1988	Small Cap Value	29.47%	Large Cap Growth	21.67%
1989	Large Cap Growth	36.40%	Small Cap Value	12.43%
1990	Large Cap Growth	0.20%	Large Cap Growth	0.20%
1991	Small Cap Growth	51.19%	Large Cap Growth	38.37%
1992	Small Cap Value	29.14%	Small Cap Growth	7.77%
1993	Small Cap Value	23.84%	Small Cap Value	23.84%
1994	Large Cap Growth	3.13%	Small Cap Value	−1.55%
1995	Large Cap Growth	38.13%	Large Cap Growth	38.13%
1996	Large Cap Growth	23.97%	Large Cap Growth	23.97%
1997	Large Cap Growth	36.52%	Large Cap Growth	36.52%
1998	Large Cap Growth	42.16%	Large Cap Growth	42.16%
1999	Small Cap Growth	43.09%	Large Cap Growth	28.25%
2000	Small Cap Value	22.83%	Small Cap Growth	−22.43%

Note: The market index for style benchmark used in the analysis: S&P 500/Barra Growth Index for large cap growth; S&P 500/Barra Value Index for large cap value; Russell 2000 Growth Index for small cap growth; Russell 2000 Value Index for small cap value.

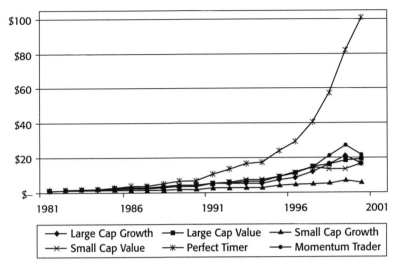

Note: The market index for style benchmark used in the analysis: S&P 500/Barra Growth Index for Large Cap Growth; S&P 500/Barra Value Index for Large Cap Value; Russell 2000 Growth Index for Small Cap Growth; Russell 2000 Value Index for Small Cap Value.

FIGURE 10.5   The investment growth of two style rotation investment strategies and various style indices (1$ invested on January 1, 1981 and ended on December 31, 2000).

TABLE 10.3   The Risk and Return Characteristics of Two Style Rotation Investment Strategies vs. Major Style Indices (January 1981–December 2000)

	Large Cap Growth	Large Cap Value	Small Cap Growth	Small Cap Value	Perfect Timer	Momentum Trader
Average Return	16.44%	16.50%	10.51%	16.13%	26.70%	17.87%
Volatility	18.08%	11.79%	20.08%	17.39%	14.06%	18.19%
Sharpe Ratio	0.63	0.98	0.27	0.64	1.54	0.71
$1 Will Grow To:	$16.48	$19.18	$5.37	$15.82	$100.69	$20.98

Note: The market index for style benchmark used in the analysis: S&P 500/Barra Growth Index for large cap growth; S&P 500/Barra Value Index for large cap value; Russell 2000 Growth Index for small cap growth; Russell 2000 Value Index for small cap value.

style indices for the twenty-year period from 1981 to 2000. As we can see, the Large Cap Value index, along with the two style rotation strategies, offered higher risk-adjusted returns than the other three style indices for the period.

Determining an Investment Portfolio's Style

As we discussed earlier, it is critical to understand an investment portfolio's style. This becomes even more important for those of us who invest in mutual funds, whether we are trying to understand the style of an individual fund (which after all is a portfolio of stocks) or that of a portfolio of funds. Style analysis is an important tool to help us understand a mutual fund's investment policy and objective. For simplicity of presentation, this section speaks of style analysis in the context of a single fund. Since every mutual fund is essentially a portfolio of various assets, the discussion of style analysis in this section should also apply to any personalized portfolio of stocks and/or funds.

The two approaches to style analysis that are most widely used by both finance practitioners and academics are characteristic or holdings-based style analysis and returns-based style analysis. Holdings-based style analysis uses actual portfolio holdings and determines the fund's style based on the portfolio's constituents. The weakness of holdings-based style analysis is that it is often difficult to access up-to-date holdings data for mutual funds. Furthermore, fund managers often have difficulty reconciling a fund's holdings and its performance. Therefore, holdings-based style analysis often yields less than reliable information.

Returns-based style analysis, on the other hand, doesn't rely on actual portfolio holdings. Rather, it uses a historical time series of a fund's returns to assess that fund's style (i.e., returns behavior) relative to major style indices. The effectiveness of this approach makes it more popular than holdings-based style analysis among financial practitioners. For that reason, our focus will be on returns-based style analysis, which we will use to analyze and investigate the style-shifting history of two famous mutual funds.

Originally developed by Nobel laureate William Sharpe, returns-based style analysis analyzes a fund's pattern of returns over time to infer the manager's investment style.[8] The returns pattern shows that the fund manager behaves as if he or she is following a particular investment style. Sharpe's returns-based style analysis is based on the covariance structure of the fund's returns with the returns of a number of style indices, and is designed to capture the fund's "effective asset mix." The major appeal of the effective asset mix approach is simplicity. It requires only the returns of the fund under investigation and the style indices representing the fund manager's portfolio selection universe. Such data are more readily available than an up-to-date and detailed list of the fund's security holdings, making the method much easier to implement.

Sharpe's returns-based style analysis technique involves running a constrained regression of the fund's returns against the returns of several style indices or benchmarks in order to determine what mix of those indices would be needed in order to replicate the historical return pattern of the fund. The constraints are imposed to enhance an intuitive interpretation of the regression coefficients. The interested reader should refer to the footnote below for the technical details.[9]

Stated simply, returns-based style analysis provides insights into

---

[8] See William F. Sharpe, "Determining a Fund's Effective Asset Mix," *Journal of Portfolio Management*, Fall 1988, pp. 49–58, and William F. Sharpe, "Asset Allocation: Management Style and Performance Measurement," *Journal of Portfolio Management*, Winter 1992, pp. 7–19.

[9] The technique involves a constrained multivariate regression that uses several style indices or benchmarks to replicate the historical return patterns of a fund portfolio. Mathematically, we want to solve the following constrained multivariate regression:

$$R_t^p = \sum_{k=1}^{N} \beta_k F_{kt} + \varepsilon_t \quad t = 1, 2, \ldots, T$$

subject to $\qquad \beta_k \geq 0$

$$\sum_{k=1}^{N} \beta_k = 1$$

where R_t^p = returns for a given fund portfolio p at period t
$\qquad \beta_k$ = sensitivity of the fund portfolio returns of factor k
$\qquad F_{kt}$ = factor return (style index or benchmark asset class) k for period t
$\qquad \varepsilon_t$ = fund portfolio residual return for period t

the sources of a fund's historical returns, expressing them as the combination of index or benchmark returns that best represents the fund's overall returns.

Of course, returns-based style analysis can be used to determine the style or returns behavior for a fund at any given point in time, but it is also quite useful in understanding how that style has evolved over time. Figure 10.6 examines the style history of the Fidelity Magellan fund from January 1995 through December 2000 using three-year trailing monthly return data. Fidelity Magellan is one of the world's largest funds in terms of asset size, and is described by Morningstar's style rating and its own fund prospectus as a U.S. large cap blend (i.e., a mix of large cap growth and large cap value). As we can see from the figure, over this time frame the fund has in fact behaved predominantly as a large cap blend fund. However, it is very interesting to note that during the period between 1996 and 1997, the fund's returns were more con-

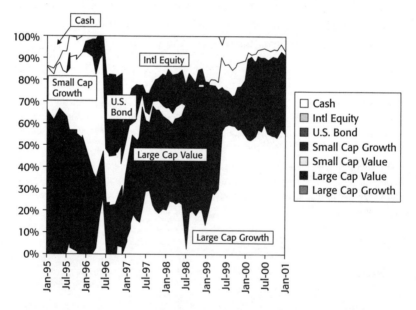

Note: The market index for style benchmark used in the analysis: S&P 500/Barra Growth Index for Large Cap Growth; S&P 500/Barra Value Index for Large Cap Value; Russell 2000 Growth Index for Small Cap Growth; Russell 2000 Value Index for Small Cap Value; Lehman Brothers Aggregate Bond Index for U.S. Bond; MSCI EAFE Index for International Equity and U.S. Three Month Treasury Bill for Cash.

FIGURE 10.6   Style history for the Fidelity Magellan Fund (1/1995–12/2000, using three-year trailing monthly returns).

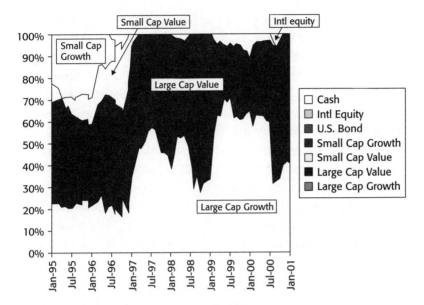

Note: The market index for style benchmark used in the analysis: S&P 500/Barra Growth Index for Large Cap Growth; S&P 500/Barra Value Index for Large Cap Value; Russell 2000 Growth Index for Small Cap Growth; Russell 2000 Value Index for Small Cap Value; Lehman Brothers Aggregate Bond Index for U.S. Bond; MSCI EAFE Index for International Equity and U.S. Three Month Treasury Bill for Cash.

FIGURE 10.7 Style history for the Legg Mason Value Trust Fund (1/1995–12/2000, using three-year trailing monthly returns).

sistent with a broad mix of small cap growth, U.S. bond, and international equity than with a large cap blend. Therefore, the fund failed to consistently exhibit its advertised large cap blend style.

Figure 10.7 examines the style history of the Legg Mason Value Trust Fund from January 1995 through December 2000, again using three-year trailing monthly return data. According to Morningstar's style rating and its own prospectus, the Legg Mason Value Trust Fund is a traditional large cap value fund. Again, as with the Fidelity Magellan fund, when the fund is analyzed using returns-based style analysis, the label doesn't necessarily fit. As the figure illustrates, for much of the late 1990s the fund behaved as though it were dominated by large cap growth, and to a lesser extent by large cap value. Therefore, from our analysis of its return patterns, the Legg Mason Value Trust Fund is not truly a large cap value fund. A better style classification might be large cap blend.

Although returns-based style analysis has proven itself as an effective technique for analyzing the true source of a fund's performance, it does have several limitations. First, since the approach relies on historical returns, it is difficult to draw any conclusions about the future risk/return profile of the fund in question or the indices against which it is being regressed. Second, returns-based style analysis rarely explains 100 percent of a fund's returns (technically speaking, it is rare for the regression to have an R-squared of 100 percent). Typically, part or all of the unexplained portion of returns will reflect the manager's active decisions (i.e., the selection effect). Third, useful and accurate results typically depend upon properly chosen style indices. Since a bad correlation structure between indices can yield misleading results, one ought to have a good understanding of style indices in order to ensure reliable results.

CHAPTER 11

Performance Attribution Analysis

I n previous chapters, we have presented key concepts of investment theory and have discussed many aspects of a disciplined investment process. Specifically:

- Chapters 1 and 2 looked at return and risk and the tradeoff between them and at portfolio diversification, both of which are cornerstones of modern portfolio theory.

- Chapters 3 and 4 presented strategic asset allocation and long-term financial planning, together providing a high-level framework for determining how we ought to be invested across major asset classes, given our tolerance for risk and the nature of the goals for which we are investing.

- Chapters 5 through 7 presented several interesting quantitative tools and techniques to help with the selection of individual stocks and/or mutual funds for our portfolio.

- Chapter 8 presented the technique of portfolio optimization, which allows us to optimally allocate our holdings across selected individual assets for the purpose of maximizing the expected return of our portfolio at any given level risk.

- Finally, for the purpose of ongoing portfolio management, Chapter 9 presented several portfolio performance measurement tools, and Chapter 10 discussed how to determine our investment style and how we can benefit from style investing.

The concepts, tools, and techniques presented thus far in this book are the key components of a disciplined, quantitative approach to planning, implementing, and managing our investments. End of story, right? Not quite.

Any of us who have been invested in the market long enough to receive a monthly or quarterly brokerage statement inevitably wonder, or should wonder, How have I achieved my investment performance and where have these returns come from? Any of us who have invested in mutual funds might also want to know whether a fund's manager delivered any added value over some index or benchmark investment. Simply speaking, if a fund performs well, we want to know whether the fund manager is smart or just lucky.

In this chapter, we take a detailed look at a technique called performance attribution analysis and provide answers to the following questions:

- What is performance attribution analysis, and why is it important?

- What are some performance attribution analysis techniques, and how do we use them to analyze our investments?

The performance attribution analysis techniques presented in this chapter help to explain to what extent an investment portfolio's return differentials (relative to an index or benchmark investment) are caused by such things as country selection, asset allocation, security or stock selection, and other attributes.[1]

Performance Attributes: A Domestic Portfolio Framework

The measurement and interpretation of performance data is a critical component of investment strategy. As superior investment performance depends upon the ability to be in the "right" geographical mar-

---

[1] As a matter of fact, the style analysis discussed in Chapter 10 is a kind of performance attribution analysis. It tries to explain which style indices will "contribute" to the returns of your portfolio. We will use the same technique for performance attribution analysis at the end of this chapter.

kets, asset classes, industry sectors, and individual securities, we need a means of monitoring our investments to ensure that our strategy remains on track. The performance measurement techniques discussed in Chapter 9 help us to understand how our investments have performed. Performance attribution analysis further enhances our understanding of performance by helping us to identify the decisions and/or factors that are likely to have contributed to our portfolio's absolute or value-added performance relative to an index or benchmark investment.

Attribution analysis begins at the broad asset class allocation level and progressively focuses with greater and greater detail on portfolio selection choices at each level of the portfolio construction process. A simple attribution analysis system, commonly applied to a domestic diversified portfolio, would decompose performance into three components, as outlined here and as illustrated in Figure 11.1:

1. Asset allocation attribution captures the impact of our decision to over- or underweight a given asset class in our portfolio.

2. Sector selection attribution does the same thing, but at the sector/industry level.

3. Security selection attribution captures the impact of security selection within each sector/industry.

Asset Allocation Attribution

Asset allocation attribution measures the impact of over- or underweighting particular asset classes, such as equity (or value equity and growth equity), fixed income, and cash (money market securities or

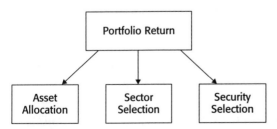

FIGURE 11.1 A simple performance attribution model for a domestic portfolio.

Treasury bills), within our portfolio by comparing the performance of a given asset class to that of the benchmark (a mix of asset classes) as a whole. In effect, it quantifies the decisions we make regarding choice of asset classes. Positive asset allocation results are achieved when a portfolio is overweighted in an asset class that outperformed the benchmark. Conversely, negative asset allocation occurs when a portfolio is underweighted in such an asset class. In the case of a balanced manager who allocates between broad asset classes such as equity and fixed income, asset allocation attribution determines to what extent the manager's over- and underweighting of those two broad classes contributed to the portfolio's excess or lagging performance relative to the benchmark. Although asset category definitions vary, the generalized model defines asset allocation in the same way. For each asset class, the asset allocation attribute is:

> Asset Class (Asset Allocation) Attribute
> = (Portfolio Weight for Asset Class
> − Benchmark Weight for Asset Class)
>   * (Portfolio Asset Class Return − Benchmark Total Return)

Note that the portfolio return is not used when calculating asset allocation; we are measuring only the impact of the asset class weighting decision.

Sector Selection Attribution

Sector selection attribution measures the impact of over- or underweighting particular sectors, such as technology or retail within the equity asset class, or corporate bonds and Treasury bonds within the fixed-income asset class. It quantifies the decisions we make regarding choice of industry or sector. Positive sector selection results are achieved when a portfolio is overweighted in a sector that outperformed the benchmark. Conversely, negative sector selection occurs when the portfolio is underweighted in such a sector. In the case of a domestic growth equity manager who selects between industry sectors such as technology and retail, sector selection attribution determines to what extent the manager's over- and underweighting of those sectors contributed to the portfolio's excess or lagging performance relative to the benchmark. For each sector the sector selection attribute within an asset class is defined as:

Sector Attribute = (Portfolio Weight for Sector
    − Benchmark Weight for Sector)
        * (Portfolio Sector Return − Benchmark Total Return)

Security Selection Attribution

Security selection attribution attempts to identify one's skill at security selection within each sector—for example, stocks selected within a particular sector such as technology or retail. Positive security selection is achieved by selecting an individual security that outperforms the sector benchmark. Negative security selection occurs when a selected security underperforms the sector benchmark.

Attribution Analysis: A Simple Example

Let's consider a hypothetical domestic diversified portfolio as an example. To keep the example as simple as possible, the portfolio is invested in stocks and bonds only. The equity portion of this managed portfolio is invested in only three sectors, the financial, retail, and technology sectors, and the fixed-income portion is invested in only two sectors, Treasury bonds and corporate bonds. The portfolio return over the period (e.g., a month or a year) is 6.50 percent. In order to conduct performance attribution analysis, we first need to set up a benchmark (called a "bogey"), which is designed to measure the returns the money manager would earn by pursuing a passive strategy. There are two levels of meaning to "passive" strategy. First, at the asset allocation level, it means that the money manager allocates funds "neutrally" across major asset classes (in this example, stocks and bonds) based on his or her investment policy and risk tolerance. Second, within each asset class, the manager invests his or her allocated money in an indexed portfolio such as the S&P 500 index for the equity allocation and the Lehman Brothers Bond Index for the fixed-income allocation. There are no sector or security selection investment decisions to be made in such a passive strategy. Any departure of the managed portfolio's return from that of the passive benchmark must be attributed to either the manager's asset allocation efforts (departure from the neutral asset class allocations) or the manager's sector and/or security bets (departure from the passive indexes within asset classes).

In Table 11.1, the bogey portfolio has been set at 60 percent equity and 40 percent fixed income. With this 60/40 weighting, it has a return of 4.38 percent for the period. The managed portfolio, with a return of 6.50 percent, has a positive excess return over the bogey portfolio of 6.50 − 4.38 = 2.12 percent. Now we need to decompose the 2.12 percent excess return and determine what part of it can be attributed to asset allocation, sector selection, and security selection.

In this hypothetical domestic portfolio, the money manager invested 80 percent in equity and 20 percent in fixed income. Table 11.2 illustrates how we can isolate the effects of the manager's asset allocation decision (i.e., to apply an 80/20 weighting of equity and fixed-income securities rather than the 60/40 weighting of the bogey portfolio) and determine what part of the 2.12 percent is attributable to the manager's over- or underweighting of equity and fixed income in the portfolio.

We begin by subtracting the benchmark (bogey) weight for a given asset class (B) from the money manager's actual portfolio weight in that class (A) to determine the excess weight in the asset class (C). We then subtract the bogey total return from the asset class return (both from Table 11.1) to determine (D). Next, we determine the asset allocation attribute (E) for each asset class by multiplying (C) * (D). Finally, we arrive at the asset allocation attribute for the entire managed port-

TABLE 11.1   Benchmark Composition and Performance

Asset Class	Benchmark (Bogey) Weight	Return of Asset Class During the Period
Equity	60.00%	6.50%
Bonds	40.00%	1.20%

Benchmark (Bogey) Return = 60% * 6.5% + 40% * 1.2% = 4.38%

Return of Managed Portfolio: 6.50%
−Return of Bogey Portfolio: 4.38%
Excess Return of Managed Portfolio: 2.12%

TABLE 11.2   Performance Attribution: Asset Allocation

Asset Class	Portfolio's Actual Weight in Asset Class (A)	Benchmark Weight in Asset Class (B)	Excess Weight in Asset Class (C)	Asset Class Return Minus Bogey Total Return (D)	Asset Allocation Attributes to Performance (E) = (C) * (D)
Equity	80.00%	60.00%	20.00%	2.12%	0.42%
Bonds	20.00%	40.00%	−20.00%	−3.18%	0.64%
				Asset Allocation Attribute:	1.06%

folio by adding up the asset allocation attributes for all asset classes represented in the portfolio.

Table 11.2 shows that 1.06 percent (half of the managed portfolio's total excess return of 2.12 percent) can be attributed to asset allocation. As we can see from Table 11.1, during the period being analyzed, the equity market, with a return of 6.5 percent, clearly outperformed fixed income, which returned a meager 1.2 percent. Therefore, the money manager was rewarded for the respective over- and under-weightings.

If 1.06 percent (i.e., half) of the excess return can be attributed to the manager's asset allocation across decisions, the remaining 1.06 percent must be attributable to sector and security selection within each asset class. Tables 11.3 and 11.4 show that sector selection within

TABLE 11.3   Performance Attribution: Sector Selection within Equity Market

Sector	Portfolio's Actual Weight in Sector at Beginning of Period (A)	Benchmark Weight in Sector at Beginning of Period (B)	Excess Weight in Sector (C)	Sector Return (D)	Sector Over/Under Performance Equity Index (E)	Sector Selection Attributes to Performance (F) = (C) * (E)
Financials	35.00%	30.00%	5.00%	6.50%	0.00%	0.00%
Retails	20.00%	30.00%	−10.00%	3.20%	−3.30%	0.33%
Technology	45.00%	40.00%	5.00%	8.98%	2.48%	0.12%
					Sector Selection Attribute:	0.45%

TABLE 11.4 Performance Attribution: Sector Selection within Fixed-Income Market

Sector	Portfolio's Actual Weight in Sector at Beginning of Period (A)	Benchmark Weight in Sector at Beginning of Period (B)	Excess Weight in Sector (C)	Sector Return (D)	Sector Over/Under Performance Bond Index (E)	Sector Selection Attributes to Performance (F) = (C) * (E)
Treasury	55.00%	60.00%	−5.00%	0.80%	−0.40%	0.02%
Corporate	45.00%	40.00%	5.00%	1.80%	0.60%	0.03%
					Sector Selection Attribute:	0.05%

the equity and fixed-income asset classes contributed 0.45 percent and 0.05 percent, respectively, to the portfolio's overall excess return of 2.12 percent.

In the case of equities (Table 11.3), for each sector, we begin by subtracting the benchmark weight in a sector at the beginning of the period (B) from the managed portfolio's actual weight in the sector (A) to determine the excess weight in the sector. Next, we subtract the return of the equity asset class (6.5 percent, from Table 11.1) from the sector's return (D) to determine that sector's over- or underperformance relative to the equity asset class (E). Next, we determine the sector selection attribute for each sector by multiplying (C) * (E). Finally, we arrive at the sector allocation attribute for the entire equity asset class by adding up the sector allocation attributes for the financial, retail, and technology sectors.

In the case of fixed income (Table 11.4), the process is identical to that for equities, except that of course we would use the return of the fixed-income asset class (1.2 percent, from Table 11.1) in calculating (E). As we can see from this table's presentation of fixed-income performance across Treasury and corporate bonds,[2] good performance or a positive attribute came from overweighting the corporate bond sector, which performed better, and underweighting the poorer-performing Treasury bond sector.

Since we have determined that 1.56 percent in excess performance can be attributed to asset allocation and sector selection within each

---

[2] Please note that we don't pay any attention to the duration of each bond sector.

TABLE 11.5   Performance Attribution: Summary

	Performance Attributes
1. Asset Allocation	1.06%
2. Sector Selection	
a. Equity	0.45%
b. Fixed Income	0.05%
3. Security Selection	0.56%
Total Excess Return of Portfolio	2.12%

asset class, we can reasonably assume that the remaining 0.56 percent was due to individual security selection within the sectors. Table 11.5 summarizes the performance attributes of asset allocation, sector selection, and security selection. Of the total excess portfolio performance of 2.12 percent, asset allocation across major asset classes contributed 1.06 percent, sector selection for both equity and fixed-income asset classes contributed 0.50 percent, and security selection contributed 0.56 percent.

As we can see from this example, half of the entire 2.12 percent excess performance differential was explained by the manager's excellent ability to allocate funds across major asset classes. About one-fourth of the overall excess performance was due to the manager's sector selection. The remaining one-fourth was due to good stock and bond selections within asset class sectors.

More meaningful performance attribution is generally conducted over longer periods of time and is often expanded to include more attributes, such as currency for an international portfolio manager and quality and duration for a fixed-income manager.

What If You Are a Global Investor?

The benefits of international diversification in terms of return and risk have been increasingly recognized since the 1970s. Deregulation, internationalization of financial markets throughout the world, and recent advances in information technology have led to easier access to information, reduced costs, and more sophisticated investors worldwide. All of these developments have made cross-currency/cross-border investing more popular. Therefore, it is important to include factors in our performance attribution that will make the analysis meaningful to the international investor.

Figure 11.2 proposes a performance attribution model for an international portfolio. In addition to asset allocation, sector selection, and security selection, this extended model also includes country selection and currency attributes. Therefore, for an international portfolio, we would decompose performance into five components, as outlined here and illustrated in Figure 11.2:

1. Asset allocation attribution captures the impact of our decision to over- or underweight a given asset class in our portfolio.

2. Sector selection attribution does the same, but at the sector/industry level.

3. Security selection attribution captures the impact of security selection within each sector/industry.

4. Country selection captures the impact of our decision to over- or underweight exposure to a given country in our portfolio.

5. Currency reflects the currency translation effect in chosen securities (implicit) and the impact of active currency management decisions, e.g., hedging (explicit).

Country Selection Attribute

Country selection attribution captures the impact of over- or underweighting a country within our portfolio by comparing the performance of the given country to that of an international benchmark. In effect, it quantifies the decisions we make relative to choice of country markets in which to invest. Positive country selection is achieved by

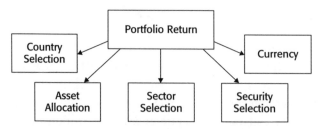

FIGURE 11.2   A performance attribution model for an international portfolio.

overweighting a portfolio in a country market that outperformed the international benchmark. Conversely, negative country selection occurs when the portfolio is underweighted in such a country market.

Currency Attribute

Currency attribution reflects the currency translation effect of the securities we hold (implicit) and the impact of active currency management decisions, e.g., hedging, (explicit). The currency attribute is measured separately and attempts to capture the effect of the currency exposures of the portfolio and the impact of forward currency contracts or currency futures. Like the asset allocation attribute, the currency attribute is measured relative to the benchmark currency return.

Attribution Analysis: Style Factor-Based Approach

The attribution analysis that we have discussed so far in this chapter focuses on using a portfolio's sector holdings information to decompose the sources of portfolio performance. However, as we discussed in Chapter 10, up-to-date holdings of mutual funds are often not accessible. Furthermore, many fund managers cannot even reconcile what the fund's holdings represent and how the fund performed.

In Chapter 10, we showed how returns-based style analysis, originally developed by Nobel laureate William Sharpe, can be used to analyze a fund's pattern of returns over time to infer the manager's investment style. In essence, the fund's return pattern or behavior suggests that the manager is following a particular investment style. The major appeal of this effective asset mix approach is simplicity. It requires only the returns of the fund under investigation and style indices representing the fund manager's portfolio selection universe. Such data are more readily available than a fund's detailed list of security holdings, making the method much easier to implement than holdings-based style analysis. It is also worth noting that Sharpe's returns-based style analysis provides insights concerning the sources of a fund's historical returns, expressing them as a combination of benchmark returns that best represents the fund's overall returns. In other words, this approach expresses performance as the weighted-average return associated with style indices or benchmarks for various style or substyle categories (i.e., value, growth, large, and small). Therefore, returns-based style analysis allows for better diagnosis of a money manager's actions and better measurement and attribution of portfolio performance.[3]

In this section, we apply returns-based style analysis to the famous Fidelity Magellan Fund. Our objective is to gain some insight, generally speaking, into what kind of market indices contributed to the fund's performance over a three-year period ending December 31, 2000. Figure 11.3 shows the results of our returns-based style performance analysis. From both, we can see that the U.S. equity market contributed the majority of the fund's return, accounting for 92.71 percent. The international equity market contributed the remaining 7.29 percent of fund performance, possibly because of its holdings in stocks that had some international exposure. Neither the U.S. bond nor the cash/money market asset class contributed to the fund's performance during the period of analysis.

Performance Attribution Analysis: Brief Summary

The goal of performance attribution analysis is to identify how and to what degree we have added value to our portfolio. If we are investing in mutual funds, the analysis helps us to uncover the fund manager's strengths and weaknesses, thus empowering us to make informed hire(buy)/retain(hold)/fire(sell) decisions. Attribution techniques break down added value into components or attributes, each of which quantifies the impact of key investment decisions.

Performance attribution analysis has great benefits to investors, allowing us to:

---

[3] For some examples of using market style indices within a multi-index model to analyze the source of portfolio performance, see Edwin Elton, Martin Gruber, Sanjiv Das, and Matthew Hlavka, "Efficiency with Costly Information: A Reinterpretation of Evidence from Manager Portfolios," *Review of Financial Studies*, Vol. 6, No. 1, 1993, pp. 1–23; William F. Sharpe, "Determining a Fund's Effective Asset Mix," *Journal of Portfolio Management*, Fall 1988, pp. 49–58; and William F. Sharpe, "Asset Allocation: Management Style and Performance Measurement," *Journal of Portfolio Management*, Winter 1992, pp. 7–19.

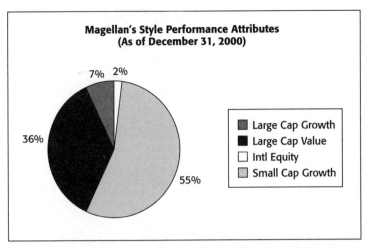

Note: Portfolio returns are as of December 31, 2000. The return-based style attribution analysis use three-year trailing monthly returns. The market index for style benchmark used in the analysis: S&P 500/Barra Growth Index for Large Cap Growth; S&P 500/Barra Value Index for Large Cap Value; Russell 2000 Growth Index for Small Cap Growth; Russell 2000 Value Index for Small Cap Value; Lehman Brothers Aggregate Bond Index for U.S. Bond; MSCI EAFE Index for International Equity and U.S. Three Month Treasury Bill for Cash.

FIGURE 11.3   Style factor-based performance attributes for Fidelity Magellan.

- Identify the detailed and key performance drivers of a portfolio.

- Highlight a potential money manager's strong and weak points, thereby facilitating our choice of manager.

- Separate those performance/risk factors that are within a money manager's control from those that might be outside his or her control as a result of a client's investment mandate or prospectus limitations.

- Ensure that our portfolio performance or our money manager's performance remains within our investment mandate.

Finally, while performance attribution holds great benefits for investors, it needs to be approached with both care and rigor. There are no standard calculations, and performance attribution methodologies and techniques will differ depending on one's investment mandate. Therefore, it is essential for investors to study in detail the calculations for each attribute and to be aware of the assumptions (such as selection of benchmark) that underlie each calculation.

Large Cap Funds that Meet Strict Selection Criteria

Selection Criteria	
Asset Class	U.S. Large Cap
Manager Tenure	Greater than or equal to 5 years
Load fees?	None
Expense Ratio	Less than or equal to 1.0%
1-year Return	Greater than or equal to the performance of the average U.S. Large Cap Fund
3-year Return	Greater than or equal to the performance of the average U.S. Large Cap Fund

Symbol	Name	Expense Ratio (%)
STLDX	Barclay's Global Investors LP 2030	0.95
PWTYX	Brinson Tactical Allocation Y	0.56
SPFIX	California Investment S&P 500 Index	0.20
DVASX	Diversified Investment Interm/Long Horizon	0.20
DGAGX	Dreyfus Appreciation	0.88
CAPEX	Eaton Vance Tax-Managed Growth 1.0	0.47
ELFNX	Elfun Trusts	0.10
FASGX	Fidelity Asset Manager: Growth	0.77

(continued)

Symbol	Name	Expense Ratio (%)
FGRIX	Fidelity Growth & Income	0.66
MGEQX	First Funds Growth & Income I	0.97
GEEDX	GE U.S Equity Y	0.58
HASYX	Hartford Stock Y	0.80
FIIIX	Invesco Equity Income Investment	0.96
LKEQX	LKCM Equity	0.80
LSCGX	Loomis Sayles Provident Fund	0.65
MVAEX	M.S.D.&T. Growth & Income	0.70
BEIAX	Northern Institutional Equity Index A	0.21
OGVFX	One Group Diversified Equity I	0.95
PAPIX	PIMCO Capital Appreciation Institutional	0.95
PSIFX	Prudential Stock Index Z	0.40
SWHGX	Schwab MarketTrack Growth	0.57
STFGX	State Farm Growth	0.11
STSEX	State Street Exchange	0.55
VINIX	Vanguard Institutional Index	0.06
VASGX	Vanguard LifeStrategy Growth	0.00
VTGIX	Vanguard Tax Managed Growth & Income	0.19
WAAYX	Waddel & Reed Adv Accumulative Y	0.80
NVDEX	Wells Fargo Diversified Equity I	1.00
NVINX	Wells Fargo Index I	0.25

Source: These funds were selected using data provided by Morningstar.com.

Small Cap Funds that Meet Strict Selection Criteria

Selection Criteria	
Asset Class	U.S. Small Cap
Manager Tenure	Greater than or equal to 3 years
Load fees?	None
Expense Ratio	Less than or equal to 1.5%
1-year Return	Greater than or equal to the performance of the average US Small Cap Fund
3-year Return	Greater than or equal to the performance of the average US Small Cap Fund

Symbol	Name	Expense Ratio (%)
ARGFX	Ariel	1.24
BRSIX	Bridgeway Ultra-Small Co Tax Advantage	0.75
CGMFX	CGM Focus	1.20
FCGFX	Fiduciary Capital Grow	1.30
GSVIX	GE Instl Small-Cap Value Equity Investment	0.70
SMCEX	Galaxy Small Cap Value Trust	0.94
LKSCX	LKCM Small Cap Equity	0.93
LRSYX	Lord Abbett Small-Cap Y	1.23

(continued)

Symbol	Name	Expense Ratio (%)
M$-BDJF	Maxim Ariel SmallCap Value	1.23
MVALX	Meridian Value	1.41
NBGAX	Neuberger Berman Genesis Advantage	1.50
NBGNX	Neuberger Berman Genesis Investment	1.21
NBGEX	Neuberger Berman Genesis Trust	1.21
RYPRX	Royce Premier	1.20
COPCX	SG Cowen Opportunity I	1.30
WSCVX	Schroder Small Cap Value Investment	1.50
RHJMX	UAM Rice Hall James Small Mid Cap	1.25
RHJSX	UAM Rice Hall James Small Cap	1.19
WGROX	Wasatch Core Growth	1.38
WPSCX	Westport Small Cap I	1.14
WPSRX	Westport Small Cap R	1.27

Source: These funds were selected using data provided by Morningstar.com.

Bond Funds that Meet Strict Selection Criteria

Selection Criteria

Asset Class	Bond, Intermediate Term
Manager Tenure	Any
Load fees?	None
Expense Ratio	Less than or equal to 1.0%
1-year Return	Greater than or equal to the performance of the average Intermediate Bond Fund
3-year Return	Greater than or equal to the performance of the average Intermediate Bond Fund

Symbol	Name	Expense Ratio (%)
BFMCX	BlackRock Core Bond Institutional	0.55
CFIYX	Conseco Fixed Income Y	0.60
MFINX	Deutsche Fixed Income Institutional	0.54
DODIX	Dodge & Cox Income	0.46
DIGFX	Dreyfus Basic GNMA	0.65
FBIDX	Fidelity U.S. Bond Index	0.31
FBDFX	Fremont Bond	0.62
FRTRX	Frontegra Total Return Bond	0.43

(continued)

Symbol	Name	Expense Ratio (%)
GSFIX	Goldman Sachs Core Fixed Income Institutional	0.54
JHABX	John Hancock Active Bond	0.60
HABDX	Harbor Bond	0.60
MWTRX	Metropolitan West Total Return Bond	0.65
MIBFX	Monetta Intermediate Bond	0.54
MPFIX	Morgan Stanley Inst Fixed Income	0.47
MPSPX	Morgan Stanley Inst Special Purpose Fixed Income	0.48
PMDRX	PIMCO Moderate Duration Institutional	0.45
PTRAX	PIMCO Total Return Administrative	0.68
PRADX	PIMCO Total Return II Administrative	0.75
PMBIX	PIMCO Total Return II Institutional	0.50
PTSAX	PIMCO Total Return III Institutional	0.50
PTTRX	PIMCO Total Return Institutional	0.43
SRBFX	Stein Roe Intermediate Bond	0.72
TAIBX	Target Intermediate-Term Bond	0.71
VBTIX	Vanguard Total Bond Market Index Institutional	0.10
WATFX	Western Asset Core	0.50
WATIX	Western Asset Intermediate	0.45

Source: These funds were selected using data provided by Morningstar.com.

International Equity Funds that Meet Strict Selection Criteria

Selection Criteria	
Asset Class	International Equity (Global Focus)
Manager Tenure	Any
Load fees?	None
Expense Ratio	Less than or equal to 2.0%
1-year Return	Greater than or equal to the performance of the average International Equity Fund with a global focus
3-year Return	Greater than or equal to the performance of the average International Equity Fund with a global focus

Symbol	Name	Expense Ratio (%)
EGLBX	Elfun International Equity	0.15
FWWFX	Fidelity Worldwide	1.04
GGEDX	GE Global Equity Y	1.06
MSGEX	Morgan Stanley Institutional Global Value Equity A	1.00
MIGEX	Morgan Stanley Institutional Global Value Equity B	1.25
MDISX	Mutual Discovery Z	1.02
PURIX	Purisima Total Return	1.50
RSPFX	RS Partners	1.90

(continued)

Symbol	Name	Expense Ratio (%)
SGLYX	Smith Barney Hansberger Global Value Y	1.06
TGADX	Templeton Growth Advantage	0.86
VHGEX	Vanguard Global Equity	0.70

Source: These funds were selected using data provided by Morningstar.com.

Comprehensive List of Available Index Funds

S&P 500 INDEX FUNDS/ LARGE CAP STOCKS

Name	Symbol	Expense Ratio (%)
ARK Equity Index A	ARKAX	0.50
Advantus Index 500 A	ADIAX	0.75
American AAdvant S&P 500 Mlg	AAFMX	0.55
American AAdvant S&P 500 Pln	AAFPX	0.55
American Cent Eq Idx Inv	ACIVX	0.49
Armada Equity Index I	AQDIX	0.34
BlackRock Index Equity Inv A	CIEAX	0.78
BlackRock Index Equity Svc	PNESX	0.59
Brinson S&P 500 Index A	PSPIX	0.60
California Invmt S&P 500 Idx	SPFIX	0.20
Deutsche Equity 500 Idx Invm	BTIEX	0.25
Dreyfus Basic S&P 500 Stock	DSPIX	0.20
Dreyfus S&P 500 Index	PEOPX	0.50
E*TRADE S&P 500 Index	ETSPX	0.32

(continued)

S&P 500 INDEX FUNDS/ LARGE CAP STOCKS (Cont.)

Name	Symbol	Expense Ratio (%)
Eclipse Indexed Equity	NIIEX	0.30
Eclipse Indexed Equity Svc	MAQSX	0.55
Fidelity Spartan 500 Index	FSMKX	0.19
First American Equity Indx A	FAEIX	0.60
Firstar Equity Index Instl	FIENX	0.37
Firstar Equity Index Ret A	FRENX	0.62
Forum Equity Index	FOEIX	0.25
Galaxy II Large Co Index Ret	ILCIX	0.47
Harris Ins Index Instl	HIDIX	0.45
Harris Ins Index N	HIDAX	0.70
INVESCO S&P 500 Index Inv	ISPIX	0.63
Kent Index Equity Invmt	KNIDX	0.67
MainStay Equity Index A	MCSEX	0.92
Mason Street Index 400 Stk A	MSIAX	0.95
Merrill Lynch S&P 500 Idx A	MASRX	0.38
Morgan Stanley S&P 500 Idx A	SPIAX	0.75
Munder Index 500 A	MUXAX	0.50
Nations Large Cap Idx Inv A	NEIAX	0.60
Northern Stock Index	NOSIX	0.55
One Group Equity Index A	OGEAX	0.60
Prudential Stock Index I	PDSIX	0.30
Prudential Stock Index Z	PSIFX	0.40
SSgA S&P 500 Index	SVSPX	0.18
Schwab S&P 500 Inv	SWPIX	0.36
Schwab S&P 500 e.Sh	SWPEX	0.29
Scudder S&P 500 Index S	SCPIX	0.40

(continued)

S&P 500 INDEX FUNDS/ LARGE CAP STOCKS (*Cont.*)

Name	Symbol	Expense Ratio (%)
Smith Barney S&P 500 Index A	SBSPX	0.59
Strong Index 500	SINEX	0.45
T. Rowe Price Equity Idx 500	PREIX	0.35
Transamerica Prem Index Inv	TPIIX	0.25
USAA S&P 500 Index	USSPX	0.18
United Assoc S&P 500 Idx II	UAIIX	0.15
Vanguard 500 Index	VFINX	0.18
Vantagepoint 500 Stock Idx I	VPFIX	0.44
Victory Stock Index A	SSTIX	0.59
Victory Stock Index G	VINGX	0.82
Wachovia Equity Index A	BTEIX	0.66
Wells Fargo Equity Index A	SFCSX	0.71

SMALL CAP INDEX FUNDS

Name	Symbol	Expense Ratio (%)
AXP Small Company Index A	ISIAX	0.97
Bridgeway Ultra-Small Tx Adv	BRSIX	0.75
California Invmt S&P SmC Idx	SMCIX	0.65
Dreyfus Small Cap Stock Idx	DISSX	0.50
Galaxy II Small Co Index Ret	ISCIX	0.41
Merrill Lynch Sm Cap Idx A	MASKX	0.50
Merrill Lynch Sm Cap Idx D	MDSKX	0.74
North American Sm-Cp Idx A	NISAX	0.83
Northern Small Cap Index	NSIDX	1.00
Schwab Small Cap Index Inv	SWSMX	0.49
Vanguard Sm Cp Gr Index	VISGX	0.27

(*continued*)

SMALL CAP INDEX FUNDS (*Cont.*)

Name	Symbol	Expense Ratio (%)
Vanguard Sm Cp Index	NAESX	0.27
Vanguard Sm Cp Val Index	VISVX	0.27
Vanguard Tax-Mgd Sm Cap Ret	VTMSX	0.20

INTERNATIONAL EQUITY INDEX FUNDS

Name	Symbol	Expense Ratio (%)
E*TRADE International Index	ETINX	0.55
Merrill Lynch Intl Index A	MAIIX	0.64
Merrill Lynch Intl Index D	MDIIX	0.89
STI Classic Intl Eqty Idx Tr	SIEIX	1.06
Schwab International Idx Inv	SWINX	0.58
Vanguard Total Intl Stk Idx	VGTSX	0.00

INTERMEDIATE BOND INDEX FUNDS

Name	Symbol	Expense Ratio (%)
Dreyfus Bond Market Idx Bas	DBIRX	0.15
Dreyfus Bond Market Idx Inv	DBMIX	0.40
E*TRADE Bond Index	ETBDX	0.35
Galaxy II U.S. Treas Idx Ret	IUTIX	0.41
Merrill Lynch Aggregate Bd A	MAABX	0.38
Merrill Lynch Aggregate Bd D	MDABX	0.63
Schwab Total Bond Market Idx	SWLBX	0.35
Vanguard Intrm-Term Bd Idx	VBIIX	0.00
Vanguard Tot Bond Mkt Idx	VBMFX	0.22
Vantagepoint Core Bond Idx I	VPCIX	0.47

Source: IndexFunds.com.

Comprehensive List of Available Exchange Traded Funds (ETFs)

ETFS ON THE S&P500/ LARGE CAPS

Name	Symbol	Expense Ratio (%)
SPDRs	SPY	0.17
iShares S&P500 Index	IVV	0.09
iShares S&P500/ Barra Growth	IVW	0.18
iShares S&P500/ Barra Value	IVE	0.18

ETFS ON SMALL CAP STOCKS

Name	Symbol	Expense Ratio (%)
iShares Russell 2000 Growth Index	IWO	0.25
iShares Russell 2000 Index	IWM	0.20
iShares Russell 2000 Value Index	IWN	0.25
iShares S&P SmallCap 600 Index	IJR	0.20
iShares S&P SmallCap 600/BARRA Growth	IJT	0.25
iShares S&P SmallCap 600/BARRA Value	IJS	0.25
streetTRACKS DJ US Small Cap Growth	DSG	0.25
streetTRACKS DJ US Small Cap Value	DSV	0.25

OTHER U.S. INDEX ETFS

Name	Symbol	Expense Ratio (%)
Diamond Series Trust I	DIA	0.12
Nasdaq 100 Trust Series I	QQQ	0.18
iShares S&P Midcap 400	IJH	0.20
iShares S&P Midcap 400/Barra Growth	IJK	0.25
iShares S&P Midcap 400/Barra Value	IJJ	0.25
iShares Russell 1000	IWB	0.15
iShares Russell 1000 Growth	IWF	0.20
iShares Russell 1000 Value	IWD	0.20
iShares Russell 3000	IWV	0.20
iShares Russell 3000 Growth	IWZ	0.25
iShares Russell 3000 Value	IWW	0.25

ETFS ON INTERNATIONAL STOCKS

Name	Symbol	Expense Ratio (%)
iShares S&P Global 100 Index	IOO	0.40
streetTRACKS DJ Global Titans	DGT	0.50

U.S. SECTOR ETFS

Name	Symbol	Expense Ratio (%)
iShares Dow Jones US Basic Mtrls	IYM	0.60
iShares Dow Jones US Chemicals	IYD	0.60
iShares Dow Jones US Cons Cyclic	IYC	0.60
iShares Dow Jones US Cons Non-Cycl	IYK	0.60
iShares Dow Jones US Energy Sec	IYE	0.60
iShares Dow Jones US Financial Sct	IYF	0.60
iShares Dow Jones US Financial Srv IYG		0.60
iShares Dow Jones US Healthcare	IYH	0.60

(continued)

U.S. SECTOR ETFS (*Cont.*)

Name	Symbol	Expense Ratio (%)
iShares Dow Jones US Industrial	IYJ	0.60
iShares Dow Jones US Internet	IYV	0.60
iShares Dow Jones US Real Estate	IYR	0.60
iShares Dow Jones US Technology	IYW	0.60
iShares Dow Jones US Telecom	IYZ	0.60
iShares Dow Jones US Total Mkt	IYY	0.20
iShares Dow Jones US Utilities	IDU	0.60
SPDR Basic Industries	XLB	0.28
SPDR Consumer Services	XLV	0.28
SPDR Consumer Staples	XLP	0.28
SPDR Cyclical/Transportation	XLY	0.28
SPDR Energy	XLE	0.28
SPDR Financial	XLF	0.28
SPDR Industrial	XLI	0.28
SPDR Mid Cap	MDY	0.25
SPDR Technology	XLK	0.28
SPDR Utilities	XLU	0.28
HOLDR B2B Internet	BHH	$0.08 per 100 shares
HOLDR Biotech	BBH	$0.08 per 100 shares
HOLDR Broadband	BDH	$0.08 per 100 shares
HOLDR Internet	HHH	$0.08 per 100 shares
HOLDR Internet Arch	IAH	$0.08 per 100 shares
HOLDR Internet Infra	IIH	$0.08 per 100 shares
HOLDR Pharm	PPH	$0.08 per 100 shares
HOLDR Reg Bank	RKH	$0.08 per 100 shares
HOLDR Semi-conductor	SMH	$0.08 per 100 shares
HOLDR TeleBras	TBH	$0.08 per 100 shares
HOLDR Telecom	TTH	$0.08 per 100 shares
HOLDR Utilities	UTH	$0.08 per 100 shares

COUNTRY OR REGIONAL ETFS

Name	Symbol	Expense Ratio (%)
iShares MSCI Australia Index	EWA	0.84
iShares MSCI Austria Index	EWO	0.84
iShares MSCI Belgium Index	EWK	0.84
iShares MSCI Brazil Index	EWZ	0.99
iShares MSCI Canada Index	EWC	0.84
iShares MSCI France Index	EWQ	0.84
iShares MSCI EMU	EZU	0.84
iShares MSCI Germany Index	EWG	0.84
iShares MSCI Hong Kong Index	EWH	0.84
iShares MSCI Italy Index	EWI	0.84
iShares MSCI Japan Index	EWJ	0.84
iShares MSCI Malaysia Index	EWM	0.84
iShares MSCI Mexico Index	EWW	0.84
iShares MSCI Netherlands Index	EWN	0.84
iShares MSCI Singapore Index	EWS	0.84
iShares MSCI Spain Index	EWP	0.84
iShares MSCI South Korea Index	EWY	0.99
iShares MSCI Sweden Index	EWD	0.84
iShares MSCI Switzerland Index	EWL	0.84
iShares MSCI Taiwan Index	EWT	0.99
iShares MSCI UK Index	EWU	0.84
iShares S&P Europe 350	IEV	0.60
iShares S&P TSE 60 Index Fund	IKC	0.50

Source: IndexFunds.com.

APPENDIX G 100 Largest Mutual Funds and Their Risk and Return Statistics

Symbol	Fund Name	Morningstar Rating	Mean	Standard Deviation	Sharpe Ratio	Beta	Alpha	R²
FMAGX	Fidelity Magellan	4-star	5.85	21.92	0.03	1.06	2.14	96.54
VFINX	Vanguard 500 Index	4-star	3.93	19.87	−0.08	1	0.02	100
AIVSX	American Funds Investment Co Amer A	4-star	9.45	16.11	0.3	0.75	4.75	91.09
AWSHX	American Funds Washington Mutual A	4-star	7.49	17.31	0.15	0.61	3.13	50.77
AGTHX	American Funds Growth Fund of Amer A	5-star	17.94	27.79	0.52	1.06	14.53	73.73
FGRIX	Fidelity Growth & Income	4-star	3.97	16.37	−0.09	0.8	−0.4	92.88
FCNTX	Fidelity Contrafund	4-star	5.19	19.55	0	0.83	1.22	72.28
PTTRX	PIMCO Total Return Instl	5-star	7.59	4.06	0.68	1.16	0.35	94.78
JANSX	Janus	3-star	5.6	30.15	0.01	1.29	3.54	78.34
ANWPX	American Funds New Perspective A	5-star	9.95	19.34	0.28	0.84	5.65	81.47
AEPGX	American Funds EuroPacific Growth A	4-star	5.89	19.79	0.04	0.78	1.93	62.2
TWCUX	American Century Ultra Inv	3-star	2.82	27.73	−0.1	1.27	0.42	84.14
VWNFX	Vanguard Windsor II	4-star	5.45	18.78	0.01	0.65	1.43	48.82
JAWWX	Janus Worldwide	5-star	3.83	27.12	−0.06	0.96	1.3	51.24
VINIX	Vanguard Institutional Index	4-star	4.05	19.88	−0.07	1	0.13	100

(continued)

Symbol	Fund Name	Morningstar Rating	Mean	Standard Deviation	Sharpe Ratio	Beta	Alpha	R^2
FDGRX	Fidelity Growth Company	4-star	14.08	41.19	0.25	1.11	14.02	37.69
FEQIX	Fidelity Equity-Income	4-star	5.93	18.59	0.04	0.75	1.81	65.88
FBGRX	Fidelity Blue Chip Growth	3-star	3.19	22.71	-0.1	1.09	-0.19	89.99
VWELX	Vanguard Wellington	4-star	8.05	11.67	0.28	0.43	3.05	54.83
FPURX	Fidelity Puritan	4-star	5.6	10.86	0.04	0.48	0.63	77
ANCFX	American Funds Fundamental Invs A	4-star	9.27	17.08	0.27	0.8	4.69	93.8
PGRWX	Putnam Fund for Growth & Income A	3-star	4.86	17.74	-0.03	0.72	0.68	65.45
VPMCX	Vanguard Primecap	5-star	15.29	26.41	0.43	1.01	11.82	70.3
AMECX	American Funds Income Fund of Amer A	4-star	6.84	9.72	0.19	0.35	1.76	52.77
VWNDX	Vanguard Windsor	4-star	9.63	23.52	0.22	0.86	6.1	59.36
VGHCX	Vanguard Health Care	5-star	23.57	19.1	1.09	0.47	18.62	32.58
PVOYX	Putnam Voyager A	3-star	6.41	30.15	0.04	1.22	4.27	70.83
JAVLX	Janus Twenty	3-star	0.97	35.16	-0.14	1.44	0.42	68.9
FUSEX	Fidelity Spartan U.S. Equity Index	4-star	3.76	19.8	-0.09	1	-0.15	99.99
VTSMX	Vanguard Total Stock Mkt Idx	3-star	3.91	20.91	-0.07	1.02	0.18	94.15
FDGFX	Fidelity Dividend Growth	5-star	10.9	19.08	0.34	0.85	6.49	86.5
VFIIX	Vanguard GNMA	5-star	6.93	3	0.66	0.79	0.31	80.95

(continued)

Symbol	Fund Name	Morningstar Rating	Mean	Standard Deviation	Sharpe Ratio	Beta	Alpha	R²
INNDX	AXP New Dimensions A	3-star	5.27	22.7	0	1.07	1.74	90.37
VBMFX	Vanguard Total Bond Mkt Index	4-star	7.02	3.45	0.6	1	0.05	98.44
FFIDX	Fidelity	4-star	3.99	22.64	−0.06	1.05	0.54	85.48
FKTFX	Franklin CA Tax-Free Income A	5-star	4.99	4.4	−0.07	0.94	−1.72	51.53
FEQTX	Fidelity Equity-Income II	4-star	4.79	17.05	−0.03	0.75	0.51	75.55
VFIAX	Vanguard 500 Index Adm							
FASMX	Fidelity Asset Manager	4-star	6.87	12.51	0.15	0.59	1.95	87.88
TEPLX	Templeton Growth A	5-star	8.7	19.04	0.21	0.68	4.51	54
CSTGX	AIM Constellation A	2-star	4.59	33.32	−0.02	1.33	3.4	68.52
PNOPX	Putnam New Opportunities A	2-star	1.25	42.07	−0.11	1.61	2.66	63.91
VWUSX	Vanguard U.S. Growth	2-star	−7.41	28.26	−0.53	1.39	−8.83	82.91
DIVBX	Morgan Stanley Dividend Growth Secs B	3-star	2.6	17.01	−0.18	0.65	−1.53	55.5
VIIIX	Vanguard Institutional Index Instl Pl	3-star	4.09	19.89	−0.07	1	0.17	100
CWGIX	American Funds Capital World Gr&Inc A	5-star	9.3	15.99	0.29	0.67	4.63	75.2
LMVTX	Legg Mason Value Prim	5-star	12.28	27.63	0.29	1.18	9.19	85.27
NYVTX	Davis NY Venture A	4-star	7.2	20.27	0.11	0.92	3.2	85.59

(continued)

Symbol	Fund Name	Morningstar Rating	Mean	Standard Deviation	Sharpe Ratio	Beta	Alpha	R^2
AVLBX	AIM Value B	3-star	3.59	23.67	−0.08	1.1	0.37	86.7
PRFDX	T. Rowe Price Equity-Income	4-star	8.63	17.03	0.23	0.54	4.19	42.42
LAFFX	Lord Abbett Affiliated A	4-star	11.03	17.62	0.38	0.7	6.46	69.59
ABNDX	American Funds Bond Fund of Amer A	4-star	5.1	4.23	−0.04	0.74	−1.28	33.37
JAMRX	Janus Mercury	4-star	12.88	40.39	0.22	1.43	12.64	63.74
SMCWX	American Funds Smallcap World A	2-star	4.11	31.57	−0.04	1.01	2.61	43.49
AVLFX	AIM Value A	3-star	4.4	23.87	−0.04	1.11	1.16	86.69
ANEFX	American Funds New Economy A	3-star	6.43	25.02	0.05	1.03	3.3	71.36
FAGOX	Fidelity Advisor Growth Opport T	2-star	−5.63	17.79	−0.72	0.93	−9.25	89.96
TEMFX	Templeton Foreign A	4-star	6.09	20.45	0.05	0.72	2.27	50.59
MIGFX	MFS Massachusetts Investors Gr Stk A	4-star	5.29	26.24	0	1.12	2.44	76.44
FRSGX	Franklin Small Cap Growth I A	3-star	14.4	48.88	0.21	1.44	16.45	47.53
FSMKX	Fidelity Spartan 500 Index	4-star	3.79	19.81	−0.09	1	−0.12	99.98
VIGRX	Vanguard Growth Index	3-star	0.87	23.39	−0.22	1.13	−2.25	88.9
PGIBX	Putnam Fund for Growth & Income B	3-star	4.09	17.62	−0.08	0.72	−0.06	65.42
FOCPX	Fidelity OTC	2-star	5.95	45.03	0.02	1.55	7.63	56.38

(continued)

Symbol	Fund Name	Morningstar Rating	Mean	Standard Deviation	Sharpe Ratio	Beta	Alpha	R^2
AMRMX	American Funds American Mutual A	4-star	7.5	14.25	0.18	0.48	2.79	45.71
VAAPX	Vanguard Asset Allocation	4-star	5.42	12.52	0.02	0.6	0.57	91.3
FDEGX	Fidelity Aggressive Growth	2-star	0.36	49.52	−0.12	1.77	4	58.37
VGSTX	Vanguard STAR	4-star	8.05	12	0.27	0.54	3.03	83.35
CAIBX	American Funds Capital Inc Builder A	5-star	5.71	9.99	0.05	0.34	0.73	44.9
HACAX	Harbor Capital Appreciation	4-star	4.81	29.89	−0.02	1.32	2.76	82.18
FAEGX	Fidelity Advisor Equity Growth T	3-star	6.34	25.79	0.05	1.14	3.31	82.16
PRITX	T. Rowe Price International Stock	3-star	−2.84	19.42	−0.49	0.81	−6.33	61.23
VQNPX	Vanguard Growth & Income	4-star	4.35	20.51	−0.05	1.02	0.52	97.41
AMCPX	American Funds Amcap A	4-star	12.98	18.95	0.47	0.83	8.45	86.96
MSIGX	Oppenheimer Main St Growth & Income A	4-star	2.86	19.86	−0.14	0.99	−0.98	95.76
JAGIX	Janus Growth & Income	5-star	9.27	24.73	0.19	1.02	5.88	74.2
TEMWX	Templeton World A	4-star	3.91	18.47	−0.08	0.76	−0.12	66.19
ABALX	American Funds American Balanced A	4-star	11.15	10.69	0.64	0.36	5.94	47.94
VWIGX	Vanguard International Growth	3-star	−0.87	17.36	−0.41	0.7	−4.76	57.89
PVOBX	Putnam Voyager B	2-star	5.61	29.89	0.01	1.22	3.49	70.82

(continued)

Symbol	Fund Name	Morningstar Rating	Mean	Standard Deviation	Sharpe Ratio	Beta	Alpha	R²
AMOBX	Morgan Stanley American Opp B	3-star	3.04	25.74	-0.1	0.78	0.32	36.82
FKUSX	Franklin U.S. Government Secs A	4-star	6.51	2.79	0.54	0.75	-0.02	84.63
UNCMX	Waddell & Reed Adv Core Investment A	4-star	5.96	16.91	0.05	0.79	1.54	88.76
VFSTX	Vanguard Short-Term Corp	5-star	6.76	2.03	0.88	0.53	0.57	79.88
MITTX	MFS Massachusetts Investors A	3-star	0.39	16.49	-0.34	0.83	-3.77	92.54
FMCSX	Fidelity Mid-Cap Stock	5-star	21.12	33.9	0.53	0.72	18.81	24.61
PRSCX	T. Rowe Price Science & Tech	2-star	4.88	59.83	-0.01	2.1	11.46	65.71
VWITX	Vanguard Interm-Term Tax-Ex	4-star	5.46	3.13	0.08	0.67	-0.87	51.64
FBALX	Fidelity Balanced	4-star	8.65	11.8	0.33	0.54	3.59	85.28
APGBX	Alliance Premier Growth B	2-star	-1.56	28.34	-0.28	1.39	-3.53	90.09
POVSX	Putnam International Growth A	5-star	5.81	24.02	0.03	0.83	2.58	49.05
ACEGX	Van Kampen Emerging Growth A	4-star	15.12	50.48	0.22	1.35	17.34	39.77
TRBCX	T. Rowe Price Blue Chip Growth	4-star	4.21	22.32	-0.05	1.09	0.68	94.79
TWCGX	American Century Growth Inv	2-star	2.95	23.9	-0.11	1.07	-0.18	78.77
FKTIX	Franklin Federal Tax-Free Income A	5-star	4.73	3.33	-0.18	0.72	-1.63	51.86
RPMGX	T. Rowe Price Mid-Cap Growth	4-star	12.53	27.24	0.31	1.11	9.4	77.21

(continued)

Symbol	Fund Name	Morningstar Rating	Mean	Standard Deviation	Sharpe Ratio	Beta	Alpha	R^2
VWINX	Vanguard Wellesley Income	4-star	7.86	7.32	0.42	0.16	2.65	20.3
FIDYX	INVESCO Dynamics Inv	4-star	7.72	43.28	0.07	1.43	8.9	52.86
PIODX	Pioneer A	4-star	6.84	17.8	0.1	0.85	2.48	93.88
PTRAX	PIMCO Total Return Admin	5-star	7.32	4.05	0.6	1.16	0.1	94.78
FMAGX	Fidelity Magellan	4-star	5.85	21.92	0.03	1.06	2.14	96.54
VFINX	Vanguard 500 Index	4-star	3.93	19.87	−0.08	1	0.02	100
AIVSX	American Funds Investment Co Amer A	4-star	9.45	16.11	0.3	0.75	4.75	91.09

Data Source: Microsoft MoneyCentral.
Original Source: Morningstar.

APPENDIX H   20 Largest Funds

PERFORMANCE

Code	Ticker	Name	Return[1]	Risk[2]	Sharpe Ratio[3]	Beta	Alpha	R^2
A	AEPGX	EuroPacific Growth	15.65%	20.89%	0.53	0.28	0.09	0.08
B	AGTHX	Growth Fund of America	28.39%	29.47%	0.81	0.82	0.17	0.32
C	AIVSX	Investment Company of America	15.40%	21.02%	0.52	0.65	0.05	0.40
D	ANWPX	New Perspective	19.73%	22.91%	0.66	0.51	0.11	0.20
E	AWSHX	Washington Mutual Investors	11.96%	23.06%	0.32	0.64	0.02	0.32
F	FBGRX	Fidelity Blue Chip Growth	16.31%	22.71%	0.52	0.93	0.04	0.70
G	FCNTX	Fidelity Contrafund	17.12%	23.90%	0.53	0.78	0.06	0.44
H	FDGRX	Fidelity Growth Company	29.80%	29.82%	0.85	1.00	0.17	0.47
I	FEQIX	Fidelity Equity-Income	10.79%	19.62%	0.32	0.66	0.01	0.47
J	FGRIX	Fidelity Growth & Income	13.04%	19.53%	0.44	0.76	0.02	0.63
K	FMAGX	Fidelity Magellan	16.37%	22.55%	0.53	0.90	0.04	0.66
L	FPURX	Fidelity Puritan	9.72%	14.94%	0.35	0.45	0.01	0.38
M	JANSX	Janus	23.74%	31.41%	0.61	1.17	0.09	0.58
N	JAWWX	Janus Worldwide	21.47%	24.37%	0.70	0.72	0.11	0.36
O	PTTRX	PIMCO Total Return Instl	7.10%	5.74%	0.45	−0.01	0.03	0.00
P	TWCUX	American Century Ultra Inv	18.62%	29.62%	0.48	1.06	0.05	0.53
Q	VFINX	Vanguard 500 Index	14.00%	20.75%	0.46	0.92	0.02	0.83
R	VINIX	Vanguard Institutional Index	14.12%	20.83%	0.46	0.93	0.02	0.84
S	VWELX	Vanguard Wellington	9.79%	15.45%	0.34	0.40	0.02	0.28
T	VWNFX	Vanguard Windsor II	10.86%	22.16%	0.29	0.64	0.01	0.35

[1] Annualized arithmetic average return from 1998–2000. [2] Annualized volatility from 1998–2000. [3] Sharpe ratio uses a risk free rate of 4.5%.

CORRELATION

	A	B	C	D	E	F	G	H	I	J	K	L	M	N	O	P	Q	R	S	T
A	1.00	0.47	0.49	0.64	0.38	0.32	0.44	0.38	0.31	0.28	0.43	0.22	0.37	0.56	0.03	0.33	0.30	0.30	0.28	0.30
B	0.47	1.00	0.76	0.82	0.64	0.64	0.71	0.75	0.64	0.59	0.74	0.51	0.78	0.68	0.10	0.73	0.62	0.59	0.53	0.61
C	0.49	0.76	1.00	0.71	0.77	0.61	0.70	0.61	0.70	0.61	0.75	0.54	0.66	0.53	0.09	0.62	0.66	0.66	0.59	0.63
D	0.64	0.82	0.71	1.00	0.63	0.50	0.63	0.62	0.59	0.48	0.64	0.45	0.68	0.73	0.14	0.64	0.51	0.48	0.50	0.58
E	0.38	0.64	0.77	0.63	1.00	0.49	0.60	0.56	0.72	0.59	0.64	0.54	0.53	0.38	0.10	0.56	0.59	0.59	0.75	0.69
F	0.32	0.64	0.61	0.50	0.49	1.00	0.72	0.79	0.65	0.93	0.85	0.76	0.75	0.62	0.00	0.72	0.84	0.84	0.45	0.54
G	0.44	0.71	0.70	0.63	0.60	0.72	1.00	0.72	0.68	0.67	0.79	0.54	0.72	0.55	0.03	0.61	0.69	0.68	0.47	0.60
H	0.38	0.75	0.61	0.62	0.56	0.79	0.72	1.00	0.57	0.70	0.76	0.51	0.77	0.68	0.06	0.75	0.71	0.68	0.49	0.51
I	0.31	0.64	0.70	0.59	0.72	0.65	0.68	0.57	1.00	0.74	0.73	0.73	0.70	0.50	0.07	0.60	0.72	0.70	0.67	0.86
J	0.28	0.59	0.61	0.48	0.59	0.93	0.67	0.70	0.74	1.00	0.80	0.87	0.69	0.55	0.04	0.68	0.82	0.80	0.56	0.63
K	0.43	0.74	0.75	0.64	0.64	0.85	0.79	0.76	0.73	0.80	1.00	0.63	0.77	0.63	0.01	0.73	0.84	0.83	0.51	0.64
L	0.22	0.51	0.54	0.45	0.54	0.76	0.54	0.51	0.73	0.87	0.63	1.00	0.57	0.46	0.15	0.56	0.66	0.64	0.55	0.62
M	0.37	0.78	0.66	0.68	0.53	0.75	0.72	0.77	0.70	0.69	0.77	0.57	1.00	0.81	0.02	0.82	0.77	0.75	0.50	0.65
N	0.56	0.68	0.53	0.73	0.38	0.62	0.55	0.68	0.50	0.55	0.63	0.46	0.81	1.00	0.00	0.73	0.61	0.60	0.36	0.45
O	0.03	0.10	0.09	0.14	0.10	0.00	0.03	0.06	0.07	0.04	0.01	0.15	0.02	0.00	1.00	0.08	-0.02	-0.01	0.29	0.12
P	0.33	0.73	0.62	0.64	0.56	0.72	0.61	0.75	0.60	0.68	0.73	0.56	0.82	0.73	0.08	1.00	0.78	0.77	0.53	0.60
Q	0.30	0.62	0.66	0.51	0.59	0.84	0.69	0.71	0.72	0.82	0.84	0.66	0.77	0.61	-0.02	0.78	1.00	0.97	0.57	0.67
R	0.30	0.59	0.66	0.48	0.59	0.84	0.68	0.68	0.70	0.80	0.83	0.64	0.75	0.60	-0.01	0.77	0.97	1.00	0.58	0.66
S	0.28	0.53	0.59	0.50	0.75	0.45	0.47	0.49	0.67	0.56	0.51	0.55	0.50	0.36	0.29	0.53	0.57	0.58	1.00	0.81
T	0.30	0.61	0.63	0.58	0.69	0.54	0.60	0.51	0.86	0.63	0.64	0.62	0.65	0.45	0.12	0.60	0.67	0.66	0.81	1.00

Correlation calculated from daily returns from 1998–2000.

APPENDIX I   20 Largest Stocks

PERFORMANCE

Code	Ticker	Name	Return[1]	Risk[2]	Sharpe Ratio[3]	Beta	Alpha	R^2
A	AIG	AMER INTL GROUP INC	38.99%	36.22%	0.95	1.04	0.26	0.35
B	AOL	AMERICA ONLINE INC	83.13%	65.46%	1.20	1.71	0.64	0.29
C	BMY	BRISTOL MYERS SQUIBB	24.95%	41.04%	0.50	0.84	0.13	0.18
D	BP	BP AMOCO ADS	12.05%	31.50%	0.24	0.32	0.05	0.04
E	C	CITIGROUP INC	32.91%	43.99%	0.65	1.43	0.16	0.44
F	GE	GEN ELECTRIC CO	30.25%	31.78%	0.81	1.11	0.16	0.51
G	GSK	GLAXOSMITHKLINE PLC ADR	12.79%	36.70%	0.23	0.76	0.02	0.18
H	IBM	INTL BUSINESS MACH	26.12%	41.70%	0.52	1.03	0.13	0.25
I	INTC	INTEL CP	33.49%	53.23%	0.54	1.54	0.16	0.35
J	JNJ	JOHNSON & JOHNSON	21.80%	30.05%	0.58	0.59	0.12	0.16
K	KO	COCA COLA CO	4.22%	35.13%	−0.01	0.54	−0.05	0.10
L	MO	PHILIP MORRIS COS	12.78%	41.36%	0.20	0.39	0.05	0.04
M	MRK	MERCK & CO INC	26.22%	33.15%	0.66	0.67	0.16	0.17
N	MSFT	MICROSOFT CP	21.08%	45.41%	0.37	1.35	0.05	0.37
O	PFE	PFIZER INC	29.87%	38.41%	0.66	0.81	0.18	0.19
P	SBC	SBC COMMUNICATIONS INC	18.89%	39.04%	0.37	0.66	0.09	0.12
Q	VOD	VODAFONE GROUP PLC ADS	42.68%	48.33%	0.79	1.09	0.29	0.21
R	VZ	VERIZON COMMUNICATIONS	12.88%	36.39%	0.23	0.54	0.04	0.09
S	WMT	WAL-MART STORES INC	43.73%	43.88%	0.89	1.21	0.29	0.32
T	XOM	EXXON MOBIL CP	16.75%	28.74%	0.43	0.34	0.09	0.06

[1] Annualized arithmetic average return from 1998–2000. [2] Annualized volatility from 1998–2000. [3] Sharpe ratio uses a risk free rate of 4.5%.

CORRELATION

	A	B	C	D	E	F	G	H	I	J	K	L	M	N	O	P	Q	R	S	T
A	0.00	0.21	0.36	0.09	0.51	0.49	0.36	0.20	0.17	0.30	0.29	0.20	0.36	0.20	0.30	0.25	0.20	0.19	0.45	0.19
B	0.21	0.00	0.19	0.04	0.34	0.38	0.24	0.28	0.35	0.12	0.08	0.06	0.14	0.38	0.21	0.09	0.28	0.06	0.28	0.03
C	0.36	0.19	0.00	0.08	0.29	0.31	0.39	0.20	0.16	0.50	0.23	0.14	0.56	0.19	0.45	0.13	0.11	0.12	0.30	0.12
D	0.09	0.04	0.08	0.00	0.11	0.08	0.14	0.06	0.06	0.11	0.09	0.06	0.13	0.16	0.10	0.12	0.01	0.15	0.12	0.57
E	0.51	0.34	0.29	0.11	0.00	0.49	0.29	0.29	0.28	0.24	0.24	0.12	0.27	0.32	0.29	0.21	.28	0.19	0.12	0.13
F	0.49	0.38	0.31	0.08	0.49	0.00	0.28	0.32	0.29	0.36	0.33	0.14	0.32	0.35	0.36	0.24	.28	0.21	0.39	0.15
G	0.36	0.24	0.39	0.14	0.29	0.28	0.00	0.20	0.22	0.39	0.21	0.14	0.44	0.17	0.37	0.22	.21	0.13	0.28	0.12
H	0.20	0.28	0.20	0.06	0.29	0.32	0.20	0.00	0.38	0.11	0.04	0.09	0.11	0.33	0.17	0.12	.21	0.06	0.21	0.09
I	0.17	0.35	0.16	0.06	0.28	0.29	0.22	0.38	0.00	0.11	0.02	0.03	0.14	0.52	0.15	0.09	.31	0.11	0.19	0.04
J	0.30	0.12	0.50	0.11	0.24	0.36	0.39	0.11	0.11	0.00	0.32	0.15	0.57	0.18	0.47	0.22	.04	0.17	0.34	0.17
K	0.29	0.08	0.23	0.09	0.24	0.33	0.21	0.04	0.02	0.32	0.00	0.18	0.29	0.09	0.25	0.25	.05	0.23	0.29	0.20
L	0.20	0.06	0.14	0.06	0.12	0.14	0.14	0.09	0.03	0.15	0.18	0.00	0.18	0.03	0.13	0.15	0.01	.09	0.10	0.10
M	0.36	0.14	0.56	0.13	0.27	0.32	0.44	0.11	0.14	0.57	0.29	0.18	0.00	0.17	0.54	0.19	0.10	0.21	0.35	0.15
N	0.20	0.38	0.19	0.16	0.32	0.35	0.17	0.33	0.52	0.18	0.09	0.03	0.17	0.00	0.20	0.12	0.29	0.12	0.24	0.14
O	0.30	0.21	0.45	0.10	0.29	0.36	0.37	0.17	0.15	0.47	0.25	0.13	0.54	0.20	0.00	0.17	0.09	0.16	0.29	0.17
P	0.25	0.09	0.13	0.12	0.21	0.24	0.22	0.12	0.09	0.22	0.25	0.15	0.19	0.12	0.17	0.00	0.13	0.57	0.21	0.19
Q	0.20	0.28	0.11	0.01	0.28	0.28	0.21	0.21	0.31	0.04	0.05	0.01	0.10	0.29	0.09	0.13	0.00	0.13	0.19	0.02
R	0.19	0.06	0.12	0.15	0.19	0.21	0.13	0.06	0.11	0.17	0.23	.09	0.21	0.12	0.16	0.57	0.13	0.00	0.16	0.16
S	0.45	0.28	0.30	0.12	0.39	0.48	0.28	0.21	0.19	0.34	0.29	0.10	0.35	0.24	0.29	0.21	0.19	0.16	0.00	0.15
T	0.19	0.03	0.12	0.57	0.13	0.15	0.12	0.09	0.04	0.17	0.20	0.10	0.15	0.14	0.17	0.19	0.02	0.16	0.15	0.00

Correlation calculated from daily returns from 1998–2000.

APPENDIX J 20 Growth Stocks in the S&P 500

PERFORMANCE

Code	Ticker	Name	Return[1]	Risk[2]	Sharpe Ratio[3]	Beta	Alpha	R²
A	AGN	ALLERGAN INC	66.99%	40.04%	1.56	0.50	0.58	0.07
B	AMGN	AMGEN INC	66.04%	53.16%	1.16	1.15	0.52	0.20
C	BAX	BAXTER INTL INC	25.46%	33.33%	0.63	0.54	0.16	0.11
D	CL	COLGATE PALMOLIVE CO	28.52%	39.24%	0.61	0.73	0.18	0.15
E	DELL	DELL COMPUTER CP	36.48%	60.93%	0.52	1.69	0.18	0.32
F	FRX	FOREST LABORATORIES	69.46%	48.07%	1.35	0.76	0.59	0.10
G	G	GILLETTE CO	-1.66%	41.37%	-0.15	0.67	-0.12	0.11
H	GDT	GUIDANT CP	32.90%	53.48%	0.53	0.98	0.20	0.14
I	HNZ	HEINZ H J	5.93%	30.94%	0.05	0.28	-0.01	0.04
J	KO	COCA COLA CO	4.22%	35.13%	-0.01	0.54	-0.05	0.10
K	MDT	MEDTRONIC INC	36.63%	40.47%	0.79	0.89	0.25	0.20
L	MXIM	MAXIM INTEGRATED PROD INC	62.23%	73.02%	0.79	2.17	0.39	0.37
M	PAYX	PAYCHEX INC	54.77%	54.44%	0.92	1.11	0.41	0.17
N	PFE	PFIZER INC	29.87%	38.41%	0.66	0.81	0.18	0.19
O	PG	PROCTER & GAMBLE CO	9.32%	39.99%	0.12	0.58	0.00	0.09
P	RAL	RALSTON PURINA CO	3.08%	36.16%	-0.04	0.43	-0.05	0.06
Q	RX	IMS HEALTH INC	8.27%	50.06%	0.08	0.88	-0.04	0.13
R	SYK	STRYKER CP	44.57%	44.76%	0.90	0.66	0.34	0.09
S	UN	UNILEVER N V ORD	6.45%	36.17%	0.05	0.73	-0.04	0.17
T	WWY	WRIGLEY WM JR CO	11.73%	27.62%	0.26	0.53	0.03	0.16

[1] Annualized arithmetic average return from 1998–2000. [2] Annualized volatility from 1998–2000. [3] Sharpe ratio uses a risk free rate of 4.5%.

CORRELATION

	A	B	C	D	E	F	G	H	I	J	K	L	M	N	O	P	Q	R	S	T
A	1.00	0.24	0.29	0.12	0.12	0.33	0.06	0.18	0.12	0.13	0.23	0.08	0.14	0.32	0.08	0.08	0.17	0.14	0.16	0.21
B	0.24	1.00	0.21	0.14	0.27	0.31	0.11	0.21	0.09	0.15	0.23	0.31	0.24	0.26	0.11	0.10	0.22	0.19	0.18	0.16
C	0.29	0.21	1.00	0.31	0.11	0.25	0.14	0.27	0.21	0.27	0.32	0.05	0.17	0.35	0.18	0.21	0.13	0.23	0.29	0.33
D	0.12	0.14	0.31	1.00	0.08	0.21	0.47	0.18	0.25	0.40	0.24	0.10	0.17	0.27	0.53	0.24	0.18	0.22	0.36	0.37
E	0.12	0.27	0.11	0.08	1.00	0.13	0.09	0.20	-0.03	-0.01	0.20	0.44	0.24	0.17	0.04	0.00	0.17	0.11	0.14	0.06
F	0.33	0.31	0.25	0.21	0.13	1.00	0.14	0.25	0.13	0.17	0.25	0.13	0.10	0.40	0.15	0.07	0.15	0.23	0.18	0.18
G	0.06	0.11	0.14	0.47	0.09	0.14	1.00	0.12	0.23	0.33	0.14	0.16	0.15	0.19	0.40	0.20	0.10	0.11	0.35	0.31
H	0.18	0.21	0.27	0.18	0.20	0.25	0.12	1.00	0.06	0.13	0.36	0.13	0.10	0.27	0.11	0.14	0.22	0.19	0.19	0.20
I	0.12	0.09	0.21	0.25	-0.03	0.13	0.23	0.06	1.00	0.36	0.09	0.06	0.07	0.19	0.24	0.23	0.08	0.12	0.33	0.42
J	0.13	0.15	0.27	0.40	-0.01	0.17	0.33	0.13	0.36	1.00	0.19	0.04	0.15	0.25	0.34	0.23	0.14	0.17	0.35	0.43
K	0.23	0.23	0.32	0.24	0.20	0.25	0.14	0.36	0.09	0.19	1.00	0.20	0.25	0.38	0.20	0.10	0.20	0.29	0.22	0.29
L	0.08	0.31	0.05	0.10	0.44	0.13	0.16	0.13	0.06	0.04	0.20	1.00	0.32	0.14	0.10	0.08	0.23	0.14	0.16	0.15
M	0.14	0.24	0.17	0.17	0.24	0.10	0.15	0.10	0.07	0.15	0.25	0.32	1.00	0.23	0.15	0.12	0.17	0.10	0.18	0.23
N	0.32	0.26	0.35	0.27	0.17	0.40	0.19	0.27	0.19	0.25	0.38	0.14	0.23	1.00	0.26	0.15	0.18	0.20	0.31	0.29
O	0.08	0.11	0.18	0.53	0.04	0.15	0.40	0.11	0.24	0.34	0.20	0.10	0.15	0.26	1.00	0.18	0.13	0.17	0.40	0.36
P	0.08	0.10	0.21	0.24	0.00	0.07	0.20	0.14	0.23	0.23	0.10	0.08	0.12	0.15	0.18	1.00	0.10	0.13	0.26	0.29
Q	0.17	0.22	0.13	0.18	0.17	0.15	0.10	0.22	0.08	0.14	0.20	0.23	0.17	0.18	0.13	0.10	1.00	0.15	0.14	0.15
R	0.14	0.19	0.23	0.22	0.11	0.23	0.11	0.19	0.12	0.17	0.29	0.14	0.10	0.20	0.17	0.13	0.15	1.00	0.20	0.16
S	0.16	0.18	0.29	0.36	0.14	0.18	0.35	0.19	0.33	0.35	0.22	0.16	0.18	0.31	0.40	0.26	0.14	0.20	1.00	0.48
T	0.21	0.16	0.33	0.37	0.06	0.18	0.31	0.20	0.42	0.43	0.29	0.15	0.23	0.29	0.36	0.29	0.15	0.16	0.48	1.00

Correlation calculated from daily returns from 1998–2000.

APPENDIX K 20 Large Value Stocks in the S&P 500

PERFORMANCE

Code	Ticker	Name	Return[1]	Risk[2]	Sharpe Ratio[3]	Beta	Alpha	R^2
A	AHC	AMERADA HESS CP	13.53%	31.98%	0.28	0.38	0.06	0.06
B	ALL	ALLSTATE CP	7.38%	41.69%	0.07	0.95	−0.05	0.22
C	APC	ANADARKO PETROLEUM CP	39.64%	48.32%	0.73	0.46	0.31	0.04
D	BNI	BURLINGTON NORTH	5.49%	37.78%	0.03	0.58	−0.04	0.10
E	CB	CHUBB CP	13.57%	35.33%	0.26	0.86	0.02	0.25
F	CCR	COUNTRYWIDE CREDIT IND	15.37%	44.43%	0.24	0.99	0.02	0.21
G	CSX	CSX CP	−13.91%	37.09%	−0.50	0.53	−0.23	0.09
H	ETR	ENTERGY CP	15.17%	31.51%	0.34	0.15	0.09	0.01
I	IR	INGERSOLL RAND CO	13.54%	42.75%	0.21	0.85	0.02	0.16
J	MET	METLIFE INC	127.76%	47.84%	2.58	0.46	1.19	0.04
K	MRO	USX-MARATHON GROUP	3.08%	39.86%	−0.04	0.44	−0.05	0.05
L	OXY	OCCIDENTAL PET	1.17%	32.11%	−0.10	0.38	−0.07	0.06
M	P	PHILLIPS PETROLEUM	12.26%	31.41%	0.25	0.41	0.04	0.07
N	REI	RELIANT ENERGY INC	24.25%	28.38%	0.70	0.26	0.18	0.04
O	S	SEARS ROEBUCK & CO	2.36%	44.37%	−0.05	0.80	−0.09	0.14
P	SPC	ST PAUL COMPANIES	19.62%	37.83%	0.40	0.86	0.08	0.22
Q	UNM	UNUMPROVIDENT CP	−5.83%	53.09%	−0.19	0.59	−0.15	0.05
R	UNP	UNION PACIFIC	0.12%	34.63%	−0.13	0.52	−0.09	0.09
S	WCOM	WORLDCOM INC	3.10%	53.75%	−0.03	1.33	−0.13	0.26
T	WY	WEYERHAEUSER CO	13.23%	40.29%	0.22	0.56	0.04	0.08

[1] Annualized arithmetic average return from 1998–2000. [2] Annualized volatility from 1998–2000. [3] Sharpe ratio uses a risk free rate of 4.5%.

CORRELATION

	A	B	C	D	E	F	G	H	I	J	K	L	M	N	O	P	Q	R	S	T
A	1.00	0.14	0.58	0.15	0.17	0.02	0.16	0.04	0.25	0.03	0.56	0.55	0.59	0.11	0.15	0.12	0.09	0.13	0.04	0.13
B	0.14	1.00	0.13	0.25	0.56	0.30	0.28	0.12	0.29	0.19	0.15	0.14	0.17	0.18	0.23	0.48	0.23	0.26	0.26	0.26
C	0.58	0.13	1.00	0.07	0.05	0.02	0.08	0.04	0.18	0.08	0.49	0.49	0.53	0.05	0.09	0.09	0.05	0.10	0.08	0.11
D	0.15	0.25	0.07	1.00	0.20	0.22	0.49	0.12	0.24	0.16	0.13	0.16	0.11	0.12	0.28	0.22	0.19	0.49	0.08	0.20
E	0.17	0.56	0.05	0.20	1.00	0.36	0.27	0.16	0.33	0.22	0.14	0.17	0.16	0.26	0.27	0.63	0.34	0.26	0.25	0.25
F	0.02	0.30	0.02	0.22	0.36	1.00	0.26	0.12	0.27	0.19	0.07	0.09	0.09	0.20	0.22	0.36	0.26	0.23	0.21	0.14
G	0.16	0.28	0.08	0.49	0.27	0.26	1.00	0.10	0.30	0.05	0.13	0.15	0.14	0.13	0.26	0.28	0.27	0.48	0.11	0.27
H	0.04	0.12	0.04	0.12	0.16	0.12	0.10	1.00	0.04	0.08	0.09	0.11	0.11	0.52	0.14	0.16	0.13	0.15	0.01	0.06
I	0.25	0.29	0.18	0.24	0.33	0.27	0.30	0.04	1.00	0.10	0.20	0.22	0.23	0.13	0.21	0.33	0.23	0.26	0.16	0.34
J	0.03	0.19	0.08	0.16	0.22	0.19	0.05	0.08	0.10	1.00	0.05	0.04	0.02	0.13	0.16	0.28	0.09	0.07	−0.01	0.00
K	0.56	0.15	0.49	0.13	0.14	0.07	0.13	0.09	0.20	0.05	1.00	0.49	0.51	0.17	0.11	0.12	0.12	0.11	0.07	0.15
L	0.55	0.14	0.49	0.16	0.17	0.09	0.15	0.11	0.22	0.04	0.49	1.00	0.52	0.21	0.12	0.16	0.13	0.19	0.06	0.19
M	0.59	0.17	0.53	0.11	0.16	0.09	0.14	0.11	0.23	0.02	0.51	0.52	1.00	0.14	0.17	0.15	0.13	0.15	0.07	0.13
N	0.11	0.18	0.05	0.12	0.26	0.20	0.13	0.52	0.13	0.13	0.17	0.21	0.14	1.00	0.11	0.24	0.19	0.13	0.06	0.13
O	0.15	0.23	0.09	0.28	0.27	0.22	0.26	0.14	0.21	0.16	0.11	0.12	0.17	0.11	1.00	0.24	0.19	0.28	0.07	0.10
P	0.12	0.48	0.09	0.22	0.63	0.36	0.28	0.16	0.33	0.28	0.12	0.16	0.15	0.24	0.24	1.00	0.35	0.25	0.06	0.13
Q	0.09	0.23	0.05	0.19	0.34	0.26	0.27	0.13	0.23	0.09	0.12	0.13	0.13	0.19	0.19	0.35	1.00	0.22	0.08	0.13
R	0.13	0.26	0.10	0.49	0.26	0.23	0.48	0.15	0.26	0.07	0.11	0.19	0.15	0.13	0.28	0.25	0.22	1.00	0.06	0.23
S	0.04	0.26	0.08	0.08	0.25	0.21	0.11	0.01	0.16	−0.01	0.07	0.06	0.07	0.07	0.06	0.25	0.08	0.06	1.00	0.12
T	0.13	0.26	0.11	0.20	0.25	0.14	0.27	0.06	0.34	0.00	0.15	0.19	0.13	0.10	0.13	0.24	0.13	0.23	0.12	1.00

Correlation calculated from daily returns from 1998–2000.

APPENDIX L 20 Small Cap Growth Stocks

PERFORMANCE

Code	Ticker	Name	Return[1]	Risk[2]	Sharpe Ratio[3]	Beta	Alpha	R^2
A	AMHC	AMER HEALTHWAYS INC	35.22%	58.24%	0.53	0.38	0.27	0.02
B	BCOR	BIACORE INTL AB ADS	177.04%	93.09%	1.85	0.54	1.68	0.01
C	CLSR	CLOSURE MEDICAL CP	43.41%	79.04%	0.49	0.45	0.35	0.01
D	COKE	COCA COLA BTLG CO CONSL	−13.25%	31.97%	−0.56	0.00	−0.18	0.00
E	CRVL	CORVEL CP	22.45%	35.66%	0.50	0.13	0.17	0.01
F	DIAN	DIANON SYSTEMS INC	78.60%	66.65%	1.11	0.57	0.69	0.03
G	DYII	DYNACQ INTL INC	109.01%	89.87%	1.16	0.22	1.03	0.00
H	EDO	EDO CP	4.52%	41.10%	0.00	0.44	−0.04	0.05
I	ENZ	ENZO BIOCHEM INC	61.11%	92.28%	0.61	1.49	0.44	0.11
J	FCN	FTI CONSULTING INC	24.80%	82.54%	0.25	0.49	0.16	0.01
K	ITRI	ITRON INC	−23.74%	85.52%	−0.33	0.61	−0.33	0.02
L	KVA	KV PHARMACEUTICAL CL A	51.74%	66.05%	0.72	0.49	0.43	0.02
M	NYFX	NYFX	−31.51%	83.71%	−0.43	1.33	−0.47	0.11
N	OPMR	OPTIMAL ROBOTICS CP	101.98%	79.78%	1.22	1.02	0.89	0.07
O	ROL	ROLLINS INC	6.48%	29.61%	0.07	0.42	−0.02	0.08
P	SGA	SAGA COMMUN INC	4.18%	39.77%	−0.01	0.22	−0.02	0.01
Q	SLNK	SPECTRALINK CP	110.04%	105.60%	1.00	0.52	1.01	0.01
R	TALX	TALX CP	153.20%	74.02%	2.01	0.38	1.45	0.01
S	TCT	TOWN & COUNTRY TRUST	15.45%	21.22%	0.52	0.27	0.09	0.07
T	TRR	TRC COMPANIES INC	59.97%	47.18%	1.18	0.23	0.53	0.01

[1] Annualized arithmetic average return from 1998–2000. [2] Annualized volatility from 1998–2000. [3] Sharpe ratio uses a risk free rate of 4.5%.

CORRELATION

	A	B	C	D	E	F	G	H	I	J	K	L	M	N	O	P	Q	R	S	T
A	1.00	0.01	0.06	-0.04	0.03	0.05	-0.05	0.05	0.13	0.03	0.05	0.08	0.09	0.07	0.08	0.00	0.05	-0.01	0.09	0.02
B	0.01	1.00	0.07	0.02	0.02	0.02	-0.03	0.06	0.28	0.08	0.00	0.07	0.11	0.04	-0.02	0.02	0.05	0.10	0.01	-0.03
C	0.06	0.07	1.00	-0.02	0.07	0.08	-0.02	0.05	0.17	-0.02	0.03	0.06	0.13	0.07	0.06	0.01	0.10	0.05	0.02	0.02
D	-0.04	0.02	-0.02	1.00	0.05	-0.05	0.06	0.04	0.00	-0.01	0.01	-0.02	0.10	0.07	0.07	0.03	0.01	0.02	0.03	0.02
E	0.03	0.02	0.07	0.05	1.00	0.02	0.01	0.10	0.01	-0.02	0.05	0.06	0.06	0.02	0.06	0.02	0.04	-0.07	0.04	-0.04
F	0.05	0.02	0.08	-0.05	0.02	1.00	-0.04	0.05	0.12	0.04	0.02	0.09	0.10	0.03	0.06	0.06	0.09	0.03	0.02	-0.01
G	-0.05	-0.03	-0.02	0.06	0.01	-0.04	1.00	0.03	-0.02	0.05	0.12	0.10	0.14	0.09	0.07	0.04	0.06	-0.07	0.05	-0.06
H	0.05	0.06	0.05	0.04	0.10	0.05	0.03	1.00	0.14	0.10	0.15	0.06	0.10	0.08	0.10	0.10	0.08	0.12	0.11	0.05
I	0.13	0.28	0.17	0.00	0.01	0.12	-0.02	0.14	1.00	0.09	0.06	0.10	0.32	0.13	0.14	0.05	0.13	0.09	0.05	0.01
J	0.03	0.08	-0.02	-0.01	-0.02	0.04	0.05	0.10	0.09	1.00	0.05	0.07	0.00	0.05	0.05	0.04	0.03	0.00	0.04	-0.02
K	0.05	0.00	0.03	0.01	0.05	0.02	0.02	0.15	0.06	0.05	1.00	0.03	0.04	0.07	0.12	0.08	0.08	-0.05	0.09	0.01
L	0.08	0.07	0.06	-0.02	0.06	0.09	0.10	0.06	0.10	0.07	0.03	1.00	0.10	0.07	0.04	0.04	0.08	0.12	0.10	0.01
M	0.09	0.11	0.13	0.10	0.06	0.10	0.14	0.10	0.32	0.00	0.04	0.10	1.00	0.21	0.24	0.03	0.18	0.14	0.12	0.11
N	0.07	0.04	0.07	0.07	0.02	0.03	0.09	0.08	0.13	0.05	0.07	0.07	0.21	1.00	0.13	0.07	0.06	0.01	0.12	0.02
O	0.08	-0.02	0.06	0.07	0.06	0.06	0.07	0.10	0.14	0.05	0.12	0.04	0.24	0.13	1.00	0.06	-0.05	0.05	0.13	0.08
P	0.00	0.02	0.01	0.03	0.02	0.06	0.04	0.10	0.05	0.04	0.08	0.04	0.03	0.07	0.06	1.00	0.08	0.06	0.07	0.13
Q	0.05	0.05	0.10	0.01	0.04	0.09	0.06	0.08	0.13	0.03	0.08	0.08	0.18	0.06	-0.05	0.08	1.00	-0.02	0.09	0.03
R	-0.01	0.10	0.05	0.02	-0.07	0.03	-0.07	0.12	0.09	0.00	-0.05	0.12	0.14	0.01	0.05	0.06	-0.02	1.00	0.08	0.12
S	0.09	0.01	0.02	0.03	0.04	0.02	0.05	0.11	0.05	0.04	0.09	0.10	0.12	0.12	0.13	0.07	0.09	0.08	1.00	0.03
T	0.02	-0.03	0.02	0.02	-0.04	-0.01	-0.06	0.05	0.01	-0.02	0.01	0.01	0.11	0.02	0.08	0.13	0.03	0.12	0.03	1.00

Correlation calculated from daily returns from 1998–2000.

APPENDIX M 20 Small Cap Value Stocks

PERFORMANCE

Code	Ticker	Name	Return[1]	Risk[2]	Sharpe Ratio[3]	Beta	Alpha	R²
A	AMN	AMERON INTL CP	−11.76%	24.55%	−0.66	0.12	−0.17	0.01
B	BANR	BANNER CP	−9.02%	35.32%	−0.38	0.33	−0.16	0.04
C	BW	BRUSH ENGINEERED MATERIALS	2.01%	41.30%	−0.06	0.44	−0.06	0.05
D	CGX	CONSL GRAPHICS INC	−26.57%	58.84%	−0.53	0.67	−0.37	0.05
E	CSS	CSS INDUSTRIES	−11.89%	20.57%	−0.80	0.14	−0.18	0.02
F	DAP	DISCOUNT AUTO PARTS INC	−32.53%	42.78%	−0.87	0.23	−0.39	0.01
G	DVI	DVI INC	9.91%	50.10%	0.11	0.38	0.02	0.02
H	IDT	IDT CORP	40.76%	89.75%	0.40	1.07	0.27	0.06
I	KWD	KELLWOOD CO	−1.48%	38.96%	−0.15	0.52	−0.10	0.07
J	MCSI	MCSI INC	43.79%	58.57%	0.67	0.68	0.34	0.06
K	MHO	M I SCHOTTENSTEIN HOMES INC	15.42%	31.11%	0.35	0.34	0.08	0.05
L	NAUT	NAUTICA ENTERPRISES INC	−0.48%	54.34%	−0.09	0.51	−0.09	0.04
M	NCH	NCH CP	−11.15%	24.91%	−0.63	0.22	−0.17	0.03
N	NEV	NUEVO ENERGY CO	−11.24%	59.99%	−0.26	0.62	−0.21	0.05
O	NTK	NORTEK INC	4.87%	42.91%	0.01	0.57	−0.05	0.07
P	RWT	REDWOOD TR INC	5.67%	35.86%	0.03	0.29	−0.01	0.03
Q	STW	STANDARD COMMERCIAL CP	−10.94%	59.95%	−0.26	0.34	−0.18	0.01
R	SXI	STANDEX INTL CP	−10.49%	32.38%	−0.46	0.28	−0.17	0.03
S	TSO	TESORO PETROLEUM	3.74%	50.84%	−0.01	0.65	−0.06	0.07
T	UFCS	UNITED FIRE & CAS	−16.66%	38.19%	−0.55	0.28	−0.24	0.02

[1] Annualized arithmetic average return from 1998–2000. [2] Annualized volatility from 1998–2000. [3] Sharpe ratio uses a risk free rate of 4.5%.

CORRELATION

	A	B	C	D	E	F	G	H	I	J	K	L	M	N	O	P	Q	R	S	T
A	1.00	0.05	0.11	0.09	0.02	0.00	0.05	0.13	0.07	-0.03	0.04	0.15	0.13	0.09	0.03	0.08	0.01	0.10	0.08	0.07
B	0.05	1.00	0.04	0.15	0.09	0.05	0.08	0.05	0.09	0.14	0.11	0.08	0.14	-0.05	0.11	0.16	-0.01	0.06	0.10	0.11
C	0.11	0.04	1.00	0.10	0.12	0.07	0.09	0.11	0.16	0.07	0.08	0.08	0.13	0.19	0.14	0.06	0.04	0.11	0.15	0.08
D	0.09	0.15	0.10	1.00	0.07	0.07	0.06	0.15	0.04	-0.01	0.12	0.12	0.05	0.07	0.05	0.01	0.10	0.11	0.14	0.00
E	0.02	0.09	0.12	0.07	1.00	0.06	0.07	-0.01	0.11	0.08	0.03	0.06	0.09	0.11	0.05	0.01	-0.02	0.09	0.11	0.14
F	0.00	0.05	0.07	0.07	0.06	1.00	0.02	0.04	0.09	0.03	0.12	0.03	0.04	0.03	0.12	0.03	0.04	0.05	0.07	0.02
G	0.05	0.08	0.09	0.06	0.07	0.02	1.00	0.02	0.05	0.09	0.08	-0.02	0.05	0.12	0.12	0.07	0.04	0.02	0.05	0.05
H	0.13	0.05	0.11	0.15	-0.01	0.04	0.02	1.00	0.00	0.09	0.07	0.08	-0.02	0.13	0.02	0.08	0.00	0.05	0.09	0.01
I	0.07	0.09	0.16	0.04	0.11	0.09	0.05	0.00	1.00	0.06	0.14	0.11	0.14	0.12	0.21	0.04	0.05	0.16	0.09	0.08
J	-0.03	0.14	0.07	-0.01	0.08	0.03	0.09	0.09	0.06	1.00	0.02	0.02	0.06	0.08	0.09	0.11	0.00	0.01	0.12	-0.03
K	0.04	0.11	0.08	0.12	0.03	0.12	0.08	0.07	0.14	0.02	1.00	0.14	0.09	0.13	0.13	0.15	0.04	0.15	0.14	0.10
L	0.15	0.08	0.08	0.12	0.06	0.03	-0.02	0.08	0.11	0.02	0.14	1.00	0.10	0.09	0.15	0.07	0.03	0.12	0.11	0.13
M	0.13	0.14	0.13	0.05	0.09	0.04	0.05	-0.02	0.14	0.06	0.09	0.10	1.00	0.11	0.14	0.10	0.03	0.10	0.07	0.11
N	0.09	-0.05	0.19	0.07	0.11	0.03	0.12	0.13	0.12	0.08	0.13	0.09	0.11	1.00	0.12	0.09	0.10	0.12	0.28	0.10
O	0.03	0.11	0.14	0.05	0.05	0.12	0.12	0.02	0.21	0.09	0.13	0.15	0.14	0.12	1.00	0.13	0.11	0.14	0.12	0.10
P	0.08	0.16	0.06	0.01	0.01	0.03	0.07	0.08	0.04	0.11	0.15	0.07	0.10	0.09	0.13	1.00	0.03	0.09	0.18	0.02
Q	0.01	-0.01	0.04	0.10	-0.02	0.04	0.04	0.00	0.05	0.00	0.04	0.03	0.03	0.10	0.11	0.03	1.00	0.05	0.05	0.05
R	0.10	0.06	0.11	0.11	0.09	0.05	0.02	0.05	0.16	0.01	0.15	0.12	0.10	0.12	0.14	0.09	0.05	1.00	0.14	0.10
S	0.08	0.10	0.15	0.14	0.11	0.07	0.05	0.09	0.09	0.12	0.14	0.11	0.07	0.28	0.12	0.18	0.05	0.14	1.00	0.04
T	0.07	0.11	0.08	0.00	0.14	0.02	0.05	0.01	0.08	-0.03	0.10	0.13	0.11	0.10	0.10	0.02	0.05	0.10	0.04	1.00

Correlation calculated from daily returns from 1998–2000.

APPENDIX N Dow Jones Industrial Stocks

PERFORMANCE

Code	Ticker	Name	Return[1]	Risk[2]	Sharpe Ratio[3]	Beta	Alpha	R^2
A	AA	ALCOA INC	33.53%	42.95%	0.68	0.59	0.24	0.08
B	AXP	AMER EXPRESS CO	31.70%	42.62%	0.64	1.35	0.16	0.42
C	BA	BOEING CO	20.25%	40.03%	0.39	0.64	0.10	0.11
D	C	CITIGROUP INC	32.91%	43.99%	0.65	1.43	0.16	0.44
E	CAT	CATERPILLAR INC	11.59%	40.48%	0.18	0.73	0.01	0.14
F	DD	DU PONT E I DE NEM	2.67%	38.36%	−0.05	0.61	−0.07	0.11
G	DIS	WALT DISNEY CO (THE)	5.50%	41.72%	0.02	0.72	−0.05	0.12
H	EK	EASTMAN KODAK CO	−6.88%	34.94%	−0.33	0.42	−0.15	0.06
I	GE	GEN ELECTRIC CO	30.25%	31.78%	0.81	1.11	0.16	0.51
J	GM	GEN MOTORS CP	5.14%	37.80%	0.02	0.82	−0.06	0.20
K	HD	HOME DEPOT INC	40.30%	46.13%	0.78	1.31	0.25	0.34
L	HON	HONEYWELL INTL INC	19.59%	44.68%	0.34	0.88	0.08	0.16
M	HWP	HEWLETT PACKARD CO	15.33%	51.84%	0.21	1.14	0.01	0.20
N	IBM	INTL BUSINESS MACH	26.12%	41.70%	0.52	1.03	0.13	0.25

(continued)

PERFORMANCE (Cont.)

Code	Ticker	Name	Return[1]	Risk[2]	Sharpe Ratio[3]	Beta	Alpha	R^2
O	INTC	INTEL CP	33.49%	53.23%	0.54	1.54	0.16	0.35
P	IP	INTL PAPER CO	10.31%	43.06%	0.13	0.61	0.01	0.08
Q	JNJ	JOHNSON & JOHNSON	21.80%	30.05%	0.58	0.59	0.12	0.16
R	JPM	JP MORGAN CHASE & CO	28.22%	43.50%	0.55	1.45	−0.09	0.48
S	KO	COCA COLA CO	4.22%	35.13%	−0.01	0.54	−0.05	0.10
T	MCD	MCDONALDS CP	17.31%	34.97%	0.37	0.63	0.07	0.14
U	MMM	MINNESOTA MINING & MFG	20.41%	32.10%	0.50	0.56	0.11	0.13
V	MO	PHILIP MORRIS COS	12.78%	41.36%	0.20	0.39	0.05	0.04
W	MRK	MERCK & CO INC	26.22%	33.15%	0.66	0.67	0.16	0.17
X	MSFT	MICROSOFT CP	21.08%	45.41%	0.37	1.35	0.05	0.37
Y	PG	PROCTER & GAMBLE CO	9.32%	39.99%	0.12	0.58	0.00	0.09

[1] Annualized arithmetic average return from 1998–2000.

[2] Annualized volatility from 1998–2000.

[3] Sharpe ratio uses a risk free rate of 4.5%.

CORRELATION

	A	B	C	D	E	F	G	H	I	J	K	L	M	N	O	P	Q	R	S	T	U	V	W	X	Y
A	1.00	0.21	0.18	0.23	0.39	0.40	0.12	0.18	0.22	0.19	0.18	0.28	0.09	0.12	0.08	0.44	0.07	0.19	0.10	0.15	0.28	0.09	0.08	0.11	0.08
B	0.21	1.00	0.22	0.65	0.29	0.31	0.23	0.17	0.55	0.32	0.43	0.27	0.20	0.27	0.24	0.25	0.30	0.52	0.32	0.29	0.30	0.14	0.28	0.28	0.26
C	0.18	0.22	1.00	0.23	0.21	0.23	0.15	0.11	0.20	0.13	0.27	0.26	0.09	0.11	0.15	0.16	0.20	0.15	0.20	0.14	0.25	0.08	0.21	0.16	0.11
D	0.23	0.65	0.23	1.00	0.30	0.29	0.24	0.17	0.49	0.32	0.43	0.28	0.24	0.29	0.28	0.20	0.24	0.57	0.24	0.23	0.28	0.12	0.27	0.32	0.24
E	0.39	0.29	0.21	0.30	1.00	0.44	0.12	0.20	0.29	0.26	0.26	0.31	0.12	0.16	0.10	0.39	0.19	0.22	0.21	0.22	0.36	0.19	0.19	0.14	0.22
F	0.40	0.31	0.23	0.29	0.44	1.00	0.09	0.22	0.28	0.24	0.24	0.30	0.08	0.08	0.07	0.42	0.15	0.23	0.24	0.20	0.47	0.15	0.19	0.06	0.28
G	0.12	0.23	0.15	0.24	0.12	0.09	1.00	0.09	0.26	0.12	0.22	0.12	0.19	0.18	0.16	0.11	0.10	0.18	0.10	0.13	0.10	0.11	0.11	0.19	0.08
H	0.18	0.17	0.11	0.17	0.20	0.22	0.09	1.00	0.10	0.14	0.14	0.16	0.12	0.11	0.16	0.20	0.11	0.16	0.14	0.11	0.21	0.17	0.15	0.10	0.15
I	0.22	0.55	0.20	0.49	0.29	0.28	0.26	0.10	1.00	0.32	0.49	0.25	0.24	0.32	0.29	0.29	0.36	0.41	0.33	0.32	0.31	0.14	0.32	0.35	0.34
J	0.19	0.32	0.13	0.32	0.26	0.24	0.12	0.14	0.32	1.00	0.27	0.18	0.16	0.20	0.26	0.21	0.11	0.32	0.15	0.18	0.24	0.09	0.16	0.24	0.16
K	0.18	0.43	0.27	0.43	0.26	0.24	0.22	0.14	0.49	0.27	1.00	0.24	0.22	0.22	0.21	0.23	0.22	0.35	0.22	0.34	0.23	0.06	0.26	0.29	0.17
L	0.28	0.27	0.26	0.28	0.31	0.30	0.12	0.16	0.25	0.18	0.24	1.00	0.17	0.20	0.16	0.27	0.15	0.19	0.13	0.18	0.31	0.15	0.24	0.25	0.17
M	0.09	0.20	0.09	0.24	0.12	0.08	0.19	0.12	0.24	0.16	0.22	0.17	1.00	0.39	0.38	0.05	0.04	0.25	0.04	0.16	0.11	0.03	0.04	0.30	0.04
N	0.12	0.27	0.11	0.29	0.16	0.18	0.11	0.11	0.32	0.20	0.22	0.20	0.39	1.00	0.38	0.03	0.11	0.22	0.04	0.17	0.13	0.09	0.11	0.33	0.03
O	0.08	0.24	0.15	0.28	0.10	0.07	0.16	0.16	0.29	0.26	0.21	0.16	0.38	0.38	1.00	0.06	0.11	0.24	0.02	0.13	0.10	0.03	0.14	0.52	0.07

(continued)

CORRELATION (*Cont.*)

	A	B	C	D	E	F	G	H	I	J	K	L	M	N	O	P	Q	R	S	T	U	V	W	X	Y
P	0.44	0.25	0.16	0.20	0.39	0.42	0.11	0.20	0.29	0.21	0.23	0.27	0.05	0.03	0.06	1.00	0.10	0.15	0.11	0.15	0.38	0.10	0.13	0.12	0.13
Q	0.07	0.30	0.20	0.24	0.19	0.15	0.10	0.11	0.36	0.11	0.22	0.15	0.04	0.11	0.11	0.10	1.00	0.14	0.32	0.27	0.17	0.15	0.57	0.18	0.36
R	0.19	0.52	0.15	0.57	0.22	0.23	0.18	0.16	0.41	0.32	0.35	0.19	0.25	0.22	0.24	0.15	0.14	1.00	0.18	0.18	0.24	0.06	0.22	0.27	0.17
S	0.10	0.32	0.20	0.24	0.21	0.24	0.10	0.14	0.33	0.15	0.22	0.13	0.04	0.04	0.02	0.11	0.32	0.18	1.00	0.29	0.21	0.18	0.29	0.09	0.34
T	0.15	0.29	0.14	0.23	0.22	0.20	0.13	0.11	0.32	0.18	0.34	0.18	0.16	0.17	0.13	0.15	0.27	0.18	0.29	1.00	0.15	0.14	0.28	0.12	0.31
U	0.28	0.30	0.25	0.28	0.36	0.47	0.10	0.21	0.31	0.24	0.23	0.31	0.11	0.13	0.10	0.38	0.17	0.24	0.21	0.15	1.00	0.15	0.19	0.06	0.22
V	0.09	0.14	0.08	0.12	0.19	0.15	0.11	0.17	0.14	0.09	0.06	0.15	0.03	0.09	0.03	0.10	0.15	0.06	0.18	0.14	0.15	1.00	0.18	0.03	0.14
W	0.08	0.28	0.21	0.27	0.19	0.19	0.11	0.15	0.32	0.16	0.26	0.24	0.04	0.11	0.14	0.13	0.57	0.22	0.29	0.28	0.19	0.18	1.00	0.17	0.32
X	0.11	0.28	0.16	0.32	0.14	0.06	0.19	0.10	0.35	0.24	0.29	0.25	0.30	0.33	0.52	0.12	0.18	0.27	0.09	0.12	0.06	0.03	0.17	1.00	0.04
Y	0.08	0.26	0.11	0.24	0.22	0.28	0.08	0.15	0.34	0.16	0.17	0.17	0.04	0.03	0.07	0.13	0.36	0.17	0.34	0.31	0.22	0.14	0.32	0.04	1.00

Correlation calculated from daily returns from 1998–2000.

APPENDIX O Dow Jones Transportation Stocks

PERFORMANCE

Code	Ticker	Name	Return[1]	Risk[2]	Sharpe Ratio[3]	Beta	Alpha	R[2]
A	ABF	AIRBORNE INC	−20.80%	56.08%	−0.45	1.05	−0.34	0.15
B	ALEX	ALEXANDER & BALDWIN INC	10.96%	38.93%	0.17	0.52	0.02	0.08
C	AMR	AMR CP	12.56%	46.39%	0.17	0.88	0.01	0.15
D	BNI	BURLINGTON NORTH	5.49%	37.78%	0.03	0.58	−0.04	0.10
E	CNF	CNF INC	10.78%	51.93%	0.12	0.77	0.00	0.09
F	CSX	CSX CP	−13.91%	37.09%	−0.50	0.53	−0.23	0.09
G	DAL	DELTA AIR LINES INC	4.14%	41.81%	−0.01	0.77	−0.07	0.14
H	FDX	FEDEX CP	18.34%	42.58%	0.33	0.83	0.07	0.16
I	GMT	GATX CP	20.31%	34.61%	0.46	0.63	0.10	0.14
J	JBHT	JB HUNT TRANSPORT SERV INC	14.59%	57.13%	0.18	0.66	0.04	0.06
K	LUV	SOUTHWEST AIRLINES CO	48.34%	44.89%	0.98	0.86	0.36	0.15
L	NSC	NORFOLK SOUTHERN CP	−17.51%	37.42%	−0.59	0.68	−0.28	0.14
M	NWAC	NORTHWEST AIRLINES CP	1.80%	59.79%	−0.05	1.17	−0.13	0.16
N	R	RYDER SYSTEMS INC	−11.76%	40.27%	−0.40	0.65	−0.22	0.11
O	ROAD	ROADWAY EXPRESS INC	12.82%	51.03%	0.16	0.48	0.04	0.04
P	U	US AIRWAYS GRP INC	8.02%	74.00%	0.05	1.18	−0.07	0.11
Q	UAL	UAL CP	−19.59%	41.44%	−0.58	0.74	−0.30	0.13
R	UNP	UNION PACIFIC	0.12%	34.63%	−0.13	0.52	−0.09	0.09
S	USFC	US FREIGHTWAYS CP	13.86%	54.76%	0.17	0.82	0.02	0.09
T	YELL	YELLOW CP	3.60%	46.66%	−0.02	0.68	−0.07	0.09

[1] Annualized arithmetic average return from 1998–2000. [2] Annualized volatility from 1998–2000. [3] Sharpe ratio uses a risk free rate of 4.5%.

CORRELATION

	A	B	C	D	E	F	G	H	I	J	K	L	M	N	O	P	Q	R	S	T
A	1.00	0.28	0.25	0.18	0.30	0.23	0.37	0.44	0.22	0.19	0.29	0.24	0.30	0.25	0.14	0.28	0.29	0.22	0.27	0.23
B	0.28	1.00	0.10	0.15	0.22	0.17	0.13	0.15	0.27	0.22	0.10	0.18	0.17	0.17	0.11	0.14	0.13	0.14	0.24	0.17
C	0.25	0.10	1.00	0.21	0.23	0.28	0.72	0.35	0.23	0.17	0.54	0.20	0.46	0.23	0.17	0.37	0.65	0.24	0.23	0.20
D	0.18	0.15	0.21	1.00	0.24	0.49	0.20	0.22	0.28	0.13	0.18	0.48	0.23	0.23	0.11	0.20	0.15	0.49	0.21	0.17
E	0.30	0.22	0.23	0.24	1.00	0.21	0.27	0.28	0.24	0.23	0.22	0.26	0.22	0.25	0.07	0.14	0.22	0.23	0.30	0.24
F	0.23	0.17	0.28	0.49	0.21	1.00	0.30	0.27	0.29	0.15	0.23	0.56	0.25	0.23	0.15	0.22	0.23	0.48	0.24	0.17
G	0.37	0.13	0.72	0.20	0.27	0.30	1.00	0.37	0.25	0.10	0.57	0.22	0.51	0.23	0.18	0.39	0.68	0.26	0.19	0.21
H	0.44	0.15	0.35	0.22	0.28	0.27	0.37	1.00	0.22	0.15	0.30	0.24	0.32	0.24	0.15	0.26	0.31	0.29	0.25	0.24
I	0.22	0.27	0.23	0.28	0.24	0.29	0.25	0.22	1.00	0.21	0.23	0.31	0.24	0.27	0.18	0.15	0.20	0.27	0.21	0.21
J	0.19	0.22	0.17	0.13	0.23	0.15	0.10	0.15	0.21	1.00	0.12	0.16	0.17	0.15	0.13	0.08	0.14	0.11	0.26	0.20
K	0.29	0.10	0.54	0.18	0.22	0.23	0.57	0.30	0.23	0.12	1.00	0.22	0.42	0.26	0.09	0.39	0.50	0.25	0.18	0.16
L	0.24	0.18	0.20	0.48	0.26	0.56	0.22	0.24	0.31	0.16	0.22	1.00	0.22	0.27	0.09	0.18	0.24	0.53	0.27	0.23
M	0.30	0.17	0.46	0.23	0.22	0.25	0.51	0.32	0.24	0.17	0.42	0.22	1.00	0.16	0.16	0.46	0.49	0.22	0.28	0.21
N	0.25	0.17	0.23	0.23	0.25	0.23	0.23	0.24	0.27	0.15	0.26	0.27	0.16	1.00	0.10	0.13	0.23	0.18	0.22	0.16
O	0.14	0.11	0.17	0.11	0.07	0.15	0.18	0.15	0.18	0.13	0.09	0.09	0.16	0.10	1.00	0.11	0.12	0.10	0.19	0.23
P	0.28	0.14	0.37	0.20	0.14	0.22	0.39	0.26	0.15	0.08	0.39	0.18	0.46	0.13	0.11	1.00	0.29	0.20	0.18	0.11
Q	0.29	0.13	0.65	0.15	0.22	0.23	0.68	0.31	0.20	0.14	0.50	0.24	0.49	0.23	0.12	0.29	1.00	0.24	0.22	0.20
R	0.22	0.14	0.24	0.49	0.23	0.48	0.26	0.29	0.27	0.11	0.25	0.53	0.22	0.18	0.10	0.20	0.24	1.00	0.22	0.22
S	0.27	0.24	0.23	0.21	0.30	0.24	0.19	0.25	0.21	0.26	0.18	0.27	0.28	0.22	0.19	0.18	0.22	0.22	1.00	0.31
T	0.23	0.17	0.20	0.17	0.24	0.17	0.21	0.24	0.21	0.20	0.16	0.23	0.21	0.16	0.23	0.11	0.20	0.22	0.31	1.00

Correlation calculated from daily returns from 1998–2000.

APPENDIX P Dow Jones Utilities Stocks

PERFORMANCE

Code	Ticker	Name	Return[1]	Risk[2]	Sharpe Ratio[3]	Beta	Alpha	R^2
A	AEP	AMER ELECTRIC PWR CO INC	4.42%	24.30%	0.00	0.23	-0.02	0.04
B	AES	AES CP (THE)	40.30%	49.47%	0.72	0.77	0.29	0.10
C	D	DOMINION RESOURCES INC NEW	23.18%	22.11%	0.84	0.15	0.17	0.02
D	DUK	DUKE ENERGY CP	21.87%	24.66%	0.70	0.19	0.16	0.02
E	ED	CONSL EDISON INC HLDG CO	5.18%	23.88%	0.03	0.20	-0.01	0.03
F	EIX	EDISON INTL	-6.35%	37.33%	-0.29	0.28	-0.13	0.02
G	ENE	ENRON CP	55.62%	41.95%	1.22	0.50	0.47	0.06
H	EXC	EXELON CP	41.69%	30.17%	1.23	0.12	0.36	0.01
I	NI	NISOURCE INC	16.18%	27.73%	0.42	0.15	0.10	0.01
J	PCG	PG&E CP	-4.14%	31.73%	-0.27	0.22	-0.11	0.02
K	PEG	PUBLIC SERV ENT GR	22.09%	23.35%	0.75	0.18	0.16	0.03
L	REI	RELIANT ENERGY INC	24.25%	28.38%	0.70	0.26	0.18	0.04
M	SO	SOUTHERN CO	16.94%	26.41%	0.47	0.17	0.11	-0.02
N	TXU	TXU CO	10.89%	25.17%	0.25	0.21	0.05	0.03
O	WMB	WILLIAMS COS INC	22.30%	43.71%	0.41	0.68	0.12	0.10

[1] Annualized arithmetic average return from 1998–2000. [2] Annualized volatility from 1998–2000. [3] Sharpe ratio uses a risk free rate of 4.5%.

CORRELATION

	A	B	C	D	E	F	G	H	I	J	K	L	M	N	O
A	1.00	0.18	0.61	0.61	0.69	0.35	0.12	0.50	0.41	0.46	0.67	0.61	0.63	0.62	0.10
B	0.18	1.00	0.14	0.18	0.15	0.12	0.20	0.14	0.08	0.11	0.20	0.21	0.16	0.10	0.14
C	0.61	0.14	1.00	0.61	0.61	0.32	0.14	0.49	0.38	0.48	0.65	0.58	0.63	0.56	0.11
D	0.61	0.18	0.61	1.00	0.63	0.39	0.16	0.50	0.36	0.51	0.59	0.57	0.65	0.53	0.15
E	0.69	0.15	0.61	0.63	1.00	0.35	0.10	0.48	0.41	0.47	0.66	0.61	0.63	0.61	0.14
F	0.35	0.12	0.32	0.39	0.35	1.00	0.08	0.28	0.21	0.54	0.41	0.29	0.41	0.43	0.07
G	0.12	0.20	0.14	0.16	0.10	0.08	1.00	0.05	0.08	0.10	0.19	0.14	0.11	0.10	0.34
H	0.50	0.14	0.49	0.50	0.48	0.28	0.05	1.00	0.34	0.36	0.49	0.46	0.46	0.46	0.06
I	0.41	0.08	0.38	0.36	0.41	0.21	0.08	0.34	1.00	0.28	0.40	0.39	0.36	0.37	0.11
J	0.46	0.11	0.48	0.51	0.47	0.54	0.10	0.36	0.28	1.00	0.51	0.43	0.48	0.42	0.14
K	0.67	0.20	0.65	0.59	0.66	0.41	0.19	0.49	0.40	0.51	1.00	0.62	0.64	0.61	0.12
L	0.61	0.21	0.58	0.57	0.61	0.29	0.14	0.46	0.39	0.43	0.62	1.00	0.58	0.59	0.15
M	0.63	0.16	0.63	0.65	0.63	0.41	0.11	0.46	0.36	0.48	0.64	0.58	1.00	0.60	0.11
N	0.62	0.10	0.56	0.53	0.61	0.43	0.10	0.46	0.37	0.42	0.61	0.59	0.60	1.00	0.10
O	0.10	0.14	0.11	0.15	0.14	0.07	0.34	0.06	0.11	0.14	0.12	0.15	0.11	0.10	1.00

Correlation calculated from daily returns from 1998–2000.

APPENDIX

Online and Offline Portfolio Optimizers

Online Optimizers

Financial Engines
http://www.financialengines.com

FinPortfolio
http://www.finportfolio.com

KickAssets
http://www.kickassets.com

Offline Optimizers

Advisory World
http://www.advisoryworld.com

Efficient Solutions
http://www.effisols.com

Ibbotson
http://www.ibbotson.com

Monte Carlo Simulation Solutions and Resources

Web-Based Solutions that Offer Monte Carlo Simulation

The following are a few of the better-known Websites that offer financial planning tools based on Monte Carlo simulation. The list is not meant to be exhaustive, and inclusion of a site in this list should not be construed as an endorsement of its products or services.

Financeware.com. Financeware offers a set of online financial planning and probability analysis tools dedicated to helping investors improve their chances of succeeding financially. Its *Historical Auditor* allows one to "backtest" a financial plan to see how it would have fared over prior historical periods; its *Wealthsimulator* simulates a variety of possible outcomes for one's financial plan utilizing randomized historical data; and its *Monte Carlo Simulator* simulates a variety of possible outcomes for one's financial plan utilizing randomized rates of return and life spans over a large number of lifetimes.

FinancialEngines.com. The *Financial Engines Investment Advisor*® service shows investors the chance that they will reach their financial goals based on personal information. It forecasts the likelihood of reaching targeted financial goals, taking into account realistic variables such as fluctuations in inflation, interest rates, and market returns. It uses simulation technology to show how much income a participant is likely to have in retirement. To improve the forecast, the Advisor service makes specific fund recommendations and shows how these recommendations could affect future outcomes.

FinPortfolio.com. FinPortfolio offers a comprehensive suite of online financial planning and investment analysis tools that are designed to guide individual investors (or advisors working with or on behalf of investors) through the entire investment decision-making process. Analytical tools include modules devoted to asset allocation, asset analysis and selection, portfolio optimization, risk analysis and style analysis. The site's *FinPlan* module is a comprehensive multiple-goal/multiple-investment financial planning tool that uses Monte Carlo simulation to show the percentage likelihood of achieving one's goal(s), given the investment(s) dedicated to them.

TRowePrice.com. T. Rowe Price's *Retirement Income Calculator* is a simple and fairly intuitive tool that uses Monte Carlo simulation to show how uncertainty affects one's planning for a steady income in retirement.

Desktop Solutions that Offer Monte Carlo Simulation

The following are a few of the better known desktop solutions that offer financial planning tools based on Monte Carlo simulation. The list is not meant to be exhaustive, and inclusion of a product in this list should not be construed as an endorsement of it.

@Risk (Palisade Corporation)   A risk analysis and Monte Carlo simulation add-in for Microsoft Excel or Lotus 123 spreadsheet software and one of five risk and decision analysis components in Palisade's Decision Tools Suite,

AASim 2.0—Asset Allocation Simulation Software (Financeware. com) A desktop software that realistically models mortality and investment risk simultaneously through the use of Monte Carlo simulation. The newest version of the application adds historical data that provides advisors guidance in assuming risk and return values for client financial plans. It also allows users to model term as well as paid-up life insurance, and features sensitivity analysis to show how contributions, withdrawals, and retirement age influence the probability that a financial plan will succeed.

Crystal Ball 2000 (Decisioneering, Inc.) A Microsoft Excel add-in tool that uses Monte Carlo simulation to help you analyze the risks and uncertainties associated with your spreadsheet models. Features include sensitivity analysis, correlation, tornado analysis, precision control, and distribution fitting to historical data.

Silver Financial Planner Version 3.6 (Money Tree Software) Developed for creating quick and simple plans that answer the question, "Will I outlive my money?", this software features a Monte Carlo simulation report, along with retirement projections, survivor insurance needs, education funding, asset allocation, estate planning, disability, and more.

Online Monte Carlo Simulation Resources

To learn more about Monte Carlo simulation and how it can be applied to financial and investment planning, we recommend the following online resources.

http://www.contingencyanalysis.com This site offers over 1,000 pages of information on financial risk management, with topics including value at risk, derivative instruments, credit risk and financial engineering. The glossary provides an excellent explanation of Monte Carlo simulation, as well as links to pages devoted to related terms and concepts.

http://www.montecarlosimulations.org Created by The Monitor Group, Inc., a Fairfax, Virginia financial and investment advisory firm, this site is intended to provide a central resource library for planners interested in learning more about Monte Carlo and other tools to deal with uncertainty.

Popular Financial Websites

AOL Personal Finance:
http://www.quicken.aol.com/

Big Charts:
http://www.bigcharts.com

Bloomberg LP:
http://www.bloomberg.com/

BusinessWeek Online:
http://www.businessweek.com/

CNNfn:
http://www.cnnfn.com

Microsoft Moneycentral:
http://www.moneycentral.com

Morningstar:
http://www.morningstar.com

Motley Fool:
http://www.fool.com/

Quicken:
http://www.quicken.com

Smart Money:
http://www.smartmoney.com

Yahoo Finance:
http://quote.yahoo.com

Glossary

Alpha   The residual return of an asset or a portfolio after taking into account beta-adjusted market return. Alpha calculates the difference between what the portfolio actually earned and what it was expected to earn given its level of systematic risk. A positive alpha suggests return of the asset or the portfolio exceeds the general market expectation. A negative alpha suggests return of the asset or the portfolio falls short of the general market expectation.

Annualized Average Return   To annualize an average return, multiply the number by a factor. For example, to annualize monthly average return, multiply the number by 12 (there are 12 months in a year). To annualize daily average return, multiply the number by 252 (there are 252 business days in a year).

Annualized Risk   To annualize risk, multiply the number by a factor. For example, to annualize monthly risk, multiply the number by the square root of 12 (there are 12 months in a year). To annualize daily risk, multiply the number by the square root of 252 (there are 252 business days in a year).

Annualized Volatility   See Annualized Risk.

Arithmetic Average Return   See Average Return.

Asset Allocation   The implementation of a financial policy by selecting asset classes, and allocating wealth to put in each of these asset classes.

Asset Allocation Attribution   It measures the impact of over or under-weighting particular asset classes, such as equity (or value equity and growth equity), fixed-income, and cash (money market or treasury bill) within our portfolio by comparing performance of a given asset class to that of the benchmark (a mix of asset classes) as a whole. In effect, it quantifies the decisions we make relative to choice of asset classes. Positive asset allocation results are achieved when a portfolio is over-weighted in an asset class that outperformed the benchmark. Conversely, negative asset allocation occurs when a portfolio is under-weighted in such an asset class.

Asset Class   The broad categories assets or securities belong to. These categories can be very general, such as U.S. Stocks, U.S. Bonds, International Equity etc., or they can be quite focused, such as U.S. Large Cap Stocks, U.S. Small Cap Stocks, U.S. Corporate Bonds, U.S. Municipal Bonds, Developed International Equity, Emerging International Equity etc.

Average Return   Arithmetic average return of an investment calculated from historical returns over a specified period of time. The average can be of different frequencies depending on the historical return data used. For example, average calculated from daily return data from the past 30 days will be daily average return. Average calculated from monthly return data from the past 36 months will be monthly average return.

Beta   A measurement of the volatility of an asset or a portfolio relative to a selected benchmark, usually a market index. A beta of 1.0 indicates the magnitude and direction of movements of return of the asset or the portfolio are the same as those of the benchmark. A higher-than-1.0 beta indicates greater volatility, while a lower-than-1.0 beta indicates less volatility when measured against a benchmark. A negative beta indicates the asset's return or the portfolio's return moves in an opposite direction relative to the benchmark.

Bond   Debt securities issued by governments or corporations. Bonds are fixed income securities because they yield interest. The U.S. bond asset class in asset allocation is represented by Lehman Brothers Aggregated Bond Index.

Capital Asset Pricing Model (CAPM)   A theory that states the expected return of an asset or a portfolio is equal to the risk-free rate plus the risk premium defined by its beta and the market excess return. A high beta would result in a high expected return according to CAPM.

Capital Gain The realized profit on the sale of an investment. For example, one has a capital gain of $1,000 if he/she purchases a stock for $2,000 and sells it for $3,000.

Cash There are two definitions of cash. Hard cash is the paper money that yields no interest. The cash asset class used in asset allocation is short-term government treasury. The return of the cash asset class can be considered the risk-free rate.

Cashflow Model A cashflow model is a means of measuring cash inflows and outflows. Of course, depending on the nature of those inflows and outflows, a cashflow model can range from simple (like a piggy bank) to complex (like an exotic derivative instrument).

Correlation A statistic figure that measures the movements of two variables—the return behaviors of two assets or two asset classes. It falls between -1 and $+1$. A correlation of -1 indicates perfect negative correlation where two assets or two asset classes move simultaneously in opposite directions. A correlation of $+1$ indicates perfect positive correlation where two assets or two asset classes move simultaneously in the same direction. A correlation of 0 indicates there is no relationship between the return behaviors of two assets or two asset classes.

Corporate Bond Bonds issued by corporations. There are different ratings of corporate bonds ranging from AAA (safe, low coupon rate) to D (close to default, high coupon rate).

Country Selection Attribution It captures the impact of over or under-weighting a country within our portfolio, by comparing performance of the given country to that of an international benchmark. In effect, it quantifies the decisions we make relative to choice of country markets in which to invest. Positive country selection is achieved by over-weighting a portfolio in a country market that outperformed the international benchmark. Conversely, negative country selection occurs when the portfolio is under-weighted in such a country market.

Currency Attribution It reflects the currency translation effect of the securities we hold (implicit) and the impact of active currency management decisions, e.g. hedging, (explicit). The currency attribute is measured separately, and attempts to capture the effect of currency exposures of the portfolio and the impact of forward currency contracts or currency futures. Like the asset allocation attribute, the currency attribute is measured relative to the benchmark currency return.

Dollar-Weighted Return (DTR)   See Internal Rate of Return.

Diversification   The process of "putting your eggs in different baskets" to reduce excessive exposure to any one source of risk. Generally speaking, a portfolio can be considered diversified with 15–20 stocks.

Diversifiable Risk   See Unsystematic Risk.

Dividend Discount Model (DDM)   A stock valuation method that estimates future dividends of a company and discounts back into a fair present value.

Drawdown   A risk measurement that is defined as the largest percentage loss within an investment period, from the highest point to subsequent lowest point.

Efficient Frontier   A curve that represents a set of portfolios that have maximum expected return at each level of portfolio risk. Each optimal portfolio on the efficient frontier also has the minimum risk at that level of portfolio expected return.

Excess Return   The remaining return of an asset or a portfolio after subtracting the risk-free rate.

Exchange Traded Fund (ETF)   Fund that is traded on an exchange and can be bought and sold throughout the day. There are Nasdaq 100's QQQ, the S&P 500's SPY, and many other country-specific and sector specific products currently offered by Barclay (iShares), Merrill Lynch (Holders), and Vanguard (Vipers). ETF provides investors with instant exposure to a group of stocks or a particular market.

Expected Return   The return expected to be generated from an investment in the future.

Folio   A new type of investment vehicle that is similar to a mutual fund but also gives investors control over capital gains taxes. There are currently three companies offering such services: FolionFn, Netfolio, and UNX.

Geometric Average Return   A method to compute historical average return by taking the effect of compounding into consideration. It will always be lower than arithmetic average return.

High-Yield Bond   Very risky bonds that have low ratings. They often carry a high coupon rate for additional risks.

Index Fund   A type of mutual fund that duplicates the returns of a particular market index, such as the S&P 500 Index.

Inflation   The increases in price of goods and service over time.

Inflation Risk   The risk of having returns on investments fall below the inflation rate. If that happens, the purchasing power of one's wealth will decrease over time.

Internal Rate of Return (IRR)   IRR measures the actual return earned on a beginning portfolio value and on any net contributions made during a given period

International Equities   Stocks that are traded outside of the United States. Developed international equities are stocks traded in foreign developed countries. Emerging market equities are stocks traded in foreign emerging countries. The international equity asset class in asset allocation is represented by the MSCI EAFE Index.

Investment Process   An investment process is a plan of action for implementing an investment philosophy. An investment process must be highly disciplined and consistently applied over time.

Jensen Alpha   See Alpha.

Junk Bond   See High-Yield Bond.

Large-Cap Stocks   Commonly defined as stocks with a market capitalization of above $5 billion. The U.S. large-cap stocks asset class in asset allocation is represented by the S&P 500 Index.

Liquidity   The ease of buying and selling an asset and the market impact it has.

M-Squared   Developed by Leah Modigliani, a U.S. stock strategist at Morgan Stanley, and her grandfather, Nobel Winner Franco Modigliani, the ratio normalizes an investment's risk level to match that of the market portfolio (S&P 500), thereby allowing for a one-to-one return comparison against that benchmark.

Market Risk   The risk or uncertainty of an investment that is attributable to the movements or changes of a broad market. Unlike firm-specific risk, market risk cannot be eliminated by owning many stocks.

Market Portfolio   A portfolio consisting of all the stocks. It is often approximated using a Wilshire 5000 Index or S&P 500 Index.

Mean-Variance Optimization   A portfolio optimization process invented by Nobel Laureate Harry Markowitz.

Modern Portfolio Theory (MPT)   MPT explores how risk-averse investors construct portfolios in order to achieve the best risk-return trade-off or to have optimal market risk against expected returns. It was invented in the 1950s by Harry Markowitz. His book, *Portfolio Selection: Efficient Diversification of Investments*, was an extension of his PhD thesis. Modern Portfolio Theory is regarded as among the most important analytical tools in 20th century finance. In 1990, Markowitz shared the Nobel Prize in Economics with Merton Miller and William Sharpe for what has become a broad theory for portfolio selection and corporate finance.

Monte Carlo Simulation   Monte Carlo simulation is a technique for calculating and accounting for uncertainty in a forecast of future events. In the context of financial planning, Monte Carlo simulation helps us to understand the likelihood of successfully achieving our goals, given the investments we have set up specifically for those goals

Mutual Fund   A portfolio of assets managed by a fund manager. Investors pay a fee for the fund manager to carry out research on individual assets, execute trades, build a portfolio, and make ongoing changes as he/she sees fit. A mutual fund provides investors instant diversification.

Naïve Asset Allocation   An asset allocation that allocates the investment to assets and asset classes equally.

Non-Diversifiable Risk   See Systematic Risk.

Normal Distribution   A type of random distribution that returns on assets or asset classes are assumed to follow.

Portfolio Optimization   The process of finding the efficient frontier.

Optimal Portfolio   A portfolio on the efficient frontier. It has the maximum possible expected return for a level of risk, and a minimum possible risk for a level of expected return.

Optimization Constraint   Different weight restrictions placed on assets during portfolio optimization. There are several types of constraints. Single constraints put limitations on single assets; for example, an asset or an asset class can make up a minimum of 10% of a portfolio, and a maximum of 50% of a portfolio. Group constraints put limitations on multiple assets; for example, three assets or three asset classes can make up no more than 60% of a portfolio. Optimization constraints can be used to control risk and improve optimization results.

Performance Attribution Analysis   The process of analyzing a portfolio's past return to understand how much each factor, such as asset allocation, market timing, and security selection, affects the portfolio's performance.

R-Squared   A statistics correlation measurement that shows the significance of any regression analysis. In linear regression to calculate beta, r-squared shows the percentage of volatility in a portfolio's return that can be explained by returns of the benchmark portfolio.

Return-Based Style Analysis   Originally developed by Nobel Prize laureate William Sharpe, returns-based style analysis analyzes the fund's pattern of returns over time to infer the manager's investment style. It analyses asset's or a portfolio's style components by running a multi-factor regression analysis against style benchmarks. Returns-based style analysis provides insights on the sources of a fund's historic returns, expressing them as the combination of index or benchmark returns that best represents the fund's overall returns. The advantage of this approach is that it is independent of a portfolio's holdings.

Return Volatility   See Risk.

Risk   In modern portfolio theory, risk is a measurement of uncertainties of expected return. It is often measured using standard deviation. Different assets have different levels of risk. A government treasury bill has very little uncertainty, or risk. A foreign emerging market stock may contain a lot of risk.

Risk-Adjusted Return   The return of an asset or a portfolio adjusted for risk. The Sharpe Ratio can be considered a form of risk-adjusted return. M-Squared can also be considered a form of risk-adjusted return.

Risk-Free Rate   The rate of return that does not have default risk. The rate of return on a Treasury bill issued by U.S. government is usually used as a risk-free rate.

Risk Tolerance   The amount of risk an individual is willing to take. It can be influenced by external financial factors. If an individual is in retirement, he/she may have very low risk tolerance because he/she cannot afford to lose a lot of money. It can also be influenced by personality. Each individual reacts differently when the value of a portfolio varies over time.

Sector Selection Attribution   It measures the impact of over or under-weighting particular sectors, such as technology or retail within the equity asset class, or corporate bond and Treasury bond within the fixed-income asset class. It quantifies the decisions we make relative to choice of industry sector. Positive sector selection results are achieved when a portfolio is over-weighted in a sector that outperformed the benchmark. Conversely, negative sector selection occurs when the portfolio is under-weighted in such a sector.

Security Selection Attribution   It attempts to identify one's skill at security selection within each sector. For example, stocks selected within a particular sector such as technology or retail. Positive security selection is achieved by selecting an individual security that outperforms the sector benchmark. Negative security selection occurs when a selected security under-performs the sector benchmark

Sharpe Ratio   A form of risk-adjusted return proposed by Nobel Laureate William Sharpe. It is a ratio of excess asset or portfolio return over its excess return volatility. The higher the Sharpe ratio, the higher the rate of return generated by taking each unit of risk. It is often beneficial to look at Sharpe ratios, in additional to total return of a portfolio, when measuring its performance.

Small-Cap Stocks   Commonly defined as stocks with a market capitalization of under $1 billion. The U.S. small-cap stocks asset class in asset allocation is represented by Russell 2000 Index.

Standard Deviation   A statistics measurement that indicates a value's variability. It is often used to measure the risk of an asset or a portfolio. Higher the standard deviation, higher the risk of an asset or a portfolio.

Strategic Asset Allocation   See Asset Allocation.

Style Analysis   The process of analyzing an asset or a portfolio's styles such as growth, value, large cap, small cap, equity, bond etc.

Style Investing   An investment process that periodically shifts the assets among style asset classes to generate better returns.

Style Rotation   See Style Investing.

Systematic Return   The return of a portfolio that can be explained by the market.

Systematic Risk   The risk of a portfolio that is attributable to market risk.

Tactical Asset Allocation   The process of selecting individual securities and allocating wealth among these securities. A common approach is to use portfolio optimization.

Time-Weighted Return (TWR)   TWR is a compound rate of return for the entire period. The rate of return for each time period can be calculated by a cash inflow or outflow.

Total Return   The overall return of an asset or a portfolio over a specific historical time period.

Treasury   Debt issued by the U.S. government. A Treasury Bill is a short-term government debt with a maturity of less than 1 year. A Treasury Note can range from 1 to 10 years. A Treasury Bond has a maturity of over 10 years.

Treynor Ratio   A risk-adjusted return measurement that is defined as the excess return of a portfolio divided by the portfolio beta.

Unsystematic Risk   The residual risk of a portfolio after subtracting systematic risk from total risk. This portion of risk is often reducible through proper diversification.

Value at Risk (VaR)   VaR is a number that expresses the maximum expected loss for a given time horizon, for a given confidence interval, and for a given position or portfolio of instruments, under normal market conditions, attributable to changes in the market price of financial instruments. To be more concrete, VaR is an amount, say 1,000 dollars, where the chance of losing more than 1,000 dollars has some probability, say 5 in 100, over some future time interval, say 1 day. This is a probabilistic statement, and therefore VaR is a statistical measure of risk exposure.

Index